Adding Value through Information and Consultation

Edited by

John Storey
The Open University Business School

in association with

First published 2005 by
PALGRAVE MACMILLAN
Houndmills, Basingstoke, Hampshire RG21 6XS and
175 Fifth Avenue, New York, N.Y. 10010
Companies and representatives throughout the world

PALGRAVE MACMILLAN is the global academic imprint of the Palgrave
Macmillan division of St. Martin's Press, LLC and of Palgrave Macmillan Ltd.
Macmillan® is a registered trademark in the United States, United Kingdom
and other countries. Palgrave is a registered trademark in the European
Union and other countries.

ISBN-13: 978–1–4039–4898–4
ISBN-10: 1–4039–4898–4

This book is printed on paper suitable for recycling and made from fully
managed and sustained forest sources.

A catalogue record for this book is available from the British Library.

Library of Congress Cataloging-in-Publication Data
Adding value through information and consultation / edited by John Storey.
      p.   cm.
   Includes bibliographical references and index.
   ISBN 1–4039–4898–4 (pbk.)
   1. Management—Employee participation—European Union countries.
   2. Communication in management—European Union countries.
   3. Strategic planning—Employee participation—European Union
   countries.   4. Management—Employee participation—Law and
   legislation—European Union countries.   I. Storey, John, 1947–
   HD5660.E9A33 2005
   658.3′152′094—dc22   2005049754

10   9   8   7   6   5   4   3   2   1
14 13 12 11 10 09 08 07 06 05

Printed and bound in China

Contents

List of contributors

Phil Beaumount   Professor of Employment Relations, School of Business and Management, University of Glasgow

Andrea Broughton   Editor, *European Industrial Relations Review*, Industrial Relations Services

William Coupar   Director, IPA

Mark Fenton-O'Creevy   Professor of Organisational Behaviour, Open University Business School

Moira Fischbacher   Senior Lecturer in Strategy, School of Business and Management, University of Glasgow

John F. Geary   Associate Professor of Industrial Relations and Human Resources, Michael Smurfit Graduate School of Business, University College Dublin

Howard Gospel   Professor of Management, King's College London; Research Associate, Centre for Economic Performance, London School of Economics; Fellow, Said Business School, University of Oxford

Colin Gray   Professor of Enterprise Development, Open University Business School President, Institute for Small Business and Entrepreneurship

Mark Hall   Principal Research Fellow, Warwick University Business School

Laurie Hunter   Honorary Research Fellow, School of Business and Management, University of Glasgow

Ian Kessler   Fellow in Human Resource Management at Templeton College and Said Business School, University of Oxford

Susan Marlow   Reader in HRM, Department of HRM, Faculty of Business and Law, De Montfort University

Judy Pate   Lecturer in Strategy, School of Business and Management, University of Glasgow

William K. Roche   Professor of Industrial Relations, Michael Smurfit Graduate School of Business, University College Dublin

Robert Stevens   Research and Information Manager, IPA

John Storey   Professor of Human Resource Management, Open University Business School

Marc Thompson   Senior Research Fellow, Employee Relations, Templeton College, University of Oxford

Sarah Veale   Head, Equality and Employment Rights Department, TUC

Peter Walton   Professor of Accounting, Open University Business School

Paul Willman   Ernest Button Professor of Management, Said Business School, University of Oxford, and Fellow of Balliol College, Oxford

Stephen Wood   Professor, Institute of Work Psychology, University of Sheffield

David Yeandle   Deputy Director of Employment Policy, EEF

Preface

This book is about the theory and practice of employee consultation. To consider these twin aspects together may seem natural and an obviously sensible thing to do. Yet in fact much of the available material is almost exclusively of one mode or the other – that is, either mainly theoretical, or mainly or wholly practical. There is a substantial theoretical literature that examines and often extols the ideas of consultation, involvement and participation, but neglects the practical meaning and implementation of these ideas. On the other hand, there are also many practical guidelines, checklists and timelines that discuss the fine detail of information and consultation guidelines but neglect the underlying rationales and purposes of all this activity.

The theory without the practice misses important elements and is open to the danger of being dismissed as 'nice ideas but unrealistic in practice'. Conversely, the fine practical detail is in danger of missing the point: the regulations, the timings and so on can become empty exercises in cunning conformance with the letter of the law while missing its essential purpose. Of course, there is the possibility that a minimalist stance is adopted following a considered analysis: minimalism may be part of a strategic employment relations approach that fits a particular business strategy. The important thing is to be clear how rationale fits with purpose, and this in turn fits with action. The aim in this book is to confront theory with practice and vice versa. By examining the two together we seek a richer insight into both – and to advance both.

In order to meet this aim, this book contains a rich mixture of theoretical analysis, carefully selected extracts from landmark documents, insights into the perspectives of key parties such as employer representatives and trade union representatives, explanations of practice and case examples. Crucially, the book also includes the results and analyses deriving from original empirical research on the processes, outcomes and consequences of different forms of information and consultation practice, and of the meaning and impact of the concept of 'high performance workplaces'. As a result of this mix of perspectives and material, managers and others have the resources on which they can take decisions using more evidence-based research rather than relying on 'gut feel' or unsubstantiated assumptions.

As the editor of this volume, I want to acknowledge first of all the work of those people who have contributed thoughtful original chapters. Taken together they reveal the range of perspectives, and they catalogue the different concerns and hopes of the various parties. I am grateful to the Involvement and Participation Association (IPA) for the decision flowchart shown in Appendix 1.

JOHN STOREY

The authors and publishers are grateful to the Taylor & Francis Group for permission to use the material in chapter 9, previously published as 'Dilemmas in Worker Representation: Information, Consultation and Negotiation', by Howard Gospel & Paul Willman in Gospel & Wood (eds), *Representing Workers: Trade Union Recognition*, Routledge, 2003.

Every effort has been made to trace all copyright holders, but if any have inadvertently been missed the publishers will be pleased to make the necessary arrangements at the first opportunity.

1

The idea of added value through information and consultation

The purpose of Part 1 is to set the whole debate in context. It does this by introducing the 'idea' of employee information and consultation, by locating it in terms of its previous historical incarnations, by summarising what is new and explaining how various interested parties are reacting, by offering a description of the new legal requirements, and then by summarising the key issues, questions and dilemmas arising. In all, this introductory chapter sets the scene and the agenda for the rest of the book.

1

Employee information and consultation: an overview of theory and practice

John Storey

The purpose of this introductory chapter is to set the scene in preparation for the more detailed, special analyses in the subsequent chapters of this book. The immediate trigger for the discussions in this book was the European Directive on Information and Consultation (I&C) for employees (EU 2002)which was subsequently enacted into UK law (or in the jargon 'transposed') in 2005 (Houses of Parliament 2004). But while these legal instruments may have provided the initial trigger for this book, the issues they raise go well beyond the specifics of these laws. Indeed, the underlying issues originate from much earlier times, and their working-through has occasioned much debate over the decades. But new times, of course, bring new twists to long-standing problems, and the controversy surrounding how best – or even whether – to 'involve' employees in organisational matters has now taken on some new forms.

The great information and consultation debate – why now?

It is widely believed that the immediate prompt for the European Commission to insist on a legally enforceable rights for employees stemmed from a couple of high profile cases where major firms announced redundancies publicly before informing or consulting their employees. Whatever the immediate 'cause', events were set in train which meant that, as from April 2005, UK enterprises employing at least 150 people are required by law to respond to a new set of rights given to employees. In quick succession the employee thresholds will reduce until by 2008 all undertakings with 50 or more employees will be subject to this new set of regulations. Apart from the immediate trigger it is also argued that the growing intensity of global economic challenges make the case for greater employee engagement a compelling one. Information and consultation, it is reasoned, are necessary elements in developing employee involvement, a shared sense of responsibility and participation. The persistent productivity gap in Britain makes the case for some new action to be taken even more compelling.

This new law is significant in two main respects. First, it is novel in bestowing new rights on employees to be informed and consulted, and second its coverage is massive – with some 75 per cent of all employees in the country within its reach. Some commentators have suggested that this law is one of the most significant pieces of employment legislation for many decades. It will, some have argued, 'transform' employment relations in the UK. One of the objectives of this book is to evaluate such a claim and to weigh the significance, possibilities and pitfalls inherent in the new set of rules.

Some participants are enthusiastic and optimistic. One set of reasons is that they see these processes as 'drivers' of a more economically vibrant business scene – and in an enlightened, progressive manner to boot. There is the argument that high commitment leads to high performance. This is the stance adopted by the Department of Trade and Industry (DTI) in its consultation papers (DTI 2002). Indeed, in much literature and in many presentations – including official consultation papers – the twin terms are elided into one: 'high commitment/high performance'. The path to 'high performance', it is argued, is to be steered via 'high commitment'. This in turn requires an informed, knowledgeable workforce, fully consulted and able to leverage its creativity and its innovation potential. In answer to the question: 'But why now?', proponents respond that in a global, competitive economy, business (and therefore jobs) will be lost unless smart products and processes are deployed. 'Offshoring', as the export of jobs to low-wage economies is now known, is currently much in evidence. Thus, in addition to the human dignity case, the business case for information and consultation stems from the analysis that smart ways of working with continual improvement and high productivity is that it represents a defence against low-wage competition. Some unions as well as some employers have made this case (see, for example, Amicus 2004). It may be a matter of surprise to some that even robust trade union leaders on the left such as Derek Simpson have embraced and endorsed the I&C regulations and seemingly accepted the logic advanced by the government. In a Foreword to the *Amicus Guide for Members* he states that good employee information and consultation is necessary for 'achieving high performance workplaces, facilitating change and building a successful economy' (Amicus 2004: 4). In other words, the case for I&C is that it is required for economic survival in a new world economic order. Similarly, the Chartered Institute of Personnel and Development (CIPD) has also stated that it believes that the new legislation will 'help promote productive employee relations through improved dialogue in the workplace'. Moreover, the CIPD also believes in the merits of a 'combination of direct and representative arrangements' (CIPD 2004: 3–4).

Not everyone is convinced. Scepticism can be found among employers, trade union representatives, employees and academic analysts. Many employers remain deeply sceptical. First, they simply find it hard to subscribe to the notion that economically valuable ideas can stem from employees. There are two sub-positions feeding into this. For some, the antipathy is essentially ideologically fuelled. At heart, they remain deeply wedded to the notion of 'management prerogative'. Put simply, they see it as managers' job to manage. The tenets of Taylorism run deep. For others, the rationale is purely pragmatic: they doubt whether the investment in the machinery and paraphernalia of I&C is economically rational. This judgement may stem from personal experience of the limited contribution from the 'tea and toilets' mode of consultation, or it may stem from a fear of the unknown. It may also indicate a lack of imagination – a difficulty in envisioning how I&C could move beyond the routine, the mundane and the game-playing. Second, many senior managers are suspicious of the 'agenda' of trade unions. They see in I&C mechanisms a potential back-door route for declining unions to mount a comeback. Moreover, the fact that the Directive comes from the EU is, for some, cause enough for suspicion and resistance.

Despite the TUC's stated position of support, some trade union representatives are also sceptical. There is a longstanding belief in some parts of the union movement that collective bargaining is the only legitimate channel for representing workers' interests. To intrude a wholly, or partially, non-union mode of representation is seen as a potentially dangerous undermining of the organised workforce approach. If I&C were to be merged into the negotiating machinery, this might dilute the nature of collective bargaining. On the other hand, to try run I&C in parallel might gradually reduce collective bargaining to very circumscribed areas – most notably pay bargaining. But while this may be seen as the vital topic, increasingly pay settlements run for two or three years, and in consequence it could become a very intermittent and incidental activity.

Employees too have their own reasons for scepticism. They have, in recent years, witnessed and been party to a range of initiatives, many of which have entailed elements of an involved, and even empowered, approach. Team working, team briefings, town hall meetings, corporate videos, quality circles, TQM (total quality management), and Six Sigma to name a few, have entailed messages about the importance of involving employees. Accordingly, the basic message about involvement is not new, and beyond these direct forms of involvement, there may be even more scepticism about representational modes. Some academic analysts are also sceptical of the outcomes of partnership as a mode of labour-management co-operation. To take just one example, following a systematic analysis of twenty-two private-sector firms reported as signing partnership agreements, John Kelly explored a whole array of outcomes and consequences. In a balanced assessment he came to the conclusion that, while such co-operation benefited employers, the impacts on employees and for unions were more mixed. In particular, he is doubtful whether such agreements offer a pathway for union renewal (Kelly 2004). Such a conclusion may, of course, give enormous encouragement to other parties.

Thus, from the above introductory remarks, it can be recognised that there are various views, expectations and feelings about the notion of I&C. Some are positive or broadly positive, and some are negative or broadly negative. Enter the new legally enforceable regulations. What difference, if any, might they make? To address this question we need to attend to ideas, to evidence, and to analyses.

Accordingly, this chapter first presents an overall description of the new legal requirements before moving on to identify and then analyse the key issues arising. The sources used for the analysis presented in this chapter are the range of secondary sources including surveys and previous research on related aspects to employee involvement and partnership, as well as a series of interviews with employers and employee representatives, along with a number of focus groups in organisations of different sizes and across a number of sectors. The core objective of this primary research was to explore with the key players their expectations, their plans and their calculations in relation to the short-, medium- and long-term prospects for the new information and consultation regulations.

The argument, in a nutshell, is that many of the players – managers, employee representatives and employees alike – expect that a likely outcome, in the medium term at least, is that organisations will introduce a series of adjustments to their current arrangements, but these will in all probability be of a 'bolt-on' nature. The expectation that a transformation of employment relations will be triggered is not high. On the other hand, there are some players who, more optimistically, see potential for the regulations to act as a catalyst for change. This interpretation envisages and hopes for a growth in mutual learning. The belief is that, as the parties engage with each other, they will discover the potential to secure mutual advantage through more meaningful consultation and information sharing.

It is possible, of course, for both of these patterns to be played out in different settings. Identifying and analysing the nature of the factors that will determine the different outcomes is the crucial work to be done. Indeed, the central purpose of this volume is to tackle these issues by drawing on theory, practice and evidence (both quantitative and case-study based). The mix of chapters featuring contemporary analyses from specialist authors is intended to enable the necessary detailed exploration and weighing of these crucial factors. It is useful to begin with a summary of the new legal requirements.

Key features of the new regulations

In terms of the new legal requirements there are two prime sources that need to be understood. The first is the European Directive, which impels member states to ensure that their laws conform with the framework specified, and the second is the UK regulations (and their attendant guidelines). In this section we deal with each of these in turn before setting out an overall analysis of the contentious issues for debate.

The European Directive

The EU Directive (2002/14/EC) is designed to 'establish a general framework for informing and consulting employees in the European Community'. Its point of departure is the Treaty which has as a 'particular objective' to 'promote social dialogue between management and labour' (para. 1). It notes that the Community Charter of Fundamental Social Rights provides among other things that information, consultation and participation for workers must be developed along appropriate lines, 'taking into account the practices in force in different Member States'. It also notes that the 'existing legal frameworks at national and Community level intended to ensure that employees are involved in the affairs of the undertaking employing them and in decisions which affect them has not always prevented serious decisions affecting employees from being taken and made public without adequate procedures having been implemented beforehand to inform and consult them' (para. 6). In consequence, it is maintained that there is a need to 'strengthen dialogue' in order to promote mutual trust; make work organisation more flexible; make employees aware of adaptation needs; and promote employee involvement in the future of undertakings, and so increase competitiveness. Special attention is paid to aspects of employment and potential threats to employment, and to the associated offsetting measures such as training, development and adaptability. The forces of globalisation are also seen as impelling the need for involvement and for new forms of work organisation.

Anticipation, prevention and employability are the watchwords. Notably, existing legal requirements – presumably those relating to redundancies – are seen as suffering from an 'excessively a posteriori' approach (para. 13). In sum, a range of economic, political and legal developments are seen to require a new legal framework 'enabling the right to be informed and consulted to be exercised' (para. 14). Notably, the Directive is 'without prejudice to those systems which provide for the direct involvement of employees as long as they are always free to exercise the right to be informed and consulted through their representatives' (para. 16).

The general framework is intended to establish a floor of 'minimum standards' and is not intended to restrict Member States from developing more favourable provisions on top. Moreover, the Directive emphasises the framework nature and allows for Member States to adapt it to their own national circumstances, and indeed stressing a leading role for agreement between employers and labour.

The Directive defines 'undertaking' to mean a public or private undertaking carrying out an economic activity whether or not operating for gain; 'employer' means the legal person party to employment contracts; and 'consultation' means the 'exchange of views and establishment of dialogue between employees' representatives and the employer'. Even with regard to the definition of information, the reference point is that of employees' representatives. Occasional references to direct involvement notwithstanding, there is thus a strong implicit intent to see employee information and consultation through representatives as perhaps being the norm.

The indicative content or subject matter of information and consultation is itemised in three categories:

(i) information on the recent and probable development of the undertaking or the establishments activities and economic situation;

(ii) information and consultation on the situation and probable development of employment – in particular, if there is a threat to employment; and

(iii) information and consultation on decisions likely to lead to substantial changes in work organisation or in contractual relations.

In terms of the setting for such information and consultation, this is to be at the 'relevant level of management' depending on the subject, and in a timely manner and with an appropriate method. It is required that employee representatives are able to meet with employers and obtain a response (and the reasons for the response), and with a 'view to reaching agreement'. Moreover, there is flexibility in that employers and labour may be 'entrusted' to reach their own arrangements for informing and consulting employees. Thus employees have rights, but they may choose not to exercise them. Confidentiality may apply to information if there is a danger of serious harm to the functioning of the undertaking. There is also to be protection of employee representatives and adequate sanctions on employers for non-compliance – sanctions which are 'effective, proportionate and dissuasive' (Article 8, para. 2).

As noted, the Directive established a 'framework' and the intent was that Member States would 'transpose' this into legal regulations suited to their own particular circumstances, sensitive, for example, to culture and existing institutions.

The UK regulations

The transposition of the EU Directive into British law was accomplished through Regulations made under Section 41 of the Employment Relations Act 2004. Intense lobbying and debate began even at the EU Directive stage. This continued and intensified when the government began to consider how it would introduce the principles and rights into law in the United Kingdom. It is worth noting that initially the government was strongly opposed to the Directive. Once it came to accept, however, that its introduction was inevitable, it bent its energies first to shaping the content so that it allowed as much flexibility as possible, and second it promoted the concept in terms of 'high performance'. The employers' organisation, the Confederation of British Industry (CBI), and the Trades Union Congress (TUC), notably entered the fray with some vigour. The government issued consultation papers and held regional 'roadshows' where participants from various lobby groups could have their say. In due course, the transposed British law was constructed around a number of key points.

The Regulations apply from 6 April 2005 to 'undertakings' with at least 150 employees; from 6 April 2007 to undertakings with at least 100 employees; and from 6 April 2008 to undertakings with at least 50 employees. The number of employees is calculated as an annual average. Employees or representatives are entitled to receive data about employee numbers. This request can be enforced by the Central Arbitration Committee (CAC).

Alternative pathways and scenarios

Given the nature of the regulations, there are a range of potential pathways or scenarios. The main ones are shown in Figure 1.1.

First, as the Figure indicates, one possibility is that no action is taken. This could occur if the employer does nothing, and no request comes from the employees.

The second possibility is that an employer negotiates a pre-existing agreement. This can occur at any time either prior to the Regulations coming into force for that size of undertaking, or at any time after the regulations come into effect. This is indicated near the top right of Figure 1.1.

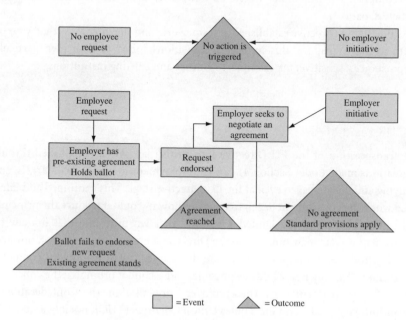

Figure 1.1 Flowchart of the process

Pre-existing agreement

The third possibility is shown in the top left of the figure; here it is the employees, or at least a proportion of them, who make the request. This is the so-called 'pulling the trigger' by employees – that is, using the rights bestowed by the new legislation. An employee trigger requires at least 10 per cent of the employees to make a request (or in appropriate circumstances, a minimum of 15 or a maximum of 2,500 employees). When this happens, if there is no suitable pre-existing agreement in place, then the employer is obligated to seek to negotiate an agreement concerning I&C. There is a six-month limit to cumulative expressions of support for such a request. The request must be in writing either to the company or to the CAC.

The alternative pathway is taken where a pre-existing agreement is in place. In this case a ballot must be held in order to determine if that agreement is endorsed by the workforce as a whole. A ballot for employee endorsement of an employee request may be held if fewer than 40 per cent of employees made the request where a 'pre-existing agreement' exists. To qualify for the status of a pre-existing agreement, such an agreement needs to meet certain criteria. It must be in writing; cover all employees of the undertaking; have been approved by employees; and must set out how the employer is to give information to employees or their representatives. All employees must be entitled to vote in the ballot. A detailed example of one such recently negotiated pre-existing agreement can be found in Appendix 2 on page 276.

If the employee request is not endorsed but instead the pre-existing agreement is sustained then that agreement stands, no further action is required, and a three-year moratorium begins which prevents further challenges during that period. If, on the other hand, the workforce endorses the employee request, then the employer is obligated to begin new negotiations in order to establish I&C arrangements. Such an endorsement requires 40 per cent of employees to vote, and a majority win by those who do vote.

Once negotiations have begun, as Figure 1.1 shows, there are two possible outcomes. The first of these is that a negotiated I&C agreement is concluded. This could allow for information and consultation directly with employees, or indirectly through representatives, or both. A negotiated agreement must meet certain minimum conditions, it must:

- be in writing;
- be signed and dated;
- cover all employees in the undertaking;
- set out the circumstances in which the employer must inform and consult employees; and
- provide for the appointment or election of representatives, or provide for information and consultation arrangements directly with employees.

Agreements are deemed to be approved if all negotiating representatives sign it, or a majority sign it and in addition it is endorsed by at least 50 per cent of the employees (by secret ballot or in writing). Agreements meeting these conditions will then be protected by the moratorium provisions. The implication is that once the I&C regulations have been triggered then the parties are constrained to abide by certain minimum standards. The parties are nominally free to agree whatever they wish (just as they were before any trigger was pulled) but whatever they agree will not be protected or deemed to be sufficient to meet the I&C requirements unless these minima are achieved. Failure to achieve them even between consenting parties render such agreements vulnerable to challenge at any time.

The second potential outcome is that no agreement is reached. In this eventuality the standard provisions apply.

Standard provisions

In effect, these standard provisions state the legal minimum requirements and they can be enforced through the Central Arbitration Committee (CAC). The standard provisions apply automatically six months from the date of the initial employee request (the trigger).

These standard provisions require the election of representatives. Further, there is an obligation to inform and consult with these representatives. The nature of this critical requirement is the subject of Regulation 20. As the DTI Guidance Notes state, this regulation is based closely on Article 4 of the EU Directive and is intended to be the same as this – that is, neither intended to exceed nor to be less than that set of requirements. Article 4 of the Directive, as we saw above, requires information and consultation covering: (i) 'information on recent and probable development of the undertaking's or the establishment's activities and economic situation'; (ii) information and consultation on 'the situation, structure and probable development of employment...in particular where there is a threat to employment'; and (iii) I&C on decisions 'likely to lead to substantial changes in work organisation or in contractual relations'. Consultation is to take place to allow sufficient time, at the relevant level of management, in such a way as to enable employee representatives to meet the employer and both to obtain a response and the reasons for that response. Notably, and this item has occasioned some considerable debate, there is a requirement for consultation to occur 'with a view to reaching agreement on decisions' (Article 20(4)).

The British regulations do indeed follow EU Article 4 closely. Regulation 20 gives the clarification that information is required on (i) above, whereas information *and* consultation with the representatives is required for (ii) and (iii) – that is, where employment matters are specifically at issue. By implication, employers are not required to consult about the undertaking's economic situation or prospects as such, though they do need to share information about these matters. With regard to the required consultation on issues concerning employment and substantial changes to work organisation, the standard provisions specify certain procedural requirements. The consultation must be:

- timely;
- comprised of appropriate content;
- on the basis of relevant information;
- conducted with the appropriate level of management;
- on the basis of opinion expressed by representatives; and
- on the basis of reasoned response from the employer to such opinion.

Moreover, with regard it seems only to the elements of regulation 20(c) – that is, 'decisions likely to lead to substantial changes in work organisation or in contractual relations' – the consultation must be conducted 'with a view to reaching agreement'. This issue of the meaning of consultation is picked up again below.

Key issues and interpretations

It may be evident from the description of the regulations above that, while certain principles are reasonably clear there is, none the less, considerable scope for inter-pretation of the meaning and implications of much of this new legislation. These spaces for ambiguity are likely to be exploited. The analysis of issues in this section is informed by primary research with managers and trade union representatives in a range of organisations, as well as discussions with other interested parties and lobby groups.

The first key issue is the nature of the channel – direct or indirect – that is, manager-led direct communication with individual employees, or indirect via repre-sentatives. This is reflective of the individual versus collective tension that has been around as an issue for some time. In some quarters it is believed that the new law equates in effect to a requirement for the introduction of 'works councils' into Britain. The connotations of this suggest ongoing, permanent bodies that engage on a collective basis with a wide range of employment-related matters and which have legal protection. In a very different camp it is maintained strenuously that there is nothing in the regulations that makes representative consultations necessary, still less a standing works council system. In one respect this part of the debate is about interpretations of what is required, or what is at least 'implicit'. In another respect it is not so much about legalistic interpretation *per se* but rather more about interpret-ation in the sense of likely trends and outcomes. The former is a legalistic analysis, the latter rather more sociological.

Much previous research suggests that *combinations* of direct and indirect forms of information and consultation deliver superior outcomes (Sako 1998; Marchington 2001; Beaumont and Hunter 2003 and Beaumont *et al*, Chapter 7 in this volume; Fenton-O'Creevy and Wood, Chapter 5 in this volume). Part of the rationale is that, to be that meaningful and to make a real difference, information and consultation has to engage with the work processes at the operational level and so the direct mode is required. Yet at the same time, this works best in an environment where indirect modes are also occurring, because this gives *legitimacy* and *confidence* in the partici- pative processes. The indirect, representative, systems allow a framework to be constructed, and they provide a mechanism to ultimately hold senior managers to account in a manner that direct channels alone would not permit.

A related issue is the degree of regulation. Some parties – usually the larger employers with their own well-developed systems – wanted as much flexibility as possible. Their main concern – to the extent that it became virtually a mantra – was to avoid the much-touted 'one size fits all' solution. They wanted space and scope to devise their own arrangements. And yet other parties, usually small businesses, seemed more inclined to want as much clarity as possible. They wanted to know with as little fuss as possible what they had to do to comply with the law. There was a clear division between requests for flexibility versus requests for simple, clear rules. The question has been asked why the government framed the regulations in such a way as to seemingly offer direct involvement as a viable option when such a path might be open to challenge at the European Court of Justice (ECJ)[1]. The Employment Minister has responded that the government wanted to allow as much flexibility as possible.

The Directive is in part instructive here, but it could also be construed as ambiguous. In the preliminaries to the Articles there is one paragraph (16) which states explicitly, 'This Directive is without prejudice to those systems which provide for the direct involvement of employees, as long as they are always free to exercise the right to be informed and consulted through their representatives.' Following that statement, the remainder of the Directive is written almost entirely on the basis of an assump- tion that the I&C rights will amount to a representative, works-council-style system. For example, in Article 1 it states, 'When defining or implementing practical arrangements for information and consultation, the employer and the employees' representatives shall work in a spirit of cooperation and with due regard of their reciprocal rights and obligations'. The rest of the document, and the British regula- tions, are written in a way which makes it clear that in the main a representative system is the assumed pathway.

Similarly, the British regulations are constructed overwhelmingly with employee representation as the assumed norm. For example, the standard provisions are all about arranging ballots for the election of the relevant number of representatives. These are supported by the right to appeal to the CAC, which can order the employer to hold a ballot. Regulation 20 makes quite clear that there is a requirement for the employer to deal with information and consultation *representatives*. Similarly, the 'spirit of cooperation' phrase is also replicated in the British regulations (21). The parties are indeed 'under a duty of cooperation' when negotiating or imple- menting a negotiated agreement or when implementing the standard provisions.

A second issue derives from the first. In those cases where a representative system is initiated or redrawn, then the question arises about the nature of the representatives' role. In particular, to what extent might these representatives adopt a trade union role? One possibility is that in some situations there could be potential for trade unions to build a new or a wider base. Alternatively, the reverse could happen – trade union representation where it persists in reduced fashion could be replaced by non-union representation. Whether union-related or not, the meaningfulness of representative democracy in undertakings can vary enormously. It could transform or could be largely irrelevant to most employees; despite the paraphernalia of elections and so on, there could be difficulties in finding volunteers to stand as employee representatives.

A third issue relates to levels and structures. The EU Directive offered a choice between undertaking or establishment as the desired level depending on the traditions in the different countries. The British government made its choice and as a result the regulations stipulate 'undertaking' as the appropriate level. Why might level matter? In fact, the level at which consultation is conducted is related to the whole question of the structuring of representation. This could be as simple or as complicated as the structure of the enterprise. In a single-site, medium sized company without multiple divisions this could be very straightforward indeed. But much of the British commercial structure is complex. Corporate groups can be divided up into many separate trading companies, which may or may not have their own legal entities, and these in turn might be grouped into broad 'divisions' or themselves even have their own separate divisions which in turn might fragment into separate business units.

In principle, a case could be made for any – or indeed all – of these entities to be considered as the sensible unit for I&C related to employment matters. The contract of employment might indeed be with an entity at any one of these levels. But the regulations suggest that this in itself is not the determining factor. What seems to matter in terms of defining an 'undertaking' from the I&C regulations point of view is that this must be a 'separately incorporated legal entity which would have its own shareholders and in the case of British companies, have a unique registration number at Companies House as distinct say from an organisational entity such as an establishment, division or business unit of a company' (DTI Guidance 6). One reason why a definition of an 'undertaking' matters is that it determines in the first instance, through the calculation of employee numbers, whether the I&C regulations apply at all. But beyond that, there are other reasons why this might matter. Different parties may have different reasons for wanting the engagement to be at one level or another.

The main rationales that were encountered were as follows. Some managers said that they wanted I&C to operate at, and in effect to be restricted to, the establishment level, because these entities had been identified by them over recent years as, in effect, the key business units. Employers were also concerned that shifting the focus to the higher, 'undertaking', level might prompt new attempts to re-establish company level bargaining. None the less, some trade union representatives were also in favour of the establishment level – mainly because this is where they had focused their organising and negotiating efforts (sometimes in response to initiatives taken by employers). On the other hand, there were some employers with joint consultative committees already in place at undertaking level, and they were anxious to focus future consultation activity at this level. In practice, the regulations do seem to allow organisations to conduct their I&C activities at any of the levels appropriate to their circumstances as long as this is agreed by the employees. The specificity of the 'undertaking' in the regulations seems more to do with determining which entities fall within or outside the regulations, and the initial triggers to requesting that I&C rights be enacted rather than the actual future conduct. None the less, the manoeuvrings, concerns and implications noted above, about who would do what at which level, and what the ramifications of these moves might be, do remain as important relevant matters, irrespective of whether or not the law has a direct bearing upon them.

Beyond structural issues, there is, fourthly, the question of the meaningfulness of the processes that eventually commence. To some extent this could be interpreted as a question of tactics. One possible approach is a minimalist, 'conformance with the law and no more' approach. The 'bolt-on' versus 'catalyst' interpretations are the notable positions. The former embraces a number of sub-stances which vary in detail – for example, resistance to the regulations, the do-nothing stance, the actively-seek-to-subvert stance, the minimal compliance stance, and the ritualistic stance. The catalyst stance can also embrace a number of positions. These range from a catalyst for a new age of mutual understanding and transformed industrial relations leading to high performance workplaces, or to a catalyst for reinvigorated trade union organisations.

The question as to what the implications might be for trade unionism has been raised by both employers and trade union representatives. A number of different interpretations – and worries – were uncovered. One side of this particular coin was the concern that I&C might assist trade unions to mount a recovery; and the other side of the coin was the concern that I&C might potentially be used as a tool to further undermine trade unions. On the first, some employers harboured apprehensions that trade union representatives would dominate the consultation machinery, that they would use the opportunity to shift the tenor of information and consultation from a painfully-won direct mode to a more collectivist mode – thus, for some, reversing a trend that has been two decades in the making. The converse concern was that I&C could be used to dilute the significance of union collective representation where it existed, or to dissipate a potential union recognition move where a union was not currently recognised. Existing collective negotiation mechanisms and agreements are offered some protection in the regulations, as confirmed in the DTI guidelines, but none the less, by a subtle process, an employer so minded might possibly weaken pre-existing union organisation by restricting its realm of activity. Evidently, developments could move in either direction, and no doubt there will be instances where both types of scenario unfold. Arguably, the I&C regulations are sufficiently unobtrusive on this matter as not to be the determining factor in either direction: events will rather unfold in specific situations rather more through the determination, relative strength and will of the parties involved in those different settings.

New consultation arrangements have to cover 'all employees'. Given that virtually no organisations at the time of writing have 100 per cent union membership, it follows that union representatives, where they exist, will probably be sitting along-side non-union representatives. The significance and consequences of this will again vary, depending on local circumstances. Some union representatives might have the opportunity to demonstrate their professional expertise and will thus potentially expand their sphere of influence. In other cases, the significance of union represen-tation may be diminished by the routine evidence of non-union employee representatives performing a role that is perceived as worthwhile. If two sets of consultative arrangements were attempted – one union and one non-union – there would be a perceived danger of confused messages. Union representatives seemed to be reconciled to the idea of one general consultative council, with non-union as well as union representatives sitting together. They did stress, however, that this was predicated on the assumption that negotiation machinery was kept strictly separate.

The fifth issue relates to the nature of the game itself. Part of Article 1 of the Directive states that the employer and the employees' representatives 'shall work in a spirit of cooperation' when defining or implementing the practical arrangements for information and consultation. Legislating for 'spirit' is, of course, problematical. In practice, various parties shift between positions of expressed – and possibly genuine– intent to co-operate, and stances of traditional adversarial and tactical manoeuvres.

This is where the meaning of the term 'consultation' again becomes an issue. When people are asked to define this it is usually not because the idea is one that is tremendously difficult to understand; it is because its implementation is potentially elastic and its meaning to different parties contested. At one extreme, consultation, even when required by law, can be tokenistic. For example, companies installing mobile telephone masts are required to 'consult' parties in the vicinity. In practice, many simply post letters of notification and routinely log and effectively ignore the replies. In the employment field, the Regulations define consultation as 'the exchange of views and establishment of dialogue'. Hence, this would seem to require more than the token box-ticking in a critical path of decision-making. But the wording still leaves unclear the stage at which the exchange of views about a proposed action should be initiated. The decision could be almost made – subject to significant new information – or it could be at a stage where numerous options are open. The Court of Appeal has already ruled previously on the matter of consultation and this seems to give weight to a requirement for the latter, more open, interpretation. It said that consultation should occur during the 'formative stage' of a proposal; that adequate information needs to be provided; that adequate time be allowed; and that 'conscientious consideration by an authority' of these responses should be demonstrated. If these four criteria are fulfilled, then consultation should be mean-ingful, and it is more likely to command respect and elicit engagement. Moreover, ultimately, employers may need to justify their consultation policies and practices before the CAC.

The maximum penalty of £75,000 has also occasioned some debate, as some employers might consider this a price worth paying to avoid disclosure in advance of commercial information about a takeover, merger or similar event that has financial implications. Regulation 25(1) holds that an employer may request an information recipient to hold in confidence – a 'protected disclosure'.

The new regulations also create a right to 'reasonable' time off for employee representatives during working time in order to perform information and consultation duties, and for this time to be remunerated at the appropriate hourly rate. There is also a new right to complain to an employment tribunal to enforce these entitlements and there is also added protection from unfair dismissal. Similarly, representatives and negotiating representatives are protected from any 'detrimental' treatment short of dismissal.

Finally, if one goes back full circle to where this discussion started – that is, with the underlying idea of the fundamental purposes of 'involving' employees through information, consultation and other participative means – then the minutiae of the law could be said to be the least important aspects. Ideally, the law is there merely as a stimulus and to provide a minimum basis of rights. But if the new law only triggers a compliance response, then the impact is likely to be limited. Beyond the letter of the law is its spirit, and responding to that spirit will require (as has been noted widely) trust. But, in turn, such trust has to be won, and that will require skilful management. Quite apart from the DTI guidelines which help to interpret the law there are the Advisory, Conciliation and Arbitration Service (ACAS) guidelines which provide valuable advice on processes – the 'good practice' guidelines to help devise effective consultation. These advise on how to provide information, and how to structure and organise consultative committees in practice. But beyond even these *practices* there are some wider strategic management considerations. A number of factors are important, but it is worth notice two in particular.

The first relates to the extent to which, and the ways in which, the senior management team embraces the interrelated ideas of employee voice, partnership, joint problem-solving, and mutual gain. The top team in most organisations is in the best position to set the tone and the expectation. The extent to which they truly buy into the idea of employees adding value through motivated and creative problem-solving will usually be critical. They are in a position to shape operational management action and they can reward or sanction behaviour. Managers usually approach and interpret this kind of issue in terms of 'performance management', 'culture change' or 'values'. But regardless of the label they use, they appreciate that, if it is to be meaningful, it has to come from the top, be role-modelled at the top and be sustained continuously. The second, key issue beyond the question of the legal minima is the issue of training. This concerns not only to the training of employee representatives but also the training and development of managers who need to give information and to consult. Both of these activities involve some skill. Some trade union representatives thought that training was required not only in consultation processes but also in handling, understanding and responding to the information provided – not least of which was financial information. (Chapter 11 in this volume assesses the kind of financial literacy employee representatives might need to have.)

A detailed, real-life example of how one multi-site company employing some 500 financial services workers has constructed a new I&C agreement (see Appendix 2 on page 276). This reveals the details of the agreed company council (termed in this case the 'I&C Forum'. It offers a useful insight into how one company that has given a great deal of thought to the relevant issues, has responded to the new Directive.

Structure of the book

The critical issues identified briefly above are explored in much more depth in the ensuing chapters in this volume. The chapters in Part 2 present the distinctive perspectives and reactions of the influential parties. These include the TUC, the Engineering Employers' Federation (EEF), and the leading independent body, the Involvement and Participation Association (IPA).

Part 3 moves from aspiration and concerns to an examination of the evidence deriving from practice to date. This evidence relates to the types of mechanisms and processes used in practice, and the various performance outcomes achieved. These carefully designed studies, which examine the connections between input variables and outputs, are important stepping stones to the practical issues and dilemmas raised in the following section.

Part 4 of the book moves to a close analysis of the range of options and to a study of the main questions arising. It also seeks to resolve some of these. It ranges from an assessment of alternative ways of informing and consulting and their implications, to a study of the implications for the public sector, for small businesses and for employee representatives.

The purpose of Part 5 is to allow comparison of practice across Europe. There is detailed analysis of the situation in Ireland, which is followed by a wide-ranging overview of practice across the twenty-five EU Member countries. Then the focus narrows again to a more detailed examination of comparative practice concerning information disclosure in Germany, France and the UK.

Part 6 uses two detailed case studies to reveal how information and consultation can be handled and used in practice. In Part 7, a short conclusion highlights some of the major issues arising from the book and points practitioners and policy-makers forward by identifying the main implications for future work.

Appendix 1 offers a decision flowchart which will be of practical use to decision-makers in many organisations. Appendix 2 gives a detailed example of a newly-minted works council (I&C Forum) agreement designed to meet the requirements of the new legislation as a 'pre-existing agreement'.

Note

1   I am grateful to John Purcell for raising this point.

References

Amicus (2004) *Information and Consultation at Work: An Amicus Guide for Members*. London: Amicus.

Beaumont, P. and Hunter, L. (2003) *Information and Consultation: From Compliance to Performance*. London: CIPD.

CIPD (Chartered Institute of Personnel and Development) (2004) *Information and Consultation: A Guide*. Wimbledon: CIPD.

DTI (Department of Trade and Industry) (2002) *High Performance Workplaces: The Role of Employee Involvement in a Modern Economy. A Discussion Paper*. London: DTI.

EU (European Union) (2002) *Directive 2002/14/EC Establishing a General Framework for Informing and Consulting Employees in the European Community*. Brussels: European Union.

Houses of Parliament (2004) *The Information and Consultation of Employees Regulations*. London: Houses of Parliament.

Kelly, J. (2004) 'Social Partnership Agreements in Britain: Labor Cooperation and Compliance', *Industrial Relations: A Journal of Economy and Society* 43(1): 267–92.

Marchington, M. (2001) *Management Choice and Employee Voice*. London: CIPD.

Sako, M. (1998) 'The Nature and Impact of Employee Voice in the European Car Components Industry', *Human Resource Management Journal*, 4(2).

Perspectives of key parties on information and consultation

The chapters in Part 2 represent the views, interpretations and preferences of some of the major stakeholders.

Chapter 2 sets out the analysis made by Sarah Veale on behalf of the TUC. She was one of the key figures who represented the TUC's position during the negotiations with the government and the CBI during the lead-up to the new legislation. The chapter reveals that the TUC is broadly supportive of and endorses the way in which the government adopted a 'partnership' approach. This is an interesting development from the position often traditionally adopted by trade unions, which resisted consultation arrangements and preferred to defend a 'single channel' – namely through collective bargaining as handled exclusively by trade unions. Sarah Veale adopts a pragmatic approach, in tune with changed circumstances. As long as existing negotiating arrangements are safeguarded, the TUC is supportive of the new consultative partnership approach.

In Chapter 3, David Yeandle of the Engineering Employers' Federation (EEF) explains the EEF's position as basically being opposed to legally-enforced frameworks for information and consultation, but in favour of the principle of employee information and consultation. He makes the case that organisations differ so much in their structures, cultures and environments that a single rigid requirement would be inappropriate for many. Hence, as he explains, intense lobbying was undertaken in the run-up to the Directive and he describes the final text of this European Directive as the 'least worst deal' that employers could have realistically hoped to have achieved.

This statement from the EEF emphasis the need for companies to use the flexibility built into the British regulations in order to devise arrangements which best suit their particular needs. Hence the negotiation of 'pre-existing agreements' is urged by the EEF on its member companies. One of the most important points made in this chapter is the observation by David Yeandle that: 'From the discussions that we have had with our members, we think it is unlikely that very many, if any, companies will already have information and consultation arrangements that meet all of the criteria for pre-existing agreements in the Regulations.' This statement makes clear that, despite the flexibility and room for manoeuvre built into the British regulations, there is still enough bite in the regulations to require further action in not just many but seemingly the majority of companies. David Yeandle goes on to clarify a number of useful steps companies are advised to take in order to be in compliance and – equally if not more importantly – to get the most out of the new arrangements.

Chapter 4 sets out the position of the Involvement and Participation Association (IPA). The IPA has subscribed to the general principles of employee involvement and participation for around 100 years. It serves as a training and advisory body to help promote the participative approach. Not surprisingly, therefore, it broadly welcomes the new legislation. The IPA has a belief in both the moral rightness of involvement and in the economic efficacy and necessity, in a modern economy, of taking into account employee voice. Thus the dual merits of the moral case and the business case are central to its position. Equally important, the IPA has ideas and expertise in aspects of implementing information and consultation, and making them work in practice over a sustained period. Its sponsorship of research – both in the form of case studies and in attempts to pin down and measure the performance outcomes, is testimony to its serious intent to find an evidence-based way forward.

2

Information and consultation: a TUC perspective on the key issues

Sarah Veale

The TUC firmly believes that the UK needs to have more high-performance workplaces. To achieve this it is necessary also to have high trust relationships between workers and employers. Hence we support the idea of workplace partnerships. The problem in the UK is the lack of any effective universal workplace institutions that can create a framework for the development of high trust relationships. In April 2005, the UK government introduced the European Community (EC) Directive on Information and Consultation of Employees into UK law. This legislation represents a radical development in the UK context, introducing for the first time a comprehensive statutory framework regulating employee information and consultation issues.

The Directive's 'universal rights' approach establishes elementary representation rights for all employees in the undertakings or establishments concerned, irrespective of union membership or recognition. The Directive therefore presents significant new opportunities to unions to strengthen their influence in unorganised workforces. At the same time, it was essential from the TUC's perspective that the enhanced employee rights provided by the Directive were introduced in a way that avoided any potential for undermining unions where they are recognised, or making recognition more difficult to secure where they are not.

Judging from past records, the government could have been expected to have taken a minimal approach, and simply introduced it more or less as it is drafted, or even amended some existing UK legislation, as they did with the Posted Workers' Directive. Possible candidates in existing legislation would be the Regulations on Collective Redundancies and Transfers, TICER (European Works Councils Regulations) and parts of the Trade Union and Labour Relations Consolidation Act 1992 – for example, on disclosure of information for collective bargaining purposes.

Or the UK government could have taken a much more prescriptive approach, as they did with the Working Time Regulations, and set out in detail how each part of the Directive would apply. Instead they chose a 'social partnership' approach, which was the TUC's preferred mode. The text of the Directive itself is not especially detailed, so the transposition has been key in terms of preparing for the new laws in the workplace. The TUC is anxious to safeguard existing arrangements where they are working well and to use new laws to build on its partnership approach to employers. The best way to ensure that an effective new employment relations settlement is achieved is for the government, employers and unions to view the new legislation as providing great partnership potential, rather than seeing it as a threat. Seeing it as a threat is not a view entirely confined to employers, however; for some in the union movement, the Directive is viewed anxiously as having the potential to undermine existing collective bargaining arrangements or to establish new, non-union structures.

The negotiations on this issue between the 'social partners' (TUC, CBI and the government) began in February 2002 and continued until July 2002. A Framework Agreement was reached which reflected agreements and disagreements between the TUC and the CBI, but it also meant that the subsequent Regulations had broad support across industry.

Significance of the Directive

The Information and Consultation Directive is potentially the most significant piece of employment relations legislation ever to be introduced in the UK. In essence, it will give all employees, in undertakings employing more than 50 people, rights to be informed and consulted systematically, through their elected representatives, on matters affecting their jobs and their future employment prospects. The 1998 Workplace Employment Relations Survey (WERS) shows the impact this could have, even in organised workplaces.

The results of the survey suggest that, in many workplaces, the union role is restricted to handling grievances, discipline, and health and safety issues. The survey also indicated that representatives were present in about a third of British workplaces with ten or more employees, but that in 30 per cent of workplaces covered by a formal recognition agreement there were no workplace representatives. WERS also looked at the views of employers on the scope of the union role on questions of recruitment, selection and work organisation in workplaces with 25-plus employees. Only 3 per cent negotiated on recruitment and selection issues, and only 6 per cent negotiated on staffing levels, redeployment and other work organisation issues.

Two conclusions might be drawn from this data. First, it is evident that the scope of joint regulation has diminished dramatically since 1980. Second, as well as being a boost to worker voice in all workplaces, the introduction of information and consultation rights will enable unions in organised workplaces to address an agenda that has been beyond their reach since the later 1990s. The importance of this cannot be understated. For the full potential of the Directive to be achieved, though, unions will need to commit considerable resources and organisational skills. It is a challenge for unions but, if met, it is a challenge with rich rewards.

Points of concern

There are a number of issues of particular concern to the TUC. The first of these is the scope and interpretation of the legislation: much of this was left to Member States to determine. Employers are obliged to inform on the 'recent and probable development' of the undertaking's or the establishment's activities and economic situation. They are obliged to inform and consult on the situation, structure and probable development of employment and any 'anticipatory' measures envisaged in the event of a threat to employment, and on decisions likely to lead to substantial changes in work organisation or contractual relations. The timing, content and method must be 'appropriate' and must be discussed at the relevant level of management and worker representation. Workers' representatives must be supplied with 'relevant' information by the employer, allowed to formulate their views and to receive a response from their employer. Where work organisation or changes in contracts are at issue the process should be 'with a view to reaching an agreement'.

The UK Regulations apply to 'undertakings' rather than 'enterprises'. This form of words would seem to allow for much greater coverage in the public sector than might otherwise have been the case, but the application in many areas of the public sector remains uncertain. Further, the introduction of the new legislation will be staged, so that it will only apply to undertakings that employ more than 150 people in 2005, then those employing more than 100 in 2007, and finally those employing more than 50 in 2008. Undertakings employing fewer than 50 will not be affected at all by the Directive. The TUC regrets this. Small firms tend to have many more employment relations problems. This may be partly because they are less likely to have human resource departments and are less likely to recognise unions. Small firms have disproportionately high numbers of claims against them in Employment Tribunals. We would argue that the need for Regulations on information and consultation are in fact far greater in small firms. We also regret that the Regulations will only cover 'employees' – that is, those with contracts of employment. Casual workers and those employed through employment agencies will be excluded. The Regulations will also permit employers to count part-time workers as 'half people' for the purposes of calculating the threshold.

An important feature of the UK Regulations is the 'trigger' mechanism. Although the new legislation will require employers to inform and consult systematically with their workforce, in the UK they can do this in whatever way they choose. Indeed, unless employees use the trigger mechanism to complain, employers can choose to do nothing. The trigger mechanism allows a challenge to be made by employees where the employer has failed to set up a system for information and consultation, or has set up one which they do not support. A minimum of 10 per cent of the employees in the undertaking are needed to support the trigger if the challenge is to proceed. The Central Arbitration Committee (CAC) will be the enforcing authority. They will check when the trigger is pulled to ensure that it has the required 10 per cent support. If it does, if there is no system in place, the employer must negotiate a procedure with elected representatives of the workforce. There is a 'default' minimal procedure in the Regulations, though it is open to the parties to negotiate a different procedure. The negotiated procedure must have the support of all the negotiating representatives, or the support of the workforce indicated in a ballot or by means of a petition. The system can be union recognition, with provisions for information and consultation, or could be a mixed system, with some union representation and some non-union. It must be ongoing and 'permanent' in the sense that it cannot be challenged again for three years.

Where there is already an information and consultation system, the employer can opt to hold a further ballot of the workforce. If fewer than 40 per cent support the challenge, it fails. If 40 per cent or more support the challenge, the employer must negotiate a new agreement with elected representatives of the workforce. The TUC supported the concept of a trigger for two reasons. First, it will ensure that if there is a challenge to an existing system that is union supported, or a union agreement, it would have to be supported by a minimum of 10 per cent of the employees. This should prevent mischievous challenges by individual employees who are disgruntled with a union for some reason. In a non-recognised workplace, it would ensure that the union had sufficient support to allow it to negotiate a lasting and workable system.

There is no *explicit* requirement in the Directive that arrangements for information and consultation should be permanent. It is implicit, however, that the arrangements should be general, permanent and statutory. Article 3 suggests that workers' representatives should be able to assess the employer's proposals and have an opportunity to respond to them. It would be difficult to achieve this in practice if there was not some kind of permanent arrangement. Consultation has to take place 'at an appropriate level', which again would need to be determined and established, rather than left to determination each time an issue arose. In Art. 9 (1.A), which deals with transposition issues, reference is made to those member states with neither general, permanent and statutory systems of information and consultation, nor representation.

The Regulations do allow for information and consultation directly with individual employees. The TUC was not happy with this, as it saw such consultation as a potential loophole that could be used to avoid the intent of the Directive, but it was a point which the CBI succeeded in winning during the negotiations. There would have to be agreement with the employees that they wanted individual consultation, as the Directive refers to consultation with *representatives of the workforce*. The TUC believes that the best way of consulting employees is through their elected representatives, though there is no harm in employers providing information directly to employees as well. As the consultation has to be with 'a view to reaching an agreement' it is hard to see how the employer could reach agreement with all the employees on an individual basis alone.

As well as flexibility in terms of the statute, there is provision for voluntary agreements at the appropriate level. Although the TUC is generally relaxed about this where unions are recognised, in some sectors and workplaces where unions are weak, it could encourage employers to do the bare minimum and not take the process seriously. Devising the constituencies, determining the numbers of representatives and conducting the elections should not be under the control of the employer. The Regulations go some way towards ensuring that this is not the case, but there are worries, for example, about those who will supervise the ballots. There is no effective provision to ensure that supervisors will be competent, or fair, or genuinely independent.

An issue on which there was some further difference between the TUC and the CBI was remedies and sanctions. Article 7 of the Directive, which deals with the question of non-compliance, only requires remedies that are 'effective, proportionate and dissuasive'. The TUC believes that the Directive should provide for injunctive relief so that companies can be made to revert to the status quo ante where they have failed to consult properly. This would mean that the employer would have to stop doing whatever it is that they should be consulting on until they have completed the consultation process. For example, if they are proposing to close a site, this would have to wait until the consultation had taken place properly. This is what happens in Belgium and the Netherlands, and it is a much more effective deterrent than a fine. In recent collective redundancies in the UK, companies were castigated publicly for failing to consult their workforce before announcing mass redundancies. In situations where consultation has taken place, it has often been possible to avoid some redundancies or to offset the worst impact on individual workers by providing support packages.

The Regulations do not provide for interventions by the CAC or the courts where there is a failure to consult. Their only enforcement power is to make a declaration that consultation did not take place and impose a fine, which cannot be more than £75,000. For a large undertaking, this would not be an 'effective, proportionate and dissuasive' remedy in the view of the TUC.

There is to be protection in law against detriment or dismissal for those employees who are elected as information and consultation representatives, which is welcome. In addition, the names of those employees who sign a petition supporting a challenge (the trigger) are sent directly to the CAC, who do not have to disclose them to the employer. This will ensure that individual employees are not victimised for challenging the employer.

There are a number of other issues for unions. To comply with European Court of Justice rulings, consultation on collective redundancies and transfers must now be conducted where there is no union recognised. The Information and Consultation Regulations have been devised in such a way as to mesh with the existing laws on collective redundancies and transfers. The employer must consult on probable changes under these Regulations. Once the stage has been reached where the employer is 'proposing' redundancies or a transfer of undertakings, they must consult with the union, where a union is recognised, or other workforce representatives, presumably the information and consultation representatives. In recognised workplaces, these may be the same representatives. Unions will want to ensure that their members are also the information and consultation representatives.

The new legislation could lead to dual or hybrid systems. This may occur where information and consultation processes are conducted with the information and consultation representatives, who may or may not also be union representatives. But collective bargaining, over, for example, pay determination, working hours and so on, may be conducted solely with the recognised union for the employees in their bargaining area. Crucially, the TUC has been advising unions to ensure that the distinction between collective bargaining and consultation remains, so that where employers set up new systems, they do not result in the dissolution or reduction in collective bargaining.

Another issue for unions is the legal enforceability of information and consultation systems set up under the Regulations. Most collective agreements in the UK (other than those few recently imposed by the Central Arbitration Committee under the new union recognition laws) are voluntary and not legally enforceable. To date, unions have favoured this approach. Agreements reached under the new Information and Consultation Regulations will be legally enforceable. This could result in some cases in the information and consultation aspects of otherwise voluntary agreements being legal, but not the rest of the agreement. The TUC is considering the issue of legal enforceability more generally, because some EU Directives, for example the Posted Worker's Directive, do provide for derogations via collective agreements, but these have to be legally enforceable, which in the UK, they are generally not.

An assessment

It is important to see the positive effects of the new laws. For example, the government is currently concerned about the increase in individual employment rights litigation. Establishing formal and permanent consultative mechanisms could encourage the development of better dispute resolution procedures in workplaces. Where the workforce has been involved in the implementation of such procedures, as recommended by ACAS, workers are likely to have more faith in the processes. This could make a considerable difference to the volume of individual litigation.

There are workplaces in the UK where unions have a significant presence, but not enough to seek statutory recognition. These new regulations will provide a means of permanent and formal involvement in such workplaces, which could encourage union growth and then lead on to recognition. It is also the case that far too few employers in the UK currently consult their workforce, even when major changes are planned. Workers today have a rightful expectation that their views on proposed changes will be listened to and respected, even if not acted on.

There are, of course, already various statutory provisions which require employers to inform and consult employees, many deriving from EU law. Until 1994, this process was conducted exclusively through recognised trade unions. However, in 1994, the European Court of Justice ruled that all employees had a right to be informed and consulted, not just those covered by a collective agreement. Consequently, the UK legislation had to be amended to require employers to provide for the election of employees to act as workforce representatives where information and consultation was obligatory, and where there was no collective agreement in place. These representatives would be elected for the sole purpose of informing and consulting on a particular issue – for example, a proposed transfer of engagements. After that process had been completed, they would no longer be representatives (unless the employer decided to retain them).

Little research has been carried out to date into how often employers have established *ad hoc* representation mechanisms for the specific purpose of complying with legislation that requires information and consultation with the workforce. The fundamental weakness in such legislation is that it does not require permanent systems. In practice, it is likely to be very difficult to ensure that employees put themselves forward to be elected as workforce representatives for specific purposes. It is not always easy to persuade union members to become representatives in companies where the union is recognised and where there is paid time off for union duties and the full backing of the union for its representatives. How much more difficult then to persuade them to do it in situations where there is no real support.

The crucial difference with the Information and Consultation legislation is that it will require employers to establish permanent systems, albeit only by law if the 'trigger' is pulled successfully. The question has to be whether there is enthusiasm among the non-unionised workforce to take on the role of being a workforce representative. The other question is whether very many groups of employees will be sufficiently disgruntled about an existing system (or the lack of one) or sufficiently knowledgeable about the new laws to start the trigger process. It may be that in reality it will only be used where a union decides to use it to try to establish a system in a workplace where there is none already in place, or to challenge a weak or employer dominated existing system.

By choosing what is essentially a voluntarist approach to the new legislation, the UK government is upholding the UK's traditions for the voluntary regulation of employment relations. As long as nobody challenges them successfully, employers can use whatever system they see fit for the purposes of compliance with the new laws. There has been no serious suggestion that all undertakings will be obliged to introduce a works council. There is a statutory fallback or default model which would be imposed in cases where the trigger had been pulled successfully and the employer had refused to negotiate or had tried to impose a system. However, if the experience of the default systems used in the statutory recognition provisions and the European Works Councils' legislation is indicative of how such provisions work in practice it may be that there will be few cases where it has to be imposed. In essence, like the recognition legislation, the impact of this new legislation may be largely reflexive.

There is some evidence that employers increasingly are seeing the value of involving their employees in decision making, albeit sometimes through non-union channels. Where this is the case, the new legislation could provide an opportunity to ensure that the process to be used meets with employee approval, stimulates employee involvement and makes a difference to the outcome. From a TUC perspective, once a proper system is established, employees may decide that they want proper independent representation, with expert backup, which they will really only get through a trade union. On the other hand, there is also a possibility that what they already have will satisfy them, making it more difficult for a union to attract members. Similarly, where there is partial union recognition, if the employer decides to provide a system to cover the whole workforce, there are opportunities for the union to extend its influence but also worries that non-union (and free) forms of representation will attract current union members. The union may worry about representing employees in areas where they are not recognised, or working with non-union representatives. They may also worry about collective bargaining and consultation becoming conflated, with non-union representatives becoming involved in collective bargaining. Much will depend on the strength and effectiveness of the union and the attitude of the employer.

There are many issues to be addressed in the coming months and years in the transposition process and in workplaces. These new laws have the potential to transform the employment relations landscape in the UK in a very positive way, as long as employers and unions view them constructively, as an opportunity not a threat. If employers and the government fail to engage constructively in the transposition at national and at workplace level, great opportunities to improve workplace relations and to give UK workers a say in how their work is organised will be wasted and, inevitably, much time and money will be spent pursuing legal challenges. The time, surely, is ripe for effective social partnership and a new employee relations settlement in the UK.

3

An employers' organisation perspective

David Yeandle

A recognition of the contribution that informing and consulting employees can make to improved business performance has been a feature of EEF policy for more than thirty years. In *The Power to Manage – A History of the Engineering Employers' Federation*, published in 1972, Eric Wigham commented that 'at the heart of the new Federation policies is the encouragement of new factory relationships based on shared responsibility'. He then went on to quote from a Federation policy paper of the day that spoke of 'modern thinking [tending] to the view that full consultation is conducive to good industrial relations'.

More than thirty years after the publication of Eric Wigham's book, EEF continues to believe that informing and consulting employees has an important role to play in enhancing business performance. In 2003, EEF published a joint report with the Chartered Institute of Personnel and Development (CIPD) *Maximising Employee Potential and Business Performance – The Role of High Performance Working*. This report stressed that involving employees in decision-making, and undertaking frequent comprehensive communications with employees, are integral elements of the suite of human resources policies organisations need to implement if they are to develop the type of high performance workplace that can lead to enhanced business performance.

There is now a growing volume of evidence from many different sources that informing and consulting employees can improve business performance. It is also EEF's practical experience from talking to members, both large and small, that an increasing number of manufacturers are using a range of methods to inform and consult with their employees. These often comprise a combination of formal and

29

informal arrangements that include direct information and consultation by managers and supervisors with individual employees, as well as indirect information and consultation through a representative structure that generally, but not always, involves union representatives.

One important message EEF members have expressed consistently is that they are firmly of the view that, in order to be successful and add value to both the company and its employees, information and consultation arrangements have to fit coherently with a range of company factors. These include the company's organisational structure, its employee relations history and environment, and its management philosophy and organisational culture.

It is EEF's view that a 'one size fits all' approach to information and consultation arrangements is therefore completely inappropriate. In our experience, from talking to members, it appears that one cannot simply transfer, 'lock, stock and barrel', information and consultation arrangements that work well from one company to another and expect the same results to be achieved, because the environments in which these information and consultation arrangements are operating will inevitably be different. Rather than a 'one size fits all' approach, EEF believes that developing and implementing information and consultation arrangements that will benefit both employers and employees is an aspect of human resource management where 'variety is the spice of life'.

EEF's view that an undifferentiated approach to information and consultation arrangements is inappropriate was one of the main reasons why EEF initially opposed the EU Directive on 'Information and Consultation at National Level'. It was felt that the legislative proposal drawn up by the European Commission, and in particular the attempts by some Members of the European Parliament (MEPs) to make this legislation even more detailed and prescriptive, was the wrong approach.

Fortunately, the extensive lobbying that EEF and other employers' organisations undertook in Brussels over many months was successful in persuading MEPs to withdraw their most damaging amendments to the draft Directive. As a consequence, the final text of this European Directive was probably the 'least worst deal' that employers could realistically have hoped to have achieved. However, the next challenge for employers was to ensure that the UK government took maximum advantage of all the flexibilities in this Directive. In particular, it was felt to be important that domestic legislation did not require EEF members to change the information and consultation arrangements that had served them and their employees well for a number of years.

Now that the Information and Consultation of Employees Regulations 2004 (the Regulations) that implement this European Directive have been published, it is encouraging to see that the Government has adopted a flexible approach. Implementing this legislation on a phased basis with the smaller companies that are covered by it not being affected directly until April 2008 is sensible, as smaller companies will inevitably find it more difficult to cope with this new legislation. EEF also believes that requiring at least 10 per cent of a company's workforce to support a request for the introduction of information and consultation arrangements before this request is formally 'triggered' will ensure that there is a real demand from employees for these arrangements.

More importantly, however, the Regulations provide employers with considerable flexibility in the content and structure of both pre-existing information and consultation agreements, and negotiated information and consultation agreements. This means that both of these types of agreement can be drawn up in a way that meets the requirements of individual companies and their employees, as well as to take into account different organisational structures, employee relations environments and management philosophies. Furthermore, the Regulations ensure that, as EEF had pressed the government to do, a much higher level of employee support than the 10 per cent 'trigger' will be required before any pre-existing information and consultation agreements that meet the legislative requirements will have to be changed.

In advance of the Regulations starting to come into force on 6 April 2005, EEF actively encouraged its member companies to give serious consideration to introducing a pre-existing information and consultation agreement and published a comprehensive practical EEF Guide on the Regulations to assist them. This is not only because of the increasing evidence that information and consultation arrangements can contribute to improved business performance, but also because these pre-existing agreements have some important benefits.

First, while the Regulations require these pre-existing agreements to be in writing, cover all employees, 'set out how the employer will give information to employees or their representatives and seek their views on such information' and be approved by employees, there is considerable flexibility in terms of the content and structure of these agreements. In particular, they enable information and consultation arrangements to be undertaken indirectly through employee representatives and/or directly with individual employees, as well as (provided all employees are covered) allow different arrangements for different parts of an organisation. For example, if a company comprises three manufacturing sites and a small head office, it would be possible for the company's pre-existing information and consultation agreement to comprise indirect information and consultation arrangements through the representatives of all employees for each of the manufacturing sites, and direct information and consultation with all the staff in the head office.

Second, if a company subsequently receives a valid employee request for the introduction of information and consultation arrangements, the company can choose to ballot the whole workforce on whether they want to retain their pre-existing information and consultation agreement, or to have different information and consultation arrangements. The company will only be required to introduce new arrangements if the fairly high hurdle of both a majority of those voting in this ballot and at least 40 per cent of the employees in the company endorse this request for new information and consultation arrangements to be introduced.

Third, the Central Arbitration Committee (CAC), the body with the principal enforcement role for the Regulations, does not have the power to examine the way in which pre-existing information and consultation agreements are operating. However, the CAC does have the power to investigate whether a pre-existing information and consultation agreement meets all the necessary criteria for such agreements, if asked to do so by employees or their representatives after a valid employee request has been made.

Where companies are considering drawing up a pre-existing information and consultation agreement, EEF is recommending that, initially, they should undertake a comprehensive audit of the way in which they currently inform and consult their employees. This includes looking at all their formal and informal information and consultation arrangements as well as the different types of direct and indirect communication arrangements they have within the company. This audit will enable them to see whether their existing arrangements meet all the criteria for pre-existing information and consultation agreements as set out in the Regulations.

From the discussions EEF has had had with its members, it is thought to be unlikely that very many, if any, companies will already have information and consultation arrangements in place that meet all the criteria for pre-existing agreements in the Regulations. For example, while a number of companies will probably have detailed information and consultation arrangements for employees who are covered by collective bargaining agreements, in EEF's experience, very few, if any, of these companies will also have information and consultation arrangements for the rest of their workforce so that, as the Regulations require, all their employees are covered.

For the relatively few companies that already have comprehensive information and consultation arrangements covering all their employees, it is likely that these are arrangements that the company has introduced of its own volition. In these circumstances, it is EEF's experience that there has rarely been, as the Regulations require, any formal employee support expressed for these arrangements. Finally, although a company's information and consultation arrangements may well have been written down when they were first introduced, there is always the possibility that, with the passage of time, the arrangements no longer reflect accurately what is happening in practice, for a number of reasons.

As a result, once companies have undertaken an audit of their current information and consultation arrangements, they will probably find that they will have either to make some changes to their existing arrangements – to ensure that they meet all the criteria for pre-existing agreements that are set out in the Regulations – or to draw up new arrangements. In the former case, this may require companies to seek formal employee endorsement for their existing arrangements covering all their employees, or to extend their existing arrangements to cover a small group of employees who, for one reason or another, are not currently covered by them.

In order to assist EEF members who want to modify their existing information and consultation arrangements, or to introduce new arrangements, EEF's Guide on the Regulations contain a 'model' information and consultation agreement that meets the criteria for pre-existing agreements that are set out in the Regulations. In line with our view that information and consultation arrangements have to fit coherently with other company factors to be successful and improve business performance, this 'model' agreement cannot, however, be used by simply putting the company's name on it. Instead, the 'model' agreement contains a number of clauses covering the issues that EEF considers should be included in such an agreement but, very importantly, it is then left to individual companies to finalise the detailed text of each clause, ideally in conjunction with one of EEF's experienced advisers, in a way that meets the specific requirements of their organisation.

So far, much of the debate about the implementation of the Regulations has been about the structure and, to a lesser extent, the content of information and consultation arrangements. The debate about the structure of information and consultation arrangements has focused largely on whether these arrangements should take place at the 'undertaking' (that is, the company) level or at the 'establishment' (that is, the operational unit) level, as well as about the relationship between information and consultation arrangements and, where they exist, a company's collective bargaining arrangements with trade unions. Discussions about the content of information and consultation arrangements have largely been focused on how these new Regulations interface with existing legislation requiring employers to consult employees and their representatives on specific issues such as collective redundancies and business transfers.

While these issues of structure and content are important, it is rather disappointing, but perhaps not all that surprising given the relatively early stage of many companies' experience of information and consultation arrangements, that there has so far been relatively little debate about the process of information and consultation arrangements. However, in the longer term it is the process of information and consultation arrangements, namely the way in which management and employee representatives behave when they are undertaking information and consultation, that will be one of the most important factors in determining whether these arrangements are a success and operate in a way that enables employers and employees to gain real tangible benefits from them.

It is through the process of information and consultation arrangements that the trust between management and employee representatives, which is so vital if these benefits are to be gained, can really be developed. In all organisations, people will inevitably have some preconceptions about the likely behaviour of others based on their past behaviour. For example, there may be an understandable concern among some senior and middle managers that introducing information and consultation arrangements might undermine what they feel is 'management's right to manage'. In companies where trade unions are already recognised, managers may also be concerned that extending information and consultation arrangements to a wider group of employees may create the opportunity for trade unions to recruit members in different parts of the organisation, and therefore create pressure for collective bargaining arrangements to be extended. In contrast, there are some trade unions that will see information and consultation arrangements as a potential threat to their established collective bargaining role. This may then be demonstrated either by resistance to becoming involved in information and consultation arrangements and/or by a reluctance to sit down alongside non-trade-union representatives in information and consultation meetings.

These potential problems will be faced by many organisations and inevitably it will take a lot of time, patience, determination and careful planning to address them and build up the necessary degree of trust between management and employee representatives for the benefits of information and consultation arrangements to occur. In many circumstances, it will probably only be when some difficult and potentially divisive issues have been tackled successfully through information and consultation arrangements that all parties will start to see the real benefits that can be achieved by them.

EEF has identified some important issues that it feels will need to be considered carefully and addressed by employers if they are to obtain the tangible business benefits that EEF believes can come from effective information and consultation arrangements. This is based on EEF's extensive experience of advising a range of companies – both large and small – on implementing, modifying and operating information and consultation arrangements.

First, the objectives of information and consultation arrangements should be set out clearly so that all those involved in them – management, employee representatives and employees – have a common understanding of why these arrangements have been introduced, and what they are seeking to achieve. For example, it is important to ensure that everyone understands what is, and what is not, meant by 'consultation', as this is a word that can often be open to different interpretations. Ensuring that there is a common understanding of the objectives of information and consultation from the start will help to minimise the chances that some people will have unrealistic expectations of what can be achieved which, if they are not realised, may create disappointment or frustration.

Second, it is important that the issues that will be the subject of information and consultation are spelt out clearly, including, for example, whether these arrangements will cover health and safety issues as well as matters relating to collective redundancies and business transfers. Equally important, the issues on which there will *not* be information and consultation should also be identified clearly. These are likely to include matters relating to individual employees and, where collective bargaining arrangements exist, issues that are the subject of negotiations between the company and its recognised trade unions. Based on EEF members' practical experience, it is probably advisable for companies to start with a relatively 'narrow' information and consultation agenda and allow this agenda to broaden naturally as trust between management and employee representatives develops, and their confidence in the value of these arrangements grows.

Third, the role of the company's senior management will be critical, and their management style will have an important bearing on whether information and consultation arrangements are successful. They will need to demonstrate that they are prepared to enter into a meaningful dialogue with employee representatives, and take properly into account any views that these representatives express. They will also need to appreciate that the introduction of information and consultation arrangements will inevitably have an impact on the way they run their business and take decisions. Furthermore, the senior management team will need to demonstrate that they are genuinely committed to these information and consultation arrangements because, if they are not, it is likely that employees will notice this, and it may lead them to press for alternative arrangements by making a formal employee request for information and consultation under the Regulations.

Fourth, employee representatives will need to be aware of their new roles and responsibilities in the company's information and consultation arrangements because, for many of them, this is likely to be a new experience or, if they are trade union representatives, one that is different from their previous experienced. For example, they will need to demonstrate to management that they are not coming to information and consultation meetings with a personal or trade union agenda but that they are there to represent and articulate the views and concerns of the employees who are their constituents.

Fifth, those companies that already recognise trade unions for some of their employees will potentially have to face issues related to tackling the interrelationship between trade union and non-trade union representatives. While some companies may want to have separate information and consultation arrangements for their unionised and non-unionised employees, others will choose to have common arrangements for all their employees. In the latter case, this means they will want trade union representatives and non-trade-union representatives to sit down together to discuss issues jointly with management. Over the years, this has often been a tricky issue for companies to tackle and, while the TUC has been making the right noises and encouraging union representatives to sit alongside non-trade-union representatives, we know from the practical experience of some EEF companies that there will inevitably be local difficulties caused by, for example, personality clashes and the desire to 'settle old scores'. However, this problem will be made more difficult for companies to resolve satisfactorily if local trade union representatives receive instructions from the leadership of any individual unions not to work alongside non-trade union representatives.

Sixth, one of the key issues identified by employers, trade unions and the government during the lengthy consultation exercise on the Regulations as being vital for achieving effective information and consultation arrangements, was training. This was seen to be important both when these arrangements are established and, thereafter on an ongoing basis. Training was also felt to be important for both employee representatives and management; indeed, this is probably an area where joint training can be valuable as, through this, other benefits such as improved interpersonal relationships can be achieved.

The training that is necessary for successful information and consultation involves training on both 'hard' and 'soft' issues. As far as the former is concerned, this involves training in, for example, financial issues and the business environment in which the company is operating, so that there is a common understanding of the framework within which information and consultation takes place. The latter involves training in interpersonal skills, problem-solving and ways of working together that will help to improve the behaviour of all those who participate in information and consultation arrangements.

Seventh, handling confidential issues within information and consultation arrangements is one of the issues about which companies often express genuine concern. EEF's practical experience from advising companies is that this is an issue that should be discussed openly by management and employee representatives before the need to handle a confidential issue has occurred. Employers should make it very clear that they consider information that is being provided to employee representatives during information and consultation meetings has to be treated on a confidential basis, and that there is no misunderstanding about this. However, it is important that employers are selective about what they regard as confidential information because, if they argue that most information is confidential and cannot be disclosed by employee representatives, this will inevitably be seen as implying a lack of trust in the representatives and therefore potentially undermining the benefits of the information and consultation arrangements.

An integral element of EEF's 'model' information and consultation agreement is an individual confidentiality agreement setting out how confidential issues should be handled by all those involved in information and consultation arrangements, and the implications for them if this is not followed. EEF's advice to member companies that make use of this individual confidentiality agreement is that serious consideration should be given to having the agreement signed by both management and employee representatives, so they can all be seen to be committed to treating confidential issues in the same way.

Eighth, it is important for a clear distinction to be drawn between information and consultation arrangements and any negotiations that take place between the company and trade union or employee representatives. This can often be as difficult for management as it is for representatives, with both of them sometimes being unsure whether they are wearing an 'information and consultation hat' or a 'negotiating hat' in a meeting. This can also be a more difficult issue for British companies than for companies in many other European countries because of the decentralised nature of the UK's pay bargaining system. Whereas in many British companies the same members of management and employee representatives will be involved in both pay negotiations and information and consultation arrangements, in countries such as Germany, where national or sectoral pay bargaining is still the norm, those involved in pay bargaining within individual companies will not usually also be involved in information and consultation arrangements.

Finally, information and consultation arrangements should be treated as any other management process and should therefore be the subject of regular review and evaluation. Management, employee representatives and employees should be involved in assessing regularly whether the company's information and consultation arrangements are working effectively and achieving the objectives that were set for them. If they are not, discussions should take place with all those involved to determine what remedial action is needed to address these concerns.

References

CIPD/EEF (2003) *Maximizing Employee Potential and Business Performance: The Role of High Performance Working*. London: CIPD/EEF.

EEF (2005) *Information and Consultation: A Practical Guide to the Law*. London: EEF.

Wigham, E. (1972) *The Power to Manage: A History of the Engineering Employers Federation*. London: Macmillan.

4

The IPA perspective

Willy Coupar and Robert Stevens

Sharing the challenge of information and consultation

The EU Directive on informing and consulting with employees has been on the agenda since the early 1990s. Strong pressure from the European Commission and the loss of the blocking majority in the Council of Ministers, coupled with high profile closures and redundancies at Rover, Vauxhall (General Motors) and Corus eventually forced the government to implement the regulations in the UK.

Employers differ in their opinions about the effectiveness of legislation in this area, and many are hostile to such a course of action. Much of the UK government's opposition stemmed from this scepticism. There are differences of opinion within the union community as well. Some see it as a threat to collective bargaining, and others as a chance to access sectors previously closed to them.

The Involvement and Participation Association (IPA) has, in the main, welcomed the Directive. Employers can gain from informing and consulting with employees about business issues. The workforce too can benefit from influencing thinking in the organisation and having a voice in decision-making.

With members in most sectors of the UK private, public and not for profit companie's, the IPA has a considerable body of knowledge of how information and consultation works in practice. This evidence has been built up since the 1980s, during which time the IPA has identified a variety of mechanisms and approaches for use in unionised and non-union workplaces. The IPA is exposed through its membership to all shades of opinion about information and consultation, varying from arch-unitarists to those who hold a strong pluralist perspective.

Much of the debate about information and consultation is bedevilled by confusion as to what the terms mean. Information and consultation are not one and the same: although interrelated, there are two distinct processes involved here. *Information sharing* means disclosure by management of relevant information to employees. It is essentially a 'top down' exercise, although upward flows of information are found as well. *Consultation*, assumes that employees are already in possession of the relevant information. 'Consultation does not remove the right of managers to manage – they must still make the final decision – but it does impose an obligation that the views of employees will be sought and considered before decisions are taken' (ACAS 2003: 4–5).

Consultation also is more than two-way communication: it does not mean telling employees what managers have already decided and inviting their reaction. Consultation is a mechanism enabling employees to voice their opinions freely and frankly. Managers need to be prepared to modify the actions they are proposing in the light of employees' views. They do not have to agree and can indeed turn down the response of employees, but they do need to demonstrate openness and flexibility.

Distinguishing consultation from negotiation is also difficult. When managers consult, the expectation is that they will seek where possible to reach an understanding around the context in which decisions are taken and the basis on which they are taken. The distinction between negotiation and consultation 'with a view to reaching agreement' as set out in the Regulations has raised eyebrows among employers and trade unionists, though for different reasons, but these processes can be kept separate and should not be used as an excuse for doing nothing.

The right to information and consultation already has statutory backing in the UK in specific areas. There are the rights to be consulted over collective redundancies, the transfer of undertakings, and health and safety. In some cases the application of the working time directive, company pension scheme alterations and workplace training are also covered.

Underlying perspectives

Within the pluralist framework, employee voice is seen as a right. It has a moral justification linked closely to the idea that employees are entitled to the free expression of their views. It is, in effect, a right of citizenship. It is thus enshrined within a framework of legislative entitlement and is not *per se* dependent for its validity on any business benefit.

Within a unitarist framework, the validity of these processes is grounded in that concept of adding value to the organisation. Informing staff – that is, the communication element – is taken as a given. It is widely agreed that there are business benefits from having a well-informed workforce who have good two-way communication with their employer. There is also a place for activities such as task groups or joint problem-solving that enable employees to have an effective impact on the way that work is organised. These consultative activities are valued because they are believed to create better solutions, and help to get more buy-in to outcomes.

Guest and Peccei's (1998) detailed investigation of IPA members found that the combined use of direct and representative participation, together with an emphasis on job design and a focus on quality, produced the most positive outcomes for all the partners. In the opinion of both managers and employee representatives, the best outcomes came where there was an approach that combined both philosophies.

Additionally, it is clear from the case studies carried out by the IPA that in practice the reality of information and consultation is both complex and fluid. At different times one process melds into the other. Different organisations will value and emphasise one element of the process over another. This reflects the culture of the workplace. A service-sector employer, with a strong culture of direct involvement, will approach representative consultation as an extension of that cultural stand-point. That will be very different from an NHS Trust with seventy years of Whitleyism behind it. Similarly, a unionised workplace with a long history of collective relationships will approach continuous improvement activity in a very different way from a retailer with no unions present. The words they use may be the same, but what they signify will be very different.

The case for employee voice cannot rest solely on either social justice or the requirements of legislation. It needs to be made on both counts – that is, the employee as citizen and the business benefits of consultation. The knowledge and experience of employees is often superior to that of management. The question is 'How best can this be tapped into?'

Information, consultation and high performance

Information and consultation has an important place in creating modern high-performance workplaces. High performance demands a vision based on differenti-ation and continuous improvement in the quality of goods or services provided to customers that takes a strategic approach to people management, work organisation and employee involvement (Stevens 2003). The Department of Trade and Industry put it this way:

> Modern, high performance workplaces ... build on the simple insight that individuals are more likely to give of their best if they feel valued and are given the opportunity to contribute their ideas; and that people who are well-prepared for change can help to intro-duce it and thereby help secure employment within the business. (DTI 2002: 13)

Searching the contents of the 'black box' that is our understanding of the relation-ship between people management and performance, reveals that employees must have the ability, motivation and opportunity to participate (Purcell *et al.*: 2003) and a large number of workplace practices have been identified as contributors to high performance in the course of research.

Guest (2000) identifies eighteen practices, and Thompson (2002) reveals over thirty. Not all are present or as important in every organisation, and researchers have learnt to live with a contingent approach, or what practitioners call 'good practice', rather than hard-and-fast definitions.

Thompson (2002) identifies three distinct but related groups of practices:

- high involvement practices, which create greater opportunities for employee involvement;
- human resource practices, which help build skill levels, motivation and ability; and
- employee relations practices, which can help build trust, loyalty and identity with the organisation (2002: 17).

And Ashton and Sung (2002: 109) present them as four dimensions or bundles:

- work design and employee involvement practices – for example, multi-skilling, quality circles, TQM, teamworking and self-directed teams;
- performance and training practices – for example, appraisal, personal development plan, job rotation/cross training, mentoring, and training for trainers;
- reward practices – for example, group-based compensation, profit sharing and employee share ownership; and
- communication- and information-sharing practices – for example, regular individual/team meetings, consultative committees and staff attitudes surveys.

'There is now evidence of a robust link between [high performance work practices], productivity and profitability' they claim (Ashton and Sung 2002: 17). However, intuition rather than causal relations drives much of the 'good practice' organisations are developing.

Towards high performance

Most versions of high-performance working give 'teamworking' and 'joint problem-solving' a pivotal role in establishing effective direct employee engagement. Allied to this is the development of 'learning organisations', and in particular the development of 'formal' and 'informal' learning opportunities and the utilisation of employees' skills, knowledge and experience.

Research shows that the incidence of groups of employees set up to 'solve specific problems or discuss aspects of performance or quality' was almost twice as great in large workplaces than small ones, and more likely to be found in workplaces with a 'personnel specialist' and/or 'an integrated employee development plan' and 'in workplaces with recognised unions' (Cully *et al.* 1999: 66). While this does not establish a causal relationship, it indicates that the use of 'bundles' of employee relations and human resources practices, including representative information and consultation, are associated with increased direct employee participation.

There is a need for more case study examples of high-performance working from a range of employment sectors. In particular, from the perspective of informing and consulting staff, there is an important debate to be had about *how* indirect and direct forms interact to produce benefits for all the stakeholders concerned.

A key role for information and consultation will be in developing a culture in which employees are motivated and given the opportunity to participate in team-work and joint problem-solving activities. Allied to this is the need to examine the extent to which employees are engaged, by assessing the opportunities for skill development available, the way in which skills are acquired, and the extent to which they are utilised (Butler *et al.* 2004).

High performance and employee voice

The values of the UK Work Organisation Network (UKWON), a network of institutions, practitioners and individuals researching and developing new ways of organising work, state that where there is the opportunity for creativity and participation, new approaches to work organisation stimulate learning and innovation. 'High quality of work life, therefore, becomes central to the success of any enterprise – with benefits in terms of organisational effectiveness and stability of employment' (UKWON 2002: 2).

Information and consultation has a key role in ensuring that teamwork and increasing autonomy do not lead to unnecessary insecurity or stress for employees. However, according to the TUC, 'the notion ... that an exclusive focus on individual employee involvement is a recipe for success' or that the main purpose of such practices should be to align worker's aspirations with those of the organisation 'undervalues the important role that workers' representatives can play in testing the logic of management proposals' (TUC 2002: 4).

Concepts of citizenship

The 'Employee as Citizen' argument starts from the premise that the individual's role at work and his/her role as a citizen are inextricably linked. Employee consultation is legitimate because it extends the voice of the citizen into the place of work.

A voice at the workplace means that workers have the opportunity, and indeed the right, to:

- have ideas, proposals and policies explained to them;
- ask questions and get answers to those questions;
- be entitled to have explanations about particular courses of action or decisions, including those where the answer is 'no'; and
- influence potential outcomes, and in particular where those outcomes will have some direct impact on them.

Ideas about workplace citizenship underpin the pluralist model of relations at work. This philosophy runs through the information and consultation directive and echoes the Nobel laureate Joseph Stiglitz, who wrote:

> We care about the kind of society we live in. We believe in democratic processes. These must entail open dialogue and broadly active civic engagement, and require that individuals have a voice in the decisions that affect them, including economic decisions. Economic democracy is an essential part of a democratic society (Stiglitz 2002: 304)

Good information and consultation processes need to reflect citizenship as well as business imperatives. As citizens, the views of employees are legitimate, both when they are aligned with those of the employer and when they are divergent. It is argued that, 'Workers continue to be citizens even after they have crossed the employer's threshold' (Coats 2003: 2).

Employee voice is also a vital element in the process through which decisions are legitimated. Legitimacy is the process by which a course of action is accepted by the workforce as being the right thing to do. This does not mean that everyone agrees with the action being taken; it does, however, mean that the outcome has been accepted. This is more likely if it is arrived at in a fair and transparent way. Participants may not like the outcome, but because their views were listened to they will go along with it.

The British workplace representation and participation survey carried out in 2001 asked a sample of 1,300 workers whether they wanted an employee voice at the workplace. It also asked them what kind of voice they wanted, and for what purpose.

The survey found that 'the majority of British workers want a greater say in workplace decisions that affect their lives. Both union and non-union workers want to resolve issues collectively' (Diamond and Freeman 2001: 3). It also observed that non-unionised workers (82 per cent in the private sector) are equivocal about the best vehicle for delivering this, but that 'most British workers are favourably inclined to works councils and want to see regular meetings of elected employee representatives with management' (ibid.: 4).

The legitimacy of employee consultation is crucially put to the test in a redundancy or closure situation. Organisations with good representative consultation are able to deal with these difficult scenarios better than those without them. In one company, plant closures were carried out over several years in areas of the country where jobs were hard to find, with no disruption. The business challenges had been shared for some time beforehand, and ways to address the loss of jobs, when they arose, had also been addressed comprehensively at an early stage. When it came to implementation, the closures and redundancies were carried out through joint working groups (IPA 1998).

The directive goes to the heart of the unitarist versus pluralist debate. For human resource (HR) managers wedded to a unitarist model, the challenge is 'How do we let go?' Having complete control of communication, and by implication the value system within the organisation, minimises the risk of discordant messages, open disagreement and conflict. These risks may be viewed as too much to contemplate for some employers.

A pluralist model means that there can be real debate with the employee stakeholder, and the employee's right to express an opinion is not dependent on demonstrating added value to the business. It is about recognising their right to be heard at their place of work, and their entitlement to an intelligent response (Coats 2003: 6).

The work the IPA has carried out in its case studies shows that this mutuality of interest is often understood intuitively. However, it is rarely articulated consciously. As one senior professional summed it up in a memorable phrase: 'as an organisation we want to be making our decisions with the voice of our workforce ringing in our ears'. The reception to what you say will depend on what is said, how you say it and what impact it will have on the performance of the organisation.

Implementing information and consultation

Whether or not employees 'pull the trigger', the content of the UK regulations has an important role in setting the context for implementing information and consultation within organisations. While neither the Directive nor the Regulations explicitly require it, the implication is that organisations should introduce a permanent 'standing body' or 'works council' arrangement.

As stated by the IPA, 'The biggest issue facing organisations who are committed to informing and consulting staff is how to safeguard existing arrangements' (IPA 2003c: 4). The arrangements in many organisations have evolved organically over a number of years, and organisations should not feel obliged to assume an information and consultation straitjacket in order to 'comply'.

The reality is that information and consultation is both complex and fluid, and the IPA has long supported a model of employee involvement and participation that involves a mix of mechanisms. The rationale for this is abundantly clear from the IPA's case studies. Indeed, the worst thing that could happen is that a compliance mentality becomes the dominant theme, when the more important questions are what works well, and why.

Nevertheless, the IPA recognises that the Regulations have an important role to play in raising the standard of employee information and consultation in a great many organisations (particularly in small, non-union workplaces and the private sector), where employers pay little or no attention to the views of employees. Direct consultation with individuals and groups is to be encouraged, but should be balanced by the concern that consultation is genuine, that it is not just a cascade of management information, and that employees' views are actively sought and considered.

Above all, training and guidance go hand in hand if information and consultation is to achieve its ultimate goal in changing the behaviour of employees, representatives and management. Commitment from the top of the organisation is a vital signal to other managers that information needs to become more open and transparent, and consultation more meaningful. As such, there is a need for the mechanisms of information and consultation to be permanent rather than *ad hoc*, if they are to achieve a level of consistency at which behaviour change becomes self-sustaining.

Representative consultation

For non-union organisations, the perceived need to 'comply' with the regulations leads many to set up representative arrangements. Creating 'fit' between new and existing information and consultation arrangements will be a key concern for practitioners, as will the apparent apathy of employees and managers towards such arrangements. They are also concerned that trade unions will try to take advantage of the consultative machinery in order to gain influence within the organisation.

The regulations are certainly an opportunity for trade unions, and the IPA encourages them to view the Regulations in this light. However, in unionised organisations, even where existing negotiating arrangements are working well, few will currently satisfy the requirements of a pre-existing agreement under the regulations, either in terms of coverage or in setting out 'how the employer is to give information to the employees or their representatives and to seek their views on such information' (Regulation 8(1)(d) of the Information and Consultation of Employees Regulations 2004).

'Coverage' and 'representativeness' are the new watchwords, particularly where union density is low (ACAS suggests a guideline of less than 30 per cent). Trade unions are already under pressure to reconsider their status as the sole channel through which employees are represented for the purpose of information and consultation.

With time and training, directly elected employee representatives can become active and capable in their representative capacity. Representative constituencies are another important development, and while representative Puritanism is to be avoided, particularly when used as a veil for undermining union influence, trade unionists should engage in representative elections and can learn a lot by emulating the relationship effective employee representatives can establish with their constituencies.

In a later section we discuss some of the practical difficulties in distinguishing consultation from negotiation, and propose a solution. Nevertheless, trade unions understandably fear their specific role as negotiators could become watered down by the introduction of non-union representatives and a broader consultative agenda.

One option is to establish a parallel consultative forum or committee, as the Peabody Trust, a London based housing association, has done (IPA 2002a). This organisation separates the processes of negotiation and consultation between a union-only joint negotiating committee; an intermediate body of employee and trade union representatives for statutory consultation; and a consultative staff forum. These arrangements have enabled the Trust to keep information, consultation and negotiation separate.

The IPA has been at the forefront of supporting 'hybrid' or dual-channel arrangements involving union and non-union representatives alongside or parallel with one another. These arrangements seem to work well, especially as in many cases non-union employees belong to occupational groups for which no union has negotiating rights. 'Trade unions have also found that their position has not been weakened – indeed, because of their training and experience, their representatives often assume a leadership role' (IPA 2001: 10).

Keeping consultation and negotiation separate also helps to prevent more adversarial negotiating techniques from dominating the consultative process. Some commentators also suggest that separate arrangements could save time and duplication where negotiation takes place at the level of the bargaining unit and consultation is conducted at an undertaking level (Hall et al. 2002).

However, some organisations, including BMW Hams Hall (IPA 2003b) and Abbey (IPA 2004a) have been happy to combine consultation and negotiation within the same arrangements. Indeed, as we shall show later, joint consultation and negotiating machinery has ultimately resulted in union and management adopting an entirely consultative relationship at the United Welsh Housing Association (IPA 2004c), albeit at an advanced level.

Employee voice

Until the regulations came into force, the UK and the Republic of Ireland were unique among the original fifteen European Union member states covered by the text of the directive in not having a 'general, permanent and statuary system' of information and consultation or employee representation at the workplace (EC Directive 2002/14/EC).

Most workplaces already adopt a range of direct information-sharing practices. Indeed, repeated Workplace Employee Relations Survey (WERS) results indicate that 'systematic use of the management chain', 'regular newsletters distributed to all employees', 'regular meetings between management and workforce' or a 'suggestion scheme' have all become more common between 1980 and 1998, while the presence of workplace-level joint consultative committees has declined overall (Cully et al. 1999).

This is qualified by an increase in joint consultation in the private sector since 1990. Surveys conducted by the Labour Research Department in 2002 and 2004 also suggest an increase in the level of representative information and consultation, and it will be interesting to see whether the new WERS (to be published in 2005) will detect any change in the frequency of representative arrangements.

Perhaps the most important point to make in this respect is that representative arrangements need not undermine the unity of employees within an organisation, indeed, representation enables the workforce to speak with a single voice, and many representative arrangements are designed with this in mind.

Box 4.1   B&Q

The multi-tiered 'Grass Roots' information and consultation framework at the retail chain B&Q (IPA 2003b), grandly reflects this desire to give a voice to all employees. Day, night and management colleagues are represented in every store by independently elected employee representatives (supervised by the IPA). Store representatives nominate one from among themselves to attend regional meetings of between five and twelve stores, who in turn nominate their own representative to divisional level meetings. A national Grass Roots meeting, consisting of one employee representative from each of the six divisional forums plus two management representatives, is the highest level in the framework.

The Grass Roots framework provides a 'bottom-up' mechanism through which employees can raise issues and receive feedback, either directly from their representative or via 'Grass Roots – Your Questions Answered', a printed pamphlet circulated to all staff at their home addresses following each national meeting.

Similarly, when the Peabody Trust (IPA 2002a), established a single-tier representative staff council, its role was to improve internal communications between its diffuse workforce and diverse organisational structure. Council members, as the elected staff representatives are called, are responsible for the development of formal communication channels, seeking the views of staff, providing support and advice on the Trust policies, and feedback to their constituencies.

Developing an information and consultation culture

Some people argue that too much emphasis is placed on the structures and processes of information and consultation, and not enough on the necessary organisational culture. The IPA's experience is very clear: 'Structures and processes are necessary for effective information and consultation – without them too much depends on personalities' (IPA 2001: 19).

The principle and practice of information and consultation has the potential to replace traditional 'command and control' ways of working with a more open and engaging culture in which teamwork, problem-solving and learning prosper. As the head of manufacturing at the Atomic Weapons Establishment (AWE) explains: 'we needed a cultural change. We did not want it to be a formal arrangement involving senior managers and union officials, which we would have to drive down through the organisation' (IPA 2002b).

Over 200 autonomous continuous improvement groups have resulted, but these have required co-ordination by local facilitators and a multi-tiered framework of arrangements extending up to the board and trade unions at company level. Indeed, the success of the bottom-up approach has left the supporting structures with some catching up to do.

Research also suggests that direct arrangements are more widespread than representative forms. However, a combination of arrangements 'is more commonly associated with various enhanced and positive measures of perceived (by management) organisational performance' (CIPD 2003).

Box 4.2   Nottinghamshire Healthcare NHS Trust

At the Nottinghamshire Healthcare NHS Trust (IPA 2004b), robust collective structures, formal agreements with the recognised trade unions and commitment from the top of the organisation have been the vital first steps in developing a new approach to the involvement of front line staff in the work of the Trust and improvements in the quality of care provided to patients.

The Trust and unions worked with the Department of Trade and Industry's Partnership at Work Fund to establish an ongoing programme of workshops, open to all employees. The workshops are an opportunity for employees to share information and opinions, and engage in informal consultation on a range of issues including:

- Trust-wide policy issues, such as organisational change, effective line-management, self-managed team working, leadership/management practices and internal communications;
- Department of Health polices, such as the NHS plan, national service frameworks, and improving working lives;
- service delivery issues, such as patient and carer involvement, clinical governance, crisis resolution and promoting mental health; and
- employment relations' issues, such as the agenda for change, equal opportunities and performance management.

Typical attendance is between 40 and 60 people. The workshop programme is co-ordinated by a small joint committee and an evaluation report is sent to the chief executive, who also often attends the meetings. The workshops have succeeded because they openly address the key issues of concerns to employees, while effective employee-side representation ensures that feedback is a priority.

Out of the workshop initiative, a cultural change has begun, resulting in more open relationships between management and employees as well as more employee involvement and autonomous working. A management development programme has also been implemented in order to help managers learn to let go of old-fashioned ways of working and support greater employee discretion and involvement in decision-making.

The regulations do not require that organisations replace existing direct information and consultation mechanisms with representative arrangements. Rather, organisations should consider how their existing arrangements can be improved and strengthened, and representative mechanisms should been seen as complementary and reinforcing to direct forms of information disclosure and consultation.

Measuring I&C and performance

The association between HR practices and organisational performance is widely accepted, but there are fewer studies that have examined the relationship between information, consultation and performance. Little work has been done on the specific question of the impact of representative processes, both on information sharing and, in particular, representative influence over decision-making, on the bottom line. This makes it difficult to identify, let alone measure, the benefits of the representative role in the workplace.

Even in organisations with well-established unions or consultative councils, these links are rarely made. Indeed, Guest and Peccei (1998) found that 'works councils' have 'no impact on reported levels of direct or indirect participation. Engagement with representatives is seen largely as a way to foster a good industrial relations climate in the workplace and little else. 'We do it because we have to' is the likeliest explanation.

Line managers remain sceptical of the value of involving representatives, and where possible, they avoid it. If they involve staff to improve performance they are most likely to favour individual or direct participation. Forms of indirect or representative participation are not seen as being linked to performance and are therefore unlikely to be pursued voluntarily as a part of a business improvement plan.

As well as recognising managerial scepticism, other difficulties need to be noted when measuring the effects of informing and consulting the workforce:

(i) it is difficult to isolate the effects of one practice, such as representative consultation, from the many other influences involved in organisational change; and

(ii) the ways in which practices and processes are managed can be just as important – indeed, more important, than the substance of the practice.

These points are borne out in a survey conducted by the IPA during 2004. The survey explored the dynamics of social dialogue, asking respondents to comment on the benefits or disadvantages of consulting with reps, and the impact of that on workplace performance.

The survey was conducted with a number of organisations known to the IPA as having devoted resources to improving information and consultation, and representing the high end of 'good practice'. They were asked about what had happened in their organisation and how they measured the effectiveness of what they were doing. The research looked at the following areas:

- improved knowledge and understanding among

    (a) representatives; and
    (b) the workforce more generally;

- acceptance of the need for change and legitimating that change;
- feedback from the workforce;
- increased participation in consultative and information-sharing activities across the workforce;
- reputation of the organisation, both internally and externally;
- problem-solving activities;
- team development among reps and the workforce; and
- conflict resolution and behaviour of participants.

The IPA survey did not set out to find direct and immediate benefits from working with representatives feeding directly to the bottom line. Rather, it sought to identify what some of those indirect outcomes of joint consultation might be.

The key findings suggested that:

- indirect performance benefits are mediated through changes in attitude and behaviour. They do not stem from information and consultation practices themselves;
- consultation is viewed positively when it brings an employee-relations benefit. Better relations with unions or representatives help to legitimise change or may create a better understanding of key business information among the team of representatives themselves;
- consulting with reps is not seen to have much impact on the day-to-day organisational process. Its value is to provide greater legitimacy to changes in work practices and thus less conflict about where the organisation is going; and
- organisational performance is being enhanced through an elimination of resistance rather than business benefits derived directly from the consultation process.

Even among those organisations we would associate with the leading edge of 'good practice', the survey indicated that there were few attempts to establish these links in any systematic way. However, it also suggested that there is a strong intrinsic belief that practices associated with information and consultation can make a difference.

These findings coincide with those of the CBI–TUC Productivity Challenge Best Practice Working Group. Its report provides some underpinning to this:

Involving individual employees or teams in decisions which affect the day to day organisation of their work helps create a culture of autonomy and responsibility. And systems for encouraging employee feedback and suggestions are key to innovation and building commitment to continuous improvement.

Collective voice is important in building a climate of trust where individual employees are confident that their contribution will be valued. Equally valuable is its role in helping to identify shared objectives and resolve conflict. The involvement of employees' representatives can create the sense of mutuality that is essential for the sustainability of new working practices – the belief that both the employer and workers are reaping real benefits from improvements in work organisation. (CBI and TUC 2001).

The challenge of consulting

Information and consultation describe two distinct and separate processes, but the debate about the Regulations has been bedevilled by what 'information' and 'consultation' will mean in practice for employers.

Information sharing

Information shared directly with employees and that shared with the representatives of employees for the purposes of indirect consultation may differ. Organisations need to decide what information they can share with all employees, and what should be confined only to representatives for the purposes of indirect consultation.

Qualitative research suggests that both employee representatives and managers have been responsible for disclosing unauthorised information, but that 'confusion and lack of clarity were frequently to blame' rather than deliberate leakage (Work Foundation 2002). Similarly, a review of the ways in which different Member States manage confidentiality within European Works Council arrangements suggests that, while breaches are rare, they can and do happen (Reid 2003). Common sense dictates that the greater the number of people who have access to price-sensitive information, the greater the chance of a leak.

By giving representatives a distinctive role and some real responsibility, a culture is created in which confidentiality will regulate itself, but the onus is on management to identify which information is confidential.

There are also some 'no-go' areas beyond the scope of information and consultation. These commonly include disciplinary and grievance cases involving individual employees and any arrangements designated as topics for negotiation with recognised trade unions. Nevertheless, information shared early in the consultation process is one of the most important measures of trust and confidence in the representative process, and cannot be underestimated.

Consultation

Designating the boundaries between information, representative consultation and negotiation has been one of the most intractable questions about the regulations.

What is clear is that the process of consultation remains for many something of a mystery, located somewhere between two-way communication and joint decision-making. In particular, distinguishing between consultation and negotiation has always been difficult, particularly where 'hard consultation' undertaken within the context of 'joint problem-solving' or 'with a view to reaching an agreement' is concerned.

According to Dix and Oxenbridge (2003) 'genuine consultation' is about a belief by management in the value of employee's contributions. Eighteen ACAS regional advisers were interviewed in the course of their research. Some supported a consultative process designed to enable joint agreement, while others presented information, consultation and negotiation on a 'consultation scale'. The latter suggested that employee representatives and managers should reach a joint understanding about each other's expectations in relation to each 'dimension'.

A report undertaken by Beaumont and Hunter (2003) recommends additional 'consultation about consultation' in dealing with difficult issues. They suggest that this can be particularly useful in reconciling the expectations of the parties from the outset, and helps to minimise the 'strategic shock' of significant management decisions that might otherwise lead to conflict or a lack of trust.

Employers and representatives should establish some ground rules for consultation. These may change depending on the issue under discussion and the level at which it is being discussed, but what is important is that the parties minimise the scope for misunderstanding from the outset. Clearly, consultation on operational matters might be expected to go much further than consultation about strategic issues or policy development and the IPA has developed a model (IPA 2002c) taking this into account (see Box 4.3).

Box 4.3   A model for when to inform and consult employees

Level 1: Strategy
Information – a broad outline is communicated to partners to build a shared understanding of business context and business drivers.
Consultation – views welcome but unlikely to change direction.

Level 2: Development of policy
Information – information is shared in some detail with partners, questions are invited and views canvassed.
Consultation – discussions may lead to alternatives being put forward which influence the outcome.

Level 3: Operational policy
Information – information is shared, views are canvassed and discussed.

Box 4.3 (Continued)

Consultation – discussion is more focused on the 'how' rather than the 'why'. Where issues have significant implications for people within the organisation options are discussed and different views taken on board. These views shape outcomes.

Level 4: Implementation and day-to-day issues
Information – information shared on a regular basis about what is happening within the business, and the views of staff.
Consultation – options are discussed, and mutually agreed outcomes are sought about how they are to be implemented. Problems are aired and resolution sought. In some cases a joint problem-solving approach is appropriate.

In general, both employers and trade unions recognise the benefits of adopting a more broadly defined dialogue. Increasingly, their agenda has expanded to cover a wider range of issues, not always documented in formal agreements. However 'consultation should not simply be seen as a weak form of "real" bargaining, it must be presented as a completely different process drawing on different resources, techniques and structures' (Terry 2003).

Earlier we identified some of the arrangements organisations have developed. These included separate or 'parallel' consultation and negotiation arrangements, merged arrangements and 'hybrid' arrangements. What also appears to be emerging is a model of consultation based on the discussion of 'options' in which representatives take an 'influential' role at an early point in the decision-making process. Yet, importantly, management remains solely responsible for the final decision.

Option-based consultation

To make option-based consultation work, management need to share information at an early stage. The importance of sharing information is often overlooked, but it is a critical process in itself, and needs to happen at the earliest opportunity to enable consultation to begin at a time when decisions are still at a formative stage.

A consultative dialogue and the discussion of options take place before a decision is taken. Critically, management, staff and/or their representatives are entitled to identify different options and examine them during the consultative process. This is in contrast to traditional consultative arrangements, where representatives are only able to make comments about the options proposed by management.

Information shared at an early stage is a vital display of trust by management in the representatives' capacity to maintain confidentiality and to use the information in a constructive way. It is also an important measure of the trust the representatives have in management to make decisions with full and fair consideration of all the options presented.

Box 4.4   United Welsh Housing Association

Since 2001, the United Welsh Housing Association (UWHA) (IPA 2004c) and Unison have been working on a joint project to introduce flexible working practices and staff involvement, in order to improve the service provided to customers and local communities.

Central to these improvements is a new partnership agreement and Code of Conduct, which are unique in placing option-based consultation, rather than negotiation, at the heart of the relationship between UWHA and Unison.

Training for managers and staff has also played an important part in overcoming a prevailing 'command and control' culture, and has enabled staff to take greater responsibility for organising their own work and engage positively in how new services are developed and delivered.

Perhaps most fundamental of all is that option-based consultation applies equally well in the workplace where employees are involved in direct consultation as it does in the context of formal representative consultation. The result is a practical process for engaging staff at every level, which, if supported by training, can change the culture of organisations. Representatives also support managers in consulting directly with their employees, in effect becoming 'business partners' or 'internal consultants' to line management and employees.

The option-based consultation model is controversial for some managers because they need to share information earlier and trust representatives to respect their confidence. It is also controversial for trade unions, as bargaining has such an important place in the identity of the trade union movement and what unions stand for. Nevertheless, consultation, and option-based consultation in particular, represent an opportunity for employers, employees and their representatives to develop a much more broadly-based engagement alongside negotiation/collective bargaining.

Conclusion

A high-level group on the economic and social implications of restructuring in the EU put the argument succinctly: 'Good forward planning and dialogue allow more effective management of industrial change.'

Dialogue can enable change to be managed more effectively. Many of the organisations quoted in this chapter would demonstrate this. It does not, however, always need to do so. Historically it has also been used as a vehicle for exercising a power of veto. There are numerous examples, such as the disputes in 2003 in the UK fire service and in the postal service, where the subtext was a long-standing process of consultation going back several years, where the representatives were focused on preventing change happening.

Critically, to be effective, representative consultation needs to be located within the management of change, *not* outside it. If a performance benefit is to be achieved, a basic level of shared commitment to the organisation's goals is needed as well.

The boundary between consultation and direct involvement processes also needs to be fluid, and activity needs to straddle that boundary. Much of the IPA evidence points to this conclusion. Organisations such as AWE (IPA 2002b), Nottinghamshire NHS Healthcare Trust (IPA 2004b) and the United Welsh Housing Association (IPA 2004c) achieve the results they do through working in ways where the boundaries between what is representative involvement and what is direct involvement become quite blurred.

Both managers and representatives in these organisations would point out that improved performance requires commitment that relies, among other things, on trust. Trust depends on the perceived legitimacy of management decisions. Consultation is one of the most tangible ways of delivering such legitimacy. The closer it is located to the dynamic of change, the greater the opportunity for better outcomes.

This suggests that the two arguments for information and consultation – the business argument and the social justice argument – are entwined. The one helps to enable the other, and the success of information and consultation is measured against both these goals.

References

ACAS (2003) *Employee Communications and Consultation*. Hayes, Middlesex: Advisory Conciliation and Arbitration Service.

Ashton, D. N. and Sung, J. (2002) *Supporting Workplace Learning for High Performance Working*. Geneva: International Labour Office.

Beaumont, P. B. and Hunter, L. C. (2003) *Information and Consultation: From Compliance to Performance*, Research Report. London: Chartered Institute of Personnel and Development.

Butler, P., Felstead, A., Ashton, A., Fuller, A., Lee, T., Unwin, L. and Walters, S. (2004) 'High performance management: A Literature Review', *Learning as Work Research Paper No. 1*. The Centre for Labour Market Studies: University of Leicester.

CBI and TUC (2001) *CBI–TUC Productivity Challenge. The Final Report of the Best Practice Working Group*, London, 16 October 2001.

Coats, D. (2003) *What Next for the Unions?* London: Unions 21.

Cully, M., Woodland, S., O'Reilly, A. and Dix, G. (1999) *Britain at Work: As Depicted by the 1998 Workplace Employee Relations Survey*. London: Routledge.

Diamond, W. and Freeman, R. (2001) *What Workers Want from Workplace Organisations*. London: Trades Union Congress.

Dix, J. and Oxenbridge, S. (2003) *Information and Consultation at Work: From Challenges to Good Practice*, Research paper. London: Advisory Conciliation and Arbitration Service.

DTI (2002) *High Performance Workplaces: The Role of Employee Involvement in a Modern Economy. A Discussion Paper*. London: Department of Trade and Industry.

Guest, D. (2000) 'HR and the Bottom Line: Has the Penny Dropped?', *People Management*, 20 July 2000, pp. 5–25.

Guest, D. and Peccei, R. (1998) *The Partnership Company: Benchmarks for the Future*. London: Involvement and Participation Association.

Hall, M., Broughton, A., Carley, M. and Sisson, K. (2002) *Works Councils for the UK? Assessing the Impact of the EU Employee Consultation Directive*. Eclipse Group Ltd and Industrial Relations Research Unit, Warwick University.

IPA (1998) *Blue Circle Cement*, in case study number 5, series 3 by Willy Coupar, London: Involvement and Participation Association.

IPA (2001) *Sharing the Challenge Ahead: Informing and Consulting with Your Workforce*. London: Involvement and Participation Association.

IPA (2002a) *Peabody Trust*, in case study number 1, series 4, May, by Robert Stevens. London: Involvement and Participation Association.

IPA (2002b) *AWE plc*, in case study number 2, series 4, December, by Robert Stevens. London: Involvement and Participation Association.

IPA (2002c) 'Experience of success should guide consultation proposals', *IPA Bulletin*, no. 22, December, by Willy Coupar. London: Involvement and Participation Association.

IPA (2003a) *B&Q – Listening to the Grass Roots*, in case study number 3, series 4, July, by Mark Hall. London: Involvement and Participation Association.

IPA (2003b) *BMW Hams Hall Plant Council*, in case study number 4, series 4, October, by Mark Hall. London: Involvement and Participation Association.

IPA (2003c) *High Performance Workplaces: Informing and Consulting Employees. The IPA's Response to the DTI's Consultation Document*. London: Involvement and Participation Association.

IPA (2004a) *Abbey*, in case study number 6, Series 4, May, by Mark Hall. London: Involvement and Participation Association.

IPA (2004b) *Nottinghamshire Healthcare NHS Trust*, in case study 7, series 4, July, by Robert Stevens. London: Involvement and Participation Association.

IPA (2004c) *United Welsh Housing Association*, in case study 8, series 4, October, by Robert Stevens. London: Involvement and Participation Association.

Purcell, J., Kinnie, N., Hutchinson, S., Rayton, B. and Swart, J. (2003) *Understanding the People and Performance Link: Unlocking the Black Box*. London: Chartered Institute of Personnel and Development.

Reid, P. (2003) 'Managing confidentiality within EWCs', *European Works Council Bulletin*, 46, July/August.

Stevens, R. (2003) 'High performance workplaces', *UK Work Organisation Journal*, 1, pp. 12–15. Nottingham: The Nottingham Trent University.

Stiglitz, J. (2002) 'Democratic developments as the fruits of Labour', in Ha-Joon Chang (ed.), *Joseph Stiglitz and the World Bank – The Rebel Within*. London: Anthem Press.

Terry, M. (2003) *Partnership Uncovered: The Implications of Partnership for Trade Unions in the UK*. London: Unions 21.

Thompson, M. (2002) *High Performance Work Organisation in UK Aerospace: The SBAC Human Capital Audit 2002*. London: Society of British Aerospace Companies.

TUC (2002) *Submission on the Government's Discussion Document: High Performance Work-places*, available at http://www.tuc.org.uk/law/tuc-5866-f0.cfm

UKWON (2002) *The UK Work Organisation Network*. Nottingham: The Nottingham Trent University.

Work Foundation (2002) *New Dialogue at Work – Making Consultation Law Work*, The Work Foundation response to the DTI discussion document: *High Performance Workplaces*, London.

part **3**

The evidence of added value through information and consultation: impact and outcomes

The chapters in Part 3 focus specifically on seeking out the evidence – and the strength and reliability of that evidence – for making a link between I&C and performance outcomes.

In Chapter 5, Mark Fenton-O'Creevy and Stephen Wood explore the relative merits of the adoption of a direct approach to I&C, and an indirect (representative) approach. They also use statistical techniques to compare each of these with a third option – that is, a multi-channel approach whereby direct involvement is supplemented by representative modes. Drawing on a study of twenty-five multinational companies with a total of 108 country operations covering all the EU countries, they compile a body of data that relates I&C practices with a number of outcome measures. While they find that direct involvement was the most common type in practice, the main finding was that the greatest positive impact on productivity occurs when a *combination* of direct and indirect involvement is used.

In Chapter 6, Marc Thompson brings the idea and its measurement into the UK context. He explores the link between employee involvement and the high perform-ance workplace concept. He does this by drawing on a detailed and systematic study of aerospace companies. Thompson provides empirical evidence on the added value that work systems incorporating involvement and participation practices bring to firms. The chapter brings together data from over 640 establishments in the UK aerospace sector, collected between 1997 and 2002. The chapter shows how three sets of practices (high involvement, human resources and employee relations) interact and work together to create an organisational context in which knowledge-driven work can be performed more effectively. This chapter is important for a number of reasons, but one of the most significant is that it makes a compelling and closely argued case based on the increased importance of knowledge – and its full utilization – in the modern economy. If knowledge really is going to constitute the main (some argue *the only*) source of sustained competitive advantage in the future, then adequate and appropriate employee information and consultation practices will be needed in support. The chapter also provides systematic data, and analysis of that data. Through the use of longitudinal data it offers unique evidence of the links between high-performance practices and value-added per employee, which is an important measure of performance in manufacturing organisations. The chapter reports that firms using a greater number of these practices may see gains of up to 37 per cent in performance.

5

Benefiting from a multi-channel approach

Mark Fenton-O'Creevy and Stephen Wood

Discussion of information and consultation is all too often polarised between, on the one hand, advocates of communicating directly with individual employees, and on the other, proponents of consulting and negotiating through formal channels. This chapter presents evidence from a cross-national study of information and consultation practices that supports the value of using both direct and representative methods of employee involvement in concert.

When Nissan (UK) experienced its first drop in demand in 1993, the car maker immediately involved all its employees in deciding how to deal with the surplus labour problem. The management could have decided unilaterally on redundancies, negotiated with union representatives to agree voluntary packages, or relied on consulting with elected members of the company council. Instead, it spent two weeks talking in small groups with almost every employee. Such direct employee involvement in the strategic matters of the business is often seen as a mark of progressive employment relations. It is also associated currently with the human resource management variant of the new industrial relations, so often linked to high performance. Consulting workers directly on matters that have an immediate effect on their working lives has long been viewed by management theorists as potentially most relevant to the needs of both individuals and the organisation. But in recent years direct methods have been touted increasingly as a genuine alternative to representative systems built around trade unions or works councils. Compared with the continental European approach to information and consultation, it might form the basis for a distinctive British way. If this is the case, will such an approach characterise British organisations' reaction to the new EU-inspired information and consultation regulations? Is it likely that, where organisations are required to set up representative processes to consult and inform, that these will be largely façades, with management relying principally on direct communication with the workforce?

In Britain since the 1980s there has indeed been a significant increase in the incidence of direct involvement practices that has coincided with a decline in union representation of employees (Millward *et al.* 2000; Poole *et al.* 2001; Forth and Millward 2002). If British employers are increasingly using direct methods, and these can be shown to be as effective in providing genuine employee involvement, can this not support the argument that any legislation on employee involvement should allow for choice? Employers may be concerned that, since unions raise labour costs, any benefits of participation may be offset by higher wages. It may also be the case that an adversarial climate that might develop in a union context makes it harder to engage in effective direct involvement.

Alternatively, are trade unions right to criticise direct involvement? Often their concern is that reliance on employer voluntarism will lead to lower overall levels of involvement. Their argument is that managers will pick and choose the issues on which they talk to employees, and that any dialogue between managers and employees will be more a matter of managers sharing selective information with employees, rather than genuine involvement and consultation.

Perhaps, though, a debate in terms of an employers' preference for direct channels of communication and trade unions for formal union representation is now out of date? Certainly there is mounting evidence that organisations are using more than one channel for informing and consulting (Gospel and Willman 2003).

Moreover, there is evidence to suggest that a multi-channel approach may enhance productivity and it can, arguably, generate more genuine involvement. Cooke (1994), in the USA, has found this to be the case for the combination of direct involvement and unionisation. He argued that employees in unionised firms are more secure and thus more confident about challenging management and requesting information from supervisors. He also suggested that the greater security provided by collective bargaining provides a bedrock for long-term employee commitment upon which direct methods can flourish. Unions provide assurance to employees that the outcomes of participation will not be used against their interests, so they are more likely to participate freely.

In a study of 891 manufacturing firms in Michigan, USA, Cooke (1994) found that direct employee involvement contributed significantly to firm performance (value added, net of labour cost per employee) in unionised firms, but not in non-unionised firms. The presence of direct involvement was associated with a 22 per cent greater level of value added per employee in unionised firms, but no significant performance effect was found in non-unionised firms. Similar results were found by Michie and Sheehan-Quinn (2001) in a study of 242 UK manufacturing establishments: direct involvement had a stronger positive impact on performance where union membership was high.

In a similar vein, research in Germany has examined the effect of direct involvement and works councils on performance The evidence on works councils alone is that they tend to have a small positive effects on productivity in medium-sized and large workplaces, but that there is a small negative effect in small workplaces (Addison *et al*. 2004). There is also evidence, however, that direct involvement has more effect where works councils are present. Zwick (2003), for example, surveyed a representative sample of 2,124 establishments across the German economy over the period 1997–2000 and found a significant positive effect of direct involvement on productivity, but only in establishments with works councils. Zwick (2003: 1) explained the result by arguing that works councils might act in two ways to influence the effects of direct involvement. First they 'facilitate an efficient implementation of participative work forms by using their collective voice function to mediate between the diverging interests of management and employees' (ibid.). Second, they may constrain management from imposing additional burdens on employees as they introduce a more participative work organisation.

The studies so far have examined the effects of dual systems, but not the effects of direct involvement, works-council-type consultation and union channels together. This was the focus of our cross-national study of employee involvement practices in the subsidiaries of UK-headquartered multinational corporations, on which we now report.

Our study

We designed a study to find out how an approach to employee relations typified by direct involvement compared with representative consultation arrangements such as mandatory works councils or traditional union arrangements. Does any one system stand out as leading to more consultation and involvement across the range of issues? How do different systems affect performance outcomes? When deciding strategy, do managers opt for direct involvement rather than trade union involvement, because of the latter's past focus on pay and conditions?

We explored these questions across the European Union (EU). The results of the study demonstrate that, in companies that use only direct methods, the overall level of employee involvement is lower than where some form of representative channel (works council or trade union) is used either alone or in combination with direct methods. Moreover, the productivity of these operations is also lower. Institutions of employment relations therefore do matter. Moreover, where direct involvement methods are used, they have a more positive effect on labour productivity when they are used in tandem with a works council or a representative committee. However, we did not find the presence of a union enhanced the impact of direct involvement.

Methods and sample

Our research involved twenty-five large, multinational companies – all with headquarters in the UK and most of them in the *Financial Times* 100. The sample was acquired from the membership of an employers' group known as the European Study Group. This not-for-profit association of companies was formed to exchange ideas on best practice for communication and consultation in the context of transnational legislation.

The research data was acquired in two stages. The first stage was through a questionnaire completed by a senior human resources (HR) manager in the headquarters of each company. The second stage involved the completion of a questionnaire by local managers of separate operations within the European Union for each of the main business streams. This concentrated on personnel practices and involvement mechanisms, along the lines of the main management survey in the UK government's Workplace Employee Relations Survey (as used for example in Cully *et al.* 1999). Follow-up interviews at all of the headquarters and in a selected number of matched pairs of operations in two countries supported the validity of the data. In particular, these confirmed that managers could distinguish readily between when they were informing, consulting and negotiating with employees or their representatives.

A total of 108 country operations, covering all EU countries, were included in the study. Of these, 29 per cent were in the UK and a further 47 per cent in Germany, the Netherlands, France or Spain.

First, we were particularly interested in whether managers involved workers in a range of business-related issues. We included the future development of the business, major new investments, mergers/acquisitions, transfers of production, cutbacks to (or closures of) establishments, employment levels in the company, and collective redundancies. We also asked questions about involvement in more traditional bargaining issues such as pay, employee benefits, the introduction of new working methods/production processes/technologies, and health and safety: Fifteen issues in all.

Second, if any companies did involve employees in such matters, we were interested in the nature of this involvement. More specifically, we looked at whether it was a matter of simply sharing information, or whether it extended to consultation, to negotiation or mutual decision-making.

Finally, we wanted to know the channels through which this involvement occurred. Was it via a union, a representative committee such as a works council, or direct communication methods such as team briefings?

Results

First, we found that the use of multiple channels was common. We identified five distinct systems of involvement through the use of cluster analysis – a statistical technique for identifying groups of cases (in this case, enterprises) in a data set. Two were where a single channel dominated, while the other three reflected the use of more than one channel for a range of issues.

The five systems were:

(i) direct involvement only, in which the direct channel predominated: this existed in 32 per cent of the sample;

(ii) representative involvement, in which the representative committee or works council dominated: 21 per cent;

(iii) union-based involvement, in which the union channel predominated, but some use was made of representative committees: 4 per cent;

(iv) Direct and representative involvement, in which both methods were used equally, but little or no use was made of union channels: 32 per cent; and

(v) Multi-channel involvement, in which all three channels were used together: 11 per cent.

By far the most frequently used systems in our sample were the first, direct involvement-only route and the fourth, a combination of direct and representative involvement systems. Some direct involvement was used in three-quarters of cases (systems (i), (iv) and (v) added together). A system in which the union was the sole means of involvement did not exist in our sample.

Adding systems (iii) and (v) together, it appears that unions are an important channel for employee involvement in only 15 per cent of the operations we studied. But 73 per cent of the 108 country operations had some union presence. This means that a considerable number of firms had a union presence but involved unions in only one or two issues. Often, these were the traditional issues of pay and working conditions.

The business issues on which managers involved employees did not vary significantly across the five systems. It is not the case, for example, that in seeking to involve employees increasingly in strategic issues, managers had forsaken representation and turned to direct communication. Firms in the direct-only cluster were no more focused on strategic issues than those in the other clusters.

Our second major finding was that those organisations that relied only on direct involvement – system (i) here – involved their employees less than those using other systems. Involvement was measured by an overall index constructed on the basis of the number of issues on which managers involved the workforce, weighted for whether this entailed negotiation, consultation or simply sharing information. The lower average level of involvement on this index for the direct-only group was both because they involved workers in fewer issues and, when they did, they were less likely to consult or negotiate rather than simply to inform them. Behaviour such as that displayed by Nissan (UK) was rare. Aside from this difference between the first system and the others, there was no significant difference in the level of involvement between the other systems.

As Figure 5.1 shows, most respondents provided information to employees on almost all of the issues. But the average number of issues on which workforces were consulted was low. Half the firms consulted on fewer than five of the fifteen issues. The number that extended consultation to bargaining or co-determination was even

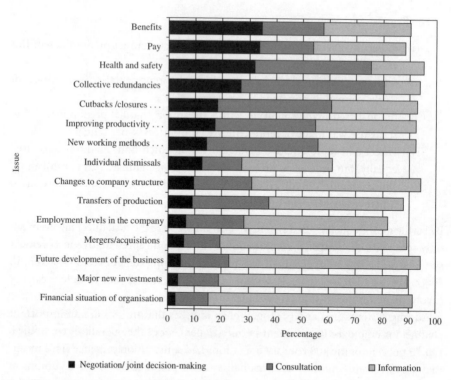

Issue

| | | | | | | | | | | |
Benefits
Pay
Health and safety
Collective redundancies
Cutbacks /closures . . .
Improving productivity . . .
New working methods . . .
Individual dismissals
Changes to company structure
Transfers of production
Employment levels in the company
Mergers/acquisitions
Future development of the business
Major new investments
Financial situation of organisation

0 10 20 30 40 50 60 70 80 90 100

Percentage

■ Negotiation/ joint decision-making   ■ Consultation   □ Information

Figure 5.1 Proportion of firms informing, consulting and negotiating on each issue

lower. More than 40 per cent of enterprises did not do this at all, while a further 10 per cent did so on only one issue. Negotiation and joint decision-making were mainly concerned with traditional bargaining issues.

Our third major finding was that, although the union tended to be used as a channel for a limited number of issues, the overall level of involvement (measured by the mean level of involvement across all issues regardless of channel) was higher on average where union influence was high. There may be several reasons for this. First, it may be that unions put managers under pressure to inform and consult via other channels. Given the links between consultative committees and trade unions, this is plausible. Members of works councils are often union appointees, and unions in some countries negotiate framework deals for works councils. Second, it is also possible that the managements of many organisations are prompted to involve employees through other channels when a union is present, in order to bypass the union. Third, it may be that managers who are favourably inclined towards unions, and hence more likely to recognise them, tend also to be positively disposed to other forms of involvement. We favour the first explanation. If the second were true, we would expect to find relatively poor relationships between employee representatives and managers where multiple channels were in use, and this was not the case. The third explanation might be more plausible in a UK-only survey, but, in most of our sample, union recognition was not a result of management discretion.

A fourth finding was that the exclusive use of direct involvement was associated with lower labour productivity. Productivity was measured by asking managers to compare their unit's labour productivity with that of their competitors, such ratings having been found to be fairly reliably related to accountancy measures of performance (see Wall *et al.* 2004). There were no marked differences in productivity between the systems that involved an element of representation.

To shed more light on the reasons for these differences between systems, in addition to our analysis of the differences between clusters, we also examined the individual and joint effects of the channels. We used moderated regression to examine the relationship with productivity; see the appendix to this chapter. First, we found that productivity was positively related to the use of the union channel for employee involvement. Second, we found that there was an interaction effect between the representative and direct involvement channels on productivity. As in several of the German studies, direct involvement was linked more positively with labour productivity where substantial use was made of the representative channel. We did not, however, find any similar interaction between the union and direct channels, or between the union and representative channels. Taken together with the cluster results, these results support the argument that employees are unlikely to engage effectively through direct involvement, and hence improve productivity, without the protection of their interests afforded by representative committees or works councils.

We also examined the impact on labour productivity of the industrial relations climate and the influence of employee representatives (both unions and works councils) on management decision-making. We found that labour productivity was higher where the industrial relations climate was positive, and lower in enterprises where union representatives had a substantial influence on management decisions than in those where influence was less, or absent. The effect of the climate was independent of the channels or system used, and the climate itself was unrelated to channel. The negative effect of union influence contrasts with the finding that high use of the union channel has a positive effect on productivity. However, it suggests that, regardless of how much the union channel is used, that productivity deteriorates if management prerogatives over key areas are reduced. But in such cases, extensive use of the union channel can act as a countervailing force, as this will always yield some productivity effects.

What about geographical differences? As we initially expected, the purely direct system of employee involvement was more concentrated in the UK than in other European countries. But there were operations in continental Europe that relied almost completely on the direct route. Direct involvement was also widely used in continental Europe in conjunction with works councils and other representative channels (system (iv)), but this approach was less prevalent in the UK (see Table 5.1).

But, regardless of the greater use of the first, direct-only system, the UK workplaces we studied did not have lower overall levels of employee involvement than did their continental European counterparts. This was for two reasons. First, the enterprises

Table 5.1   Distribution of systems, labour productivity and involvement, by country

Country	Percentage of enterprises with each system					Mean	
	1	2	3	4	5	Labour productivity	Involvement
France	17.6	29.4	0.0	41.2	11.8	3.8	1.4
Germany	23.1	15.4	0.0	53.8	7.7	3.9	1.8
Netherlands	33.3	33.3	0.0	33.3	0.0	4.3	1.4
Spain	16.7	33.3	0.0	50.0	0.0	3.7	1.2
UK	48.4	16.1	3.2	16.1	16.1	3.6	1.5
Other	33.3	16.7	12.5	25.0	12.5	3.9	1.5

that relied solely on direct involvement in the UK had higher levels of involvement than did those in this cluster from counties with more legally-mandated involvement. Second, the use of the fifth, multi-channel system was also disproportionately higher in the home bases of these British multinationals than in their European operations. Systems in which representative involvement were important (systems (ii) and (iv)) were especially prominent in Germany, France, Netherlands and Spain, but also existed in the UK (see Table 5.1). But these countries did not have greater overall levels of involvement. The only statistically significant difference here was between Germany and Spain. However, it was not the case that the effects of representative channels on performance simply reflected better economic performance in countries where their use was high, as the mean rating of labour productivity was not significantly different in any of the countries in the sample.

Conclusions

Our study suggests that employment involvement based solely on direct methods is not a genuine alternative to representative systems built on trade unions or works councils. While direct methods *per se* are not associated with lower levels of employee involvement, this is significantly lower where there is *exclusive* reliance on the direct approach. This demonstrates that institutions such as works councils and trade unions matter.

The greater prevalence of such direct-only workplaces in the UK sample may suggest a distinctive 'British' way. However, they are far from unique to Britain, and the significance of the result is lessened by the fact that UK direct-only enterprises have higher levels of involvement than do similar enterprises elsewhere.

Union influence also has a significant effect on the level of involvement, regardless of the type of system or country. This reinforces the significance of institutions. Just as the direct-only system is associated with lower levels of involvement, so is it associated with lower productivity. This again underlines the significance of institutions. It suggests that both works councils and unions are beneficial for at least this highly important dimension of performance. Moreover, the presence of a works council or similar consultative arrangement can intensify the effect of direct methods, or vice versa. Unions are not associated with the same effects, at least in our sample. These results suggest that certain types of representative institutions, sometimes placed under the label of non-union, do provide a context in which employees are more secure about engaging in management-driven direct methods in ways that can enhance productivity and that perhaps also have benefits for employees. The trade union does not appear to have this effect (nor does it reinforce any effect of the representative institution, and a heavy union influence may reduce productivity). However, high use of the union channel can have positive effects on productivity. In addition, regardless of channel usage, the quality of industrial relations is associated with productivity.

The implication of our findings is that both direct and representative forms of involvement should be encouraged and seen as being complementary. Effecting cultural change in relationships between employers, employees and their representatives is also critical. Public policy could be directed at encouraging multi-channel use and the style of management that is increasingly being placed under the partnership label. For managers, trade unions and employees, the results imply that, properly applied, the provisions for information and consultation in the UK government's information and consultation regulations offer opportunities for improving both levels of employee involvement and productivity. Most economic benefit is likely to be gained where organisations adopt a multi-channel approach, accepting that the benefits of direct involvement are most likely to be achieved in the context of effective representative participation. In implementing the provisions of the Information and Consultation Regulations, all parties have the most to gain if representative and direct approaches to informing and consulting employees are integrated effectively. However, managers need to work to ensure representative arrangements provide employees with adequate assurance that their commitment to productivity gains will not be damaging to their own interests.

References

Addison, T. J., Schnabel, C. and Wagner, J. (2004) 'The course of research into the economic consequences of German works councils', *British Journal of Industrial Relations* 42(2): 255–81.

Cooke, N. W. (1994) 'Employee participation programs, group-based incentives, and company performance: A union–nonunion comparison', *Industrial and Labor Relations Review* 47(4): 594–609.

Cully, M., Woodland, S., O'Reilly, A. and Dix, G. (1999) *Britain at Work: As Depicted by the 1998 Workplace Employee Relations Survey*. London: Routledge.

Forth, John and Neil Millward (2002) *The Growth of Direct Communication*. London: Chartered Institute of Personnel and Development.

Godard, J. (2004) 'A critical assessment of the high-performance paradigm', *British Journal of Industrial Relations* 42(2): 349–78.

Gospel, H. and Willman, P. (2003) 'Dilemmas in Worker Representation: Information, Consultation and Negotiation', in H. Gospel and S. Wood (eds) *Representing Workers: Trade Union Recognition and Membership in Modern Britain*. London: Routledge, pp. 144–65.

Michie, J. and Sheehan-Quinn, M. (2001) 'Labour market flexibility, human resource management and corporate performance', *British Journal of Management* 12(4): 207–306.

Millward, Neil, Bryson, Alex and Forth, John (2000) *All Change at Work? British Employment Relations 1980–1998, as Portrayed by the Workplace Industrial Relations Survey Series*. London: Routledge.

Poole, M., Lansbury, R. and Wailes, N. (2001) 'A comparative analysis of developments in industrial democracy', *Industrial Relations*, 40(3): 490–525.

Wall, T. D., Michie, J., Patterson, M., Wood, S. J., Sheehan, M., Clegg, C. W. and West, M. (2004) 'On the validity of subjective measures of company performance', *Personnel Psychology* 57(1): 95–118.

Zwick, T. (2003) 'Works councils and the productivity impact of direct employee participation'. *Discussion Paper No. 03–47*. Mannheim: Centre for European Economic Research/ZEW.

Appendix

Table 5.A1   Moderated regression on labour productivity

	Stage 1		Stage 2	
	Standardised regression coefficient	t-value	Standardised regression coefficient	t-value
Relationship between management and union	0.31	2.59*	0.28	2.37*
Trade union influence on management decisions	−0.49	−3.67**	−0.49	−3.78***
Involvement via union	0.32	2.84**	0.27	2.45*
Involvement via works council/ representative committee (IWC)	0.08	0.71	−0.79	−2.16*
Direct involvement (DI)	0.11	1.06	−0.57	−1.98*
IWC×DI			1.04	2.48*
R^2	0.19**		0.25***	
Change in R^2			0.06*	

Notes: * p < 0.05; ** p < 0.01; *** p < 0.001; N = 99.

6

High-performance workplaces: learning from aerospace

Marc Thompson

This chapter provides empirical evidence on the added value that work systems which incorporate involvement and participation practices bring to firms. It draws on data from over 640 establishments in the UK aerospace sector, collected in three waves between 1997 and 2002. These data have also enabled the construction of a unique panel of some ninety establishments to address a number of important questions about the consequences of high performance work practices for organisational effectiveness.

The chapter begins by arguing that high performance work practices are an essential component of the successful aerospace organisation of the future. We focus specifically on the role of knowledge in new models of value creation, and how innovative work practices can enable and support knowledge-driven work. In a network-based industry becoming more reliant on its stakeholders in order to co-produce value, the quality of the relationship with employees is of critical importance. Next, we differentiate three sets of practices that can help to create and sustain a high-performing, knowledge-driven workplace. We argue that these practices (high involvement, human resources and employee relations) interact and work together to create an organisational context in which knowledge-driven work can be performed more effectively. We look at this in the context of the emerging dominant lean production paradigm, and argue that both researchers and practitioners need to frame involvement and participation practices not only within the context of high performance work systems but also in relation to the dominant production logic in a sector.

Knowledge-driven work: the need for involvement and participation

Many commentators have argued that we are now entering a new economic era defined not by the possession of assets or technology, which can easily be matched, but one where competitiveness rests on organisations' knowledge and capabilities (Teece 1998). The future will be defined by an organisation's ability to develop, utilise and protect knowledge. The economy of tomorrow (and today) is one based on knowledge solutions, where firms need to attend to a range of stakeholder relationships in order to produce value. Far from contemporary pressures reinforcing the neoclassical model of the firm, the need is for more openness and connectedness within and between firms and their range of stakeholders, including customers and employees. Delivering complex solutions, innovating in business models and customer offerings are increasingly dependent on how firms create the conditions for co-production with their key stakeholders (Normann and Ramirez 1994). The coming of the knowledge-based economy has long been heralded, but there is increasing evidence of its arrival. This is evident in how stock markets value enterprises and the growing importance of intangible assets that typically include elements such as know-how, relationships and brand equity. In 2000, intangibles accounted for more than 85 per cent of the market value of US firms, whereas eighteen years earlier they accounted for only 38 per cent. Furthermore, analysis of different classes of asset has found that the rates of return are much higher for intangibles. The average annual rate of return was 10.7 per cent for intangibles, 7 per cent for tangibles and only 4.5 per cent for financial assets (Baruch 2000).

Social capital, or the quality of relationships, is an increasingly important feature of intangible assets, and firms value creation models. For example, it is estimated that 60 per cent of the future value created in the pharmaceutical sector will be from alliances, partnerships and other forms of co-operative relationships (de Man and Duysters (2003)). A key driver of these new network models of value creation is the simultaneous deepening and widening of the knowledge base required to enable customer solutions. In this world, no single firm can vertically integrate the knowledge needed to produce complex solutions. Future value will come increasingly from the spaces between organisations and the goodwill of customers, allies, partners and, last but not least, employees. In the new business model, relationships matter and the firm can no longer rely on command and control systems based on hierarchy and authority. However, evidence suggests that firms find it difficult to optimise these relationships and many end in failure.

At one level, there are an increasing number of job roles that require individuals and teams to look outwards and cross firm boundaries to create value. On another level, these pressures are also forcing firms to look inwards and review their current models of work organisation to support knowledge creation and responsiveness to an increasingly unstable external environment. One implication is that the traditional job based on narrow task definitions and a largely transactional relationship is no longer tenable. Where knowledge is critical for product as well as process improvement, firms need to create the opportunities for employees to apply, develop and share their knowledge. This means designing jobs in ways that give employees more information, and opportunities for participation and involvement.

However, the way in which knowledge is conceptualised has implications for firm-level policies. There are three possible ways of looking at knowledge – the strategic management approach; the evolutionary economics approach; and the social-anthropology of learning approach (Amin and Cohendet 2004). Each framework is rooted in a different understanding of knowledge, and as a consequence has different implications for organisations. In the first two approaches, knowledge is seen as something that people possess, or in the words of Cook and Brown (1999), there is an 'epistemology of possession of knowledge'. In the social-anthropology approach, knowledge is seen as emerging from individual and group practices. Rather than knowledge being seen as an asset or possession held by individuals, the emphasis is on the epistemology of practice. As a consequence, knowledge is shaped by the practices in communities and the behaviour and attitudes these produce. If we recognise knowledge as being rooted in practice (for example, the practices that enable teams of multi-professionals to solve complex problems) this means that we focus on a different set of questions to understand how knowledge can be created and shared.

If we frame knowledge from a practice perspective, this privileges the role of organisational systems, routines and practices in enabling knowledge-driven work. For example, a recent review of knowledge-based firms argues that 'forgetting, through employee rotation, new training and the establishment of new work routines, helps to weed out practices that may no longer be suitable for changing market or operational circumstances' (Amin and Cohendet 2004: 115).

Because knowledge is socially produced and embedded in the social relations of the firm internally and externally, the task of managers (and communities within firms) is to create practices that can stimulate high levels of interaction. For example, these interactions can be encouraged through practices such as job rotation which bring employees into contact with others, as well as different contexts where their 'knowing' can be stimulated. Various forms of team working – for example, semi-autonomous teams, or continuous improvement teams – can devolve greater responsibility and accountability for problem-solving, and link employee knowledge with problems through a unit of practice. Problem-solving and the greater alignment of employees to customer demands can also be encouraged through more widely available information on business strategy, customer needs and competitors. Practices such as open-book management, regular team briefings and the dissemination of business information can enrich employees' understanding of the organisation's business and market environment.

However, it needs to be emphasised that these forms of direct involvement are just one part of a high-performance work system. New forms of working require a deepening and widening of employee skills, knowledge and capabilities. While some of these goals are achieved through new forms of job design outlined above, there is also a need for the firm to put in place human resource practices that can support knowledge-driven work. For example, the firm may need to ensure a good fit between the person and the job through the use of more sophisticated recruitment and selection techniques. This can help to reduce employee turnover and align employee expectations with job demands. Employee feedback mechanisms such as performance appraisal are needed to develop skills and competencies as well as to communicate performance expectations. These systems are likely to demand higher levels of training and development both at work and outside the job. However, because of the new job designs, these skills are likely to be firm-specific and of greater value to the organisation. Incentive systems may need to be aligned with team-based forms of working and the requirement to reach higher levels of quality, cost reduction or on-time delivery. Wider reward structures can help to provide opportunities for progression linked to knowledge and skills.

The high-performance work model, as set out by Applebaum *et al.* (2000) is one where an organisation has 'adopted a cluster of practices that provide workers with the incentives, skills and, above all, the opportunity to participate in decisions to improve the plant's performance' (ibid.: 9). However, while this model and approach has been very valuable in understanding the work practices that enable greater levels of ability, motivation and opportunity, it does not deal with the other set of practices that are also important in designing a knowledge-driven work environment in the future. In tandem with Godard (2004: 307) we contend that employee relations practices need to be embraced within any such model. These indirect involvement and participation practices embodied in either trade unions or non-union entities, such as staff or works councils, provide a mechanism through which wider collective issues can be aired and potentially resolved. Providing an institutional process for worker voice at the firm level can produce a number of benefits for the knowledge-based business. First, it can capture a range of issues that may be important for organisational effectiveness (such as input on business strategy and models). Second, it can create a higher-trust work environment where employees develop a greater sense of psychological safety, and this in turn can support the greater sharing of knowledge. For example, collective channels can also give employees an input into the design of more direct forms of participation, which in turn can foster trust and in its turn supports knowledge-sharing. Finally, indirect participation and involvement can help to reinforce identification with and commitment to the firm, which is important for discretionary behaviour (Purcell *et al.* 2003).

To recap, we propose that the emphasis on knowledge as a key defining feature of post-industrial capitalism further enhances the salience of involvement and participation practices. We view knowledge as being socially enacted and embedded in relations between individuals in groups with common interests at the firm (or inter-firm) level, or in smaller sub-units within the firm. Furthermore, we contend that work organisation practices can engender behaviour and attitudes that facilitate and enable knowledge-sharing and problem-solving. As Allport (1945) stated 'people have to be active in order to learn'. Three specific sets of practices, which we term high involvement, human resources and employee relations interact to support the development, application and appropriation of knowledge in the firm. These sets of practices are linked through their emphasis on different forms of participation and involvement at both individual and collective levels.

Research on involvement and participation has focused traditionally on individual practices such as quality circles or self-directed work teams. However, in the high-performance work systems approach, a broader view of involvement and consultation dominates. Organisational and employee benefits arise from the way in which these practices interact: 'innovative HR practices affect performance not individually but as interrelated elements in an internally consistent HR "bundle" or system; and that these HR bundles contribute most to assembly plant productivity when they are integrated with manufacturing policies under the "organisational logic" of flexible production systems' (MacDuffie 1995: 217). The importance of both consistency between practices and integration with firm level strategies is a defining feature of the high performance workplace (Huselid and Becker 1996; Baron and Kreps 1999). Furthermore, some writers (for example, Lowe et al. 1997) have argued that high performance in manufacturing is the result of sources other than HR practices such as benefits from economies of scale and automation.

Our research in the UK aerospace sector seeks to address a number of specific questions in relation to involvement and participation in the context of knowledge-driven, high-performance work systems. First, is there any evidence that firms using these practices achieve higher comparative levels of performance? Our focus on one sector provides a unique insight and enables us to control for the heterogeneity from which multi-industry studies have suffered. Second, if knowledge-driven work is becoming more important, does the use of high-performance practices lead to more human capital investment? The longitudinal dimension of our research can address this causal dimension and explore whether high-performance practices increase the demand for skills, and third, it also allows us to address the extent to which high-performance work practices are important for other forms of workplace innovation such as lean practices?

The aerospace context

Reforms in work practices need to be understood against the backdrop of macroeconomic and global competitive forces which, because of their uncertainty, can cause severe shocks to any industry. Civil aerospace experienced one of these dramatic shocks after the attack on the World Trade Center in New York in September 2001 lead to a contraction in the market. Some 12,000 direct and 40,000 indirect jobs were lost as a result (SBAC 2002) and it is probably the case that a number of firms were opportunistic and used this event to bring forward, and indeed speed up, restructuring plans during this period.

The industry comprises three main areas – aircraft and systems, engines, and equipment – with the bulk of UK turnover (49 per cent) accounted for by aircraft and systems. The UK aerospace sector as a whole employs around 122,000 people directly, and indirectly supports a further 150,000 jobs. With a turnover of £17 billion per year, 60 per cent of which is exported, it makes a net contribution to the exchequer of £3 bn a year. Productivity in the industry has risen by nearly 7 per cent per annum since the mid-1980s and EEF research suggests that aerospace is one of the few UK manufacturing industries to have achieved productivity levels as good if not better than those in the rest of Europe (EEF 2002).

Although most people think that aerospace in the UK means BAE Systems, which employs over 50,000 people in the UK, there are reckoned to be around 1,500 companies in the sector, with 47 per cent of these employing fewer than 250 people – 51 per cent are single site businesses and over three-quarters of companies are UK-owned. It is a high-skill industry, with over a third of all employees holding a degree or equivalent qualification, and around 15 per cent of the workforce involved in R&D. As such it is at the forefront of the 'knowledge economy' and creates high-skill, high-value-added jobs. It still employs a large proportion of manual (though not necessarily low-skill) workers, but there is evidence of a growing shift towards high-skill work of a non-manual kind. Trade unions retain a reasonably strong presence within the sector, with around 45 per cent of firms having recognition agreements, which is unusual given the large number of SMEs in the sector. The main unions are Amicus and the TGWU.

The aerospace manufacturers have characteristics that often differ from those of other advanced manufacturing environments such as automotive producers. Within the aerospace industry, prime contractors deal with products that are highly techno-logical, complex, and are manufactured in low volumes according to irregular demand patterns. These have been termed high-variety, low-volume products (Jina *et al.* 1997) or super-value goods (James-Moore and Gibbons, 1997). By comparison, many mainstream automotive producers set out to compete by providing a low-cost solution. Such differences in competitive priorities have implications for their oper-ational and human resource management strategies. It could be argued that the complexity of parts and the high variety of products signal a much higher knowledge and skills base than other sectors, such as automotive. Furthermore, the strong craft base and tradition in the industry underlines the importance of the tacit knowledge of employees.

However, cost is becoming a key driver of value in operations with some very bold targets outlined in the recent Aerospace Innovation and Growth Team (AeIGT) report on the future of the industry to 2020 (SBAC 2003). In the next three to four years, the goal is to reduce waste in the supply chain by 75 per cent, cut new product introduction time by 75 per cent, and reduce lead-time by 75 per cent. The heavily regulated nature of the industry and the focus on high safety standards means that there is little room for low-quality manufacturing practices and emphasis is placed on standardised, trackable and repeatable processes. Moreover, the potentially disastrous consequences of poor quality means that companies do not have opportunities to make too many mistakes. Such challenges demand and require the knowledge and commitment of employees, which can be harnessed through high involvement and participation practices.

While quality standards and regulatory pressure call for high-quality production, the pressure for cost reduction means that firms are seeking to standardise processes and ensure that any changes or modifications in the production system made by employees can be embedded within the system as a whole and not only in one area, as the craft model tends to amplify. The challenge for operations managers is to leverage individual workers' tacit knowledge, make this explicit and codify it in the standard operating procedures to achieve goals such as cost, quality and delivery (CQD). This challenge emphasises further the need for higher levels of employee involvement.

In addition to demands for CQD, firms in the industry are being called upon increasingly to provide 'complete solutions'. While aerospace is not alone in having to provide customers with complete solutions, the complexity of aerospace systems greatly exacerbates the challenge. Increasingly, contracts are being won through the innovative bundling of products with related services. Changes in defence procurement and an increase in customer interest in lifecycle management are also opening up new opportunities. The Ministry of Defence (MoD), for example, is outsourcing pilot training and the management of airbases. In such ways firms are increasingly competing on 'width' as well as 'depth'. These and other challenges all require new ways of working and high levels of knowledge, skills and competence from employees at all levels. The result is that the command and control culture, the separation of the conception and execution of tasks, is no longer economically viable. For firms to prosper they need to engage employees in knowledge-driven work and high-performance work practices become critical in driving value-creation in the industry.

The research and data

The research was carried out under the auspices of the Society of British Aerospace Companies (SBAC), the key employer body in the sector, and funded by the Department of Trade and Industry (DTI). Three establishment-level surveys were conducted between 1997 and 2002, and this research draws on the results from the 1999 and 2002 surveys. In addition, a number of detailed case studies were undertaken across a sample of establishments, but for the purposes of this chapter the focus is primarily on the survey data.

Our sample frame included all establishments within the sector drawn from a range of sources including the SBAC, the DTI, the Office of National Statistics (ONS) and a publisher's database (Findlays), which produces a range of sector-specific publications. The establishment data from each source was cross-checked for duplications and accuracy of addresses. A postal survey design was deployed and sent to the managing director at each establishment. Analysis of returns found that 45 per cent had been completed by MDs in 1999 and 50 per cent in 2002.[1] Fewer than 10 per cent of respondents described themselves as human resource (HR) or personnel professionals across both surveys. Given that previous research suggests that non-HR managers are less optimistic in their assessment of HR practices and their effectiveness (Wright *et al.* 1998), our results are, if anything, likely to play down the reporting of HR practices in these firms.

The potential for measurement error in using single-source organisational surveys has been debated widely among SHRM researchers (Huselid and Becker 1996; Becker and Huselid 1998; Gerhart *et al.* 2000; Huselid and Becker 2000). A particular concern has been the potential error when a corporate-level respondent of a multi-establishment firm tries to estimate the total proportion of employees affected by a specific HR practice. Given the wide range of product and labour market conditions facing establishments in different business units within such firms, the reliability of such estimates has been found to be low (Gerhart *et al.* 2000). In contrast to previous studies where the average size of firm has been large (Huselid 1995 reported an average of 4,413 employees), the mean size of establishments in our panel was 396 employees (median 90) and 82 per cent were single-site firms.[2] Analysis by Gerhart *et al.* (2000) of responses collected at company and plant level in a study of oil refineries, found that reliability was much higher at plant level. These factors increase our confidence in the accuracy of the data. Furthermore, we used several other techniques in order to minimise measurement problems. The survey instrument was developed on the basis of prior research in the industry, including detailed interviews with managers in twelve different firms from across the industry value chain. Furthermore, the questionnaire was piloted extensively amongst thirty firms and discussed with a group of senior managers, who formed the steering group for the study. Together, these processes ensured that the questionnnaire contained questions that were both context-specific and understood by respondents (Becker and Gerhart, 1996).

Measuring high-performance work systems

Our measure of a high-performance work system comprises three different dimensions that connect to the concept of knowledge-driven work (see Figure 6.1). First, the high involvement dimension, which includes practices that enable employee direct involvement such as different forms of team working, problem-solving activities, provision of information (such as via briefings and information cascades), and the extent of job rotation within and between teams. These practices provide employees with opportunities to apply their skills and knowledge. Second, the human resource (HR) dimension, which includes those practices that can shape the quality of the psychological contract between employee and organisation as well as to develop

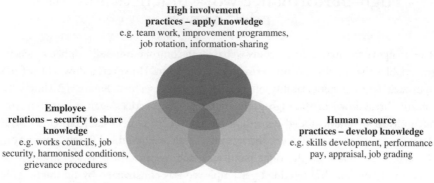

**High involvement
practices – apply knowledge**
e.g. team work, improvement programmes,
job rotation, information-sharing

**Employee
relations – security to share
knowledge**
e.g. works councils, job
security, harmonised conditions,
grievance procedures

**Human resource
practices – develop knowledge**
e.g. skills development, performance
pay, appraisal, job grading

Figure 6.1   High-performance work organisation and knowledge-driven work
Source: Thompson (2002)

employee capabilities that can support higher levels of involvement. For example, skills-based payment systems can support the acquisition of skills and knowledge for problem-solving or job rotation. Broader job grading structures can also provide a context within which greater task flexibility is able to develop, and sophisticated recruitment methods can select people whose attitudes and behaviour align most closely with those of the firm.

Finally, the third dimension, employee relations, includes practices that cover collective forms of voice. These include formal trade union relations but also non-union forms of consultation such as works councils. We also include practices that seek to reduce the status barriers between employees (such as common terms and conditions) as well as practices that minimise the scope for procedural injustice such as formalised grievance and systems, and formal sex and race discrimination procedures. These practices can increase levels of trust within the organisation and provide a context within which employees may be more prepared to share knowledge. Our approach differs from other research (for example, MacDuffie 1995; Osterman 1994) because we introduce an employee relations practice dimension over and above human resource and high-involvement practices.

A high-performance work system can be specified in a number of ways, but the two simplest are an additive or multiplicative approach. Following MacDuffie (1995) we opted for an additive approach and created an additive index of all practices. It should be remembered that in the case of high involvement and HR practices we captured both the presence and extent of use. To capture extent of use we looked at the mean proportion of employees covered by each practice and included those establishments above the mean. This provides a more refined measure of the potential impact of each practice. The practices were then divided into quartiles to differentiate between firms with low and high use of these practices. This approach enables us to address simple questions such as whether firms that use more of these practices and more intensively have higher levels of performance. In other words – is more, better?

High-performance work practices and their effectiveness

The strength of a single industry study is that it can control more easily for heterogeneity in variables that might explain performance variation. However, a downside of this approach is the generalisability of findings to other sectors. Figure 6.2 shows the quartile breakdown of the high-performance work practices against our perform-ance measure – value-added per employee for the 90 panel establishments in our database for 1999 and 2002. On the left-hand scale, value-added figures come from the 2002 data, while on the right-hand scale the measure of practices are derived from the 1999 data. Value-added per employee was constructed by subtracting the value of bought-in goods from the total turnover of the establishment, and dividing this by the total number of employees. This measure captures how well people are being utilized to transform materials into finished products in a manufacturing environment.

The analysis represented in the figure shows a 62 per cent variation (£26 k) in value-added per employee between those firms with low levels of high-perform-ance practices (that is, in the first quartile) and those with high levels (fourth quar-tile). By focusing on the 90 panel establishments and regressing measures of practices in one time period with performance data three years later, we were able to bring a longitudinal perspective to debates on the relationship between HR and performance. However, it should be noted that our measure of practices in 1999 was not able to capture whether these practices were newly introduced or had been in place for some time. Consequently, it is possible that effect sizes may be explained by omitted variable bias. In order to address this issue, we repeated the regression controlling for a number of potential confounding factors that prior literature indicated might influence the relationship, including prior performance,

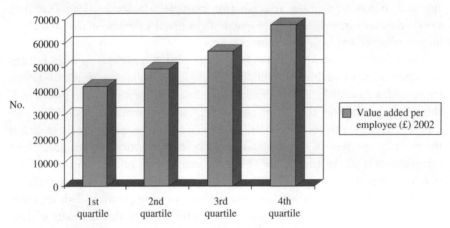

Figure 6.2 High-performance work practices and value-added per employee
Source: Thompson (2002)

foreign ownership, exposure to international markets and firm size. However, even with these controls included in the regression model, high-performance work practices still explained 37 per cent of the variance in value-added per employee. These data provide further evidence of the role that practices designed to enhance employee involvement and participation can have, as part of a high-performance work system, on organisational effectiveness.

High-performance work practice and lean implementation

The aerospace sector has been moving towards a lean production model for a number of years, but there has been some debate as to whether the low-volume, high-variety operations environment is necessarily conducive to lean practices that have been developed in a high-volume, medium-to-low-variety product market such as automotive (James-Moore and Gibbons, 1997). Lean production models look for worker commitment by paying greater attention to the social context of work and attempting to enhance social relations through involvement and participation. The thrust in the lean production system is not on variety and novelty, as under the craft model, but on standardisation and reduction of capriciousness in processes.

Within the automotive sector, research by MacDuffie *et al.* (1996) found some support for the argument that both lean practices and high-performance work practices facilitated the absorption of higher levels of product variety. Furthermore, MacDuffie (1995), using the same research evidence, emphasised the importance of high-performance work practices in the context of production systems, suggesting that there is an underlying production logic that selects certain types of practices over others and developed the concept of 'bundles' of practices that align with these logics. From this point of view, there is likely to be strong patterns of variation between sectors in their choice of practices, and between firms. In aerospace, for example, suppliers make distinctions between the Rolls-Royce and the Airbus production system, and these flagship firms are likely to shape the evolution of practices within an industry or at least a specific segment of that industry. Thus any understanding of the potential for employee involvement and participation in a mature industry may need to take into account the specific models of key players. This is certainly the case in the better-documented automotive sector, where Fordism and Toyotism have been dominant models.

From a performance perspective, previous work (MacDuffie, 1995) has shown that high-performance work practices, when combined with lean production, can lead to higher comparative productivity gains. In other words, operations strategies and technologies are necessary but not sufficient conditions for high-performance production facilities. Real benefits accrue when managers also pay attention to the social system and think through the integration of work practices with the prevailing technical and operational environment.

We build upon this insight in the aerospace sector and explore the extent to which the implementation of lean practices is linked to our three bundles of high-performance practices. The lean model suggests a strong correlation between direct involvement practices (such as job rotation, teams and information sharing), and lean practices. Research such as MacDuffie's underlines the importance of human resource practices in developing knowledge and skills for continuous improvement. We argue that while involvement is necessary for lean practices to be effective, this alone is insufficient. Firms need to address simultaneously both HR and employee relations practices, as these have significant indirect effects on lean practice implementation.

We explored this question using data from our 2002 establishment-level survey, which captured both lean and high-performance practices. In order to understand the relationship between the three bundles of practices and lean implementation we used structural equation modelling. This statistical approach allows a simultaneous estimation of a complex model where the path effects can be understood. It also takes into account any measurement error of the latent variables that might skew the analysis. The results are presented in Figure 6.3 and show that employee relations practices which provide opportunities for collective voice and procedural justice have an important indirect influence on the success of both HR and high-involvement practices. As expected, the path model shows that the strongest correlation is between direct involvement practices and lean implementation, followed by the HR practices. Indeed, the HR practices also have a direct effect on lean implementation but this is stronger through its relationship with high-involvement practices. There is no direct effect between employee relations practices and lean implementation, but a significant indirect effect through HR and high-involvement practices. Together, these results provide further evidence that organisations need to consider the role of collective voice and indirect representational mechanisms when they are building a high-performance organisational architecture.

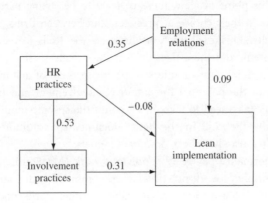

Chi-square = 24.195
Cmin/df 24.195/1

Figure 6.3   Lean implementation and high-performance work organisation
Source: Further analysis of Thompson (2002) data.

The findings provide empirical evidence supporting the conclusions of a CBI–TUC Report on the UK Productivity Challenge (2001) which argued that 'collective voice is important in building a climate of trust where individual employees are confident that their contribution will be valued', and went on to add that 'the involvement of employee representatives can create the sense of mutuality that is essential for the sustainability of working practices'. In other words, collective voice mechanisms can provide a context of legitimacy for the other practices being deployed to leverage employee knowledge and skills.

This analysis of the implementation of lean practices in aerospace, underlines the importance of both direct and indirect forms of employee involvement. In its more limited form, the lean model focuses on addressing workers' social needs through providing voice in relation to improvements in the production system immediately relevant to each individual, typically through off-line teams. However, an expanded model of lean production would embrace indirect forms of voice that can cover wider sets of issues at workplace level rather than be restricted to issues at the cell or production team level. However, this may require a considerable leap of faith by operations managers who fear that wider involvement may risk their desire for control of the overall production system and the achievement of the standardization of processes. As Niepce and Molleman (1998) have argued, 'The essential question is whether we believe that average human beings have the capacity to learn about complex production systems and manage them and should be given the opportunity to do so.' Clearly, collective voice mechanisms provide an important route through which this capacity can be developed.

Collective voice mechanisms have been shown to facilitate and enable more effective responses to environmental changes and enable companies to retain knowledge, skills and the commitment of remaining employees to innovation and workplace reform (Freeman and Medoff 1984; Heller *et al.* 1988). Indeed, Airbus worked with its unions to ensure that they could respond to the market uncertainty caused by the events of 9/11. Amicus worked with the company to moderate the impact of the downturn in business on employment levels and agreed to a wage freeze, a ban on overtime, a change in shift patterns and a reduction in the working week from 37.5 to 35 hours. At the time the company was very concerned about losing skills and knowledge in the short-term which would affect its ability to adjust to a predicted upturn in demand for its products. This was in contrast to the Rolls-Royce response, where the company used the opportunity to achieve reductions in workforce size that it had been planning as part of its wider review of its operational strategy. Here the employment relations strategy was initially not to involve unions in the restructuring process and to present job losses as a fait accompli. As a result, the company has had greater difficulty in pursuing subsequent workplace reforms in its brownfield sites because its actions led to a decrease in levels of employee trust.

A new facility Rolls-Royce has opened in Inchinnan provides, on the other hand, a blueprint for a new employee relations model that is likely to be replicated in new factories that the company has planned for the UK. The company developed a new employee relations framework jointly with Amicus and the GMB, based on a statement of sixteen principles, many of which relate to new ways of working and new values such as openness and communication. This new understanding has also led to the development of a joint management–union consultative group called 'Working Together', made up of senior management and trade union representatives. This forum shares business information and future plans, providing a context within which employees can see a link between business drivers and the need for innovations in work practices. A wide range of new practices provide the bedrock for the new model, including single-status, a 37-hour working week and higher levels of training investment. It remains to be seen how this new model performs, and how well the new consultative forum deals with crises such as a downturn (or indeed strong upturn) in business. There is evidence[3] from other Rolls brownfield sites that promised higher levels of training have not been delivered, as operations managers have focused on delivering volume in a rising market.

Conclusions

The research evidence presented in this chapter indicates that high-performance work practices are an important route to the development of higher-performing establishments and are influential in the implementation of innovations such as lean manufacturing. Through the use of longitudinal data we have provided unique evidence in one sector on the links between these practices and value-added per employee, an important measure of performance in manufacturing organisations. In simple terms, firms that use a greater number of these practices may see gains of up to 37 per cent in performance (after controlling for a number of confounding variables such as prior performance). This is not insignificant. Furthermore, we also found that the wider use of lean practices was associated with the adoption of a high-performance work model. What is important is that the employee relations dimension (that is, collective voice mechanisms) needs to be considered as part of this high-performance work model, particularly in the context of lean production.

These findings suggest that, if firms want to build knowledge-driven work systems, they need to recognise the importance of different interests in the workplace and develop channels and mechanisms for these interests to be represented. The prize for organisations is that in doing so, they are likely to attain the goals they value most highly in terms of a flexible, responsive and problem-solving workforce. Returning to our emphasis on knowledge as a key driver in value-creation in contemporary organisations, we need to recognise that 'knowing' occurs through the practices of communities, and that these communities (cells, production units and so on) need to be linked to the collective knowledge of the enterprise to enable sustainable and productive enterprises to be developed (Rolls-Royce's Working Together consultative process may be one such example). Such linkages and interactions can be crafted, and it is here that indirect representation may play a crucial role in integrating micro and macro knowledge for mutual benefit.

This means that firms need to develop a more sophisticated view of how the knowledge of disparate communities can be leveraged and integrated within a new governance regime that respects knowing as embedded in the firm as a community and in its sub-communities. This requires a pluralist model of the workplace which recognises that the different interests of workers requires a management mature and sophisticated enough to understand how collective voice can also serve to improve organisational effectiveness. As Cohen-Rosenthal (1997) has observed: 'a polymorphic understanding of the workplace rather than a singular conception of the best design linked to a singular power centre is a richer, more sustainable and more realistic alternative'.

The different interests of labour and capital cannot be wished away or ignored. Rather, taking a knowledge-based perspective of the firm, such diversity opens up endless opportunities for innovation. Managers need to recognize that the diversity of views, knowledge and insight within their organisations can be harnessed to build a more effective, satisfying and sustainable work context. However, the extent to which such an exhortation is likely to be listened to is doubtful. Managers are too wedded to market-driven efficiency and short-termism to raise their heads and consider new and different futures. When markets fail, public policy needs to step in to provide incentives as well as compulsion for firms to seek new efficiencies through involvement and participation which can create the conditions for knowledge exploitation and exploration. As such, the Involvement and Participation Directive may be something far-sighted firms can use to underpin new models of organisation based on knowledge and knowing.

Notes

1 Respondents were asked to give their job title when completing the questionnaire.
2 It is important to distinguish between 'firms' and 'establishments'. A firm may comprise several establishments (or 'facilities' as they are more generally termed in the USA) whereas an establishment will always be at a single, specific geographical location. Establishments do not generally report profit and loss figures.
3 Discussion point at a workshop held by the Midlands Aerospace Association at Rolls-Royce's Derby learning centre.

References

Allport, G. (1945) 'The psychology of participation', in *The Nature of Personality: Selected Papers*.
Amin, A. and Cohendet, P. (2004) *Architectures of Knowledge: Firms, Capabilities and Communities* (OUP).

Applebaum, E., Bailey, T., Berg, P. and Kalleberg, A. L. (2000) *Manufacturing Advantage: Why High Performance Work Systems Pay Off*. Economic Policy Institute: ILR/Cornell paperbacks.

Baron, J. and Kreps, D. R. (1999) 'Consistent human resource practices', *California Management Review* 41(3).

Baruch, Lev (2000) *Intangibles – Management, Measurement and Reporting*. Brookings Institution Press.

Becker, B. E. and Gerhart, B. A. (1996) 'The impact of human resource management on organisational performance: progress and prospects', *Academy of Management Journal* 39(4): 779–801.

Becker, B. E. and Huselid, M. A. (1998) 'High performance work systems and firm performance: a synthesis of the research and managerial implications', *Research in Personnel and Human Resource Management* 16: 53–101.

CBI/TUC (2001) *The UK Productivity Challenge*. CBI/TUC Submission to the Productivity/Initiative.

Cohen-Rosenthal, E. (1997) 'Socio-technical systems and unions: nicety or necessity?', *Human Relations* 50(5).

Cook, S. D. N. and Brown, J. S. (1999) 'Bridging epistemologies: the generative dance between organisational knowledge and organisational knowing', *Organisation Science* 10(4): 381–400.

de Man, Ard-Pieter and Duysters, Geert (2003) 'Collaboration and innovation: a review of the effect of mergers, acquistions and alliances on innovation.' Working Paper, Eindhoven Institute of Technology.

Engineering Employers Federation (2002) *Catching Up with Uncle Sam*. London: EEF.

Freema, R. and Medoff, J. (1984) *What do Unions do*? New York: Basic Books.

Gerhart, B., Wright, P. and McMahan, G. (2000) 'Measurement error in research on the human resources and firm performance relationship: further evidence and analysis', *Personnel Psychology* 53.

Godard, J. (2004) 'A critical assessment of the high performance paradigm', *British Journal of Industrial Relations* 42(2).

Heller, F., Pusic, E., Strauss, G. and Wilpert, B. (1998) *Organisational Participation: Myth and Reality*. Oxford University Press. Oxford

Huselid, M. A. (1995) 'The impact of human resource management practices on turnover, productivity, and corporate financial performance', *Academy of Management Journal* 38: 635–73.

Huselid, M. A. and Becker, B. E. (1996) 'Methodological issues in cross-sectional and panel estimates of the human resource-firm performance link', *Industrial Relations* 35: 400–22.

Huselid, M. A. and Becker, B. E. (2000) 'Comment on "Measurement error in research on human resources and firm performance: how much error is there and how does it effect size estimates?", *Personnel Psychology* 53(4).

James-Moore, S. M. and Gibbons, A. (1997) 'Is lean manufacture universally relevant? An investigative methodology', *International Journal of Operations and Production Management* 17(9):.

Jina, J., Bhattacharya, A. K. and Walton, D. R. (1997) 'Applying lean principles for high product variety and low volumes', *Logistics Information Management* 10(1).

Lowe, J., Delbridge, R. and Oliver, N. J. (1997) 'High performance manufacturing: evidence from the automotive components industry', *Organisation Studies* 18(5).

MacDuffie, J. P. (1995) 'Human resource bundles and manufacturing performance: organisational logic and flexible production systems in the world auto industry', *Industrial and Labor Relations Review* 48: 197–221.

MacDuffie J. P., Sethuraman, K. and Fisher, M. L. (1996) 'Product variety and manufacturing performance: evidence from the international automotive assembly plant study', *Management Science* 42(3).

Niepce, W. and Molleman, E. (1998) 'Work design issues in lean production from a socio-technical systems perspective: neo-Taylorism or the next step in sciotechnical design', *Human Relations* 51(3).

Normann, R. and Ramirez, R. (1994) *Designing Interactive Strategy: From Value Chain to Value Constellation*. Wiley.

Osterman, P. (1994) 'How common is workplace transformation and who adopts it?', *Industrial and Labor Relations Review*, 47: 173–88.

Purcell, J., Kinnie, N. and Swart, J. (2003) *Understanding the People and Performance Link: Unlocking the Black Box*. Chartered Institute of Personnel and Development.

SBAC (Society of British Aerospace Companies) (2002) *UK Aerospace Facts and Figures*. London: SBAC.

SBAC (Society of British Aerospace Companies) (2003) *Aerospace Innovation and Growth Team Report*. London: SBAC.

Teece, D. (1998) 'Capturing value from knowledge assets: the new economy, markets for know-how and intangible assets', *California Management Review* 40(3).

Thompson, M. (2002) *High Performance Work Organisation in UK Aerospace: The SBAC Human Capital Audit 2002*. Excutive Research Briefing, Templeter College, University of Oxford.

Wright, P. M., McMahan, G. C., McCormick, B. and Sherman, S. W. (1998) 'Strategy, core competence, and HR involvement as determinants of HR effectiveness and refinery performance', *Human Resource Management* 37: 17–29.

part 4

Options, issues and questions arising

The chapters in Part 4 move the analyses in the book forward by identifying and scrutinising closely a whole array of critical issues and key questions arising in the light of the contemporary moves to advance employee information and consultation practices. We saw in Part 3 evidence that information and consultation can deliver performance outcomes. However, these are not automatic. They are subject to a number of potential pitfalls and obstacles. The purpose of Part 4 is to examine these.

In Chapter 7, Phil Beaumont, Moira Fischbacher, Laurie Hunter and Judy Pate analyse a critical issue in relation to the effective working of I&C – namely, the issue of 'trust'. Using a number of case studies and action research interventions, the authors tease out the crucial elements necessary for building and maintaining trust. The chapter, in addition to its theoretical contribution, has important practical implications: it presents a 'road map' that practitioners can use to help move to a trusting relationship at work. It points out pitfalls along the way and gives hints about how to avoid them.

Chapter 8 by Ian Kessler focuses on the implications of I&C requirements for the public sector. The chapter notes the relative neglect of the public sector in most of the debate about the I&C Directive. Kessler notes the continuing ambiguity about the extent to which the legal requirements embrace large segments of the public sector. Furthermore, and arguably more positively, this sector already has a legacy of well-established I&C practices. How these will be affected by the new arrangements is not entirely clear, but the chapter identifies a number of critical pressure points.

In Chapter 9, Howard Gospel and Paul Willman explore the challenges and opportunities I&C offers to the various ways in which employee voice is heard or could be heard. The chapter compares the range of mechanisms and channels. Its prime focus is not on productivity or high performance, but rather on the implications for worker representation. The flow of the argument moves from what workers have traditionally had in this regard, what they currently get, how this compares with provision in other European countries, what British workers say they want, and finally the chapter speculates, in the light of recent legislative changes, what British workers are likely to get in the future.

In Chapter 10, Susan Marlow and Colin Gray assess the implications of the I&C Regulations for small and medium-sized firms. Finally, in Chapter 11, Peter Walton examines the critical question of what kinds of financial literacy employee representatives might need if they are to play an effective part in a representative works council. Many employee representatives identified this subject as one that was important to them, and yet it tends to be largely ignored in most discussions about the I&C Regulations. Using a worked example, Walton identifies the key issues and then moves on to offer a number of points of practical advice.

7

Explorations in building trust in joint consultation*

Phil Beaumont, Moira Fischbacher, Laurie Hunter and Judy Pate

It is a very safe bet that any academic conducting a series of contemporary case studies concerning the workings and effectiveness of joint consultation arrangements (whatever their form) will repeatedly hear the phrase 'it all depends on trust'. This has certainly been our recent experience. In the course of numerous case study visits and discussions with practitioners (both employees and management) we have typically heard contentions such as: 'in the absence of trust, no set of consultation arrangements will work' or 'if trust is undermined, the existing arrangements will achieve very little'. We accept completely the important role of trust in the process of consultation, but feel that the term is all too often used in a rather vague and general way. Specifically, we feel that there has been too little attention given to:

(i)   the *focus* or *focal* points of the trust relationship (between whom does it need to exist?); and

(ii) identifying the key *determinants* of trust, and the extent to which they are under the control of the representatives directly involved in the consultation process.

Accordingly, we seek here to develop a more finely-grained treatment of the notion of trust in the context of the joint consultation process. This is done by drawing on the insights obtained from a number of completed and ongoing case studies in which we have been engaged over recent years. These case studies variously have involved interviews with managers, union and employee representatives, focus group exercises with employees and the completion of a number of short questionnaire

---

*   The case study research drawn upon here was funded by the CIPD.

exercises. The material both sought and generated by the case studies has, in turn, been informed by a number of the leading propositions generated by the existing body of research on the notion of trust. The contents of Box 7.1 provide a summary statement of the propositions we extracted from this literature, which seemed the most relevant in the context of joint consultation.

Box 7.1   Some key relevant observations from the literature on trust

1 Researchers from a number of disciplines and subject areas have written about trust, variously viewing it as a function of personality differences, an institutional phenomenon or as involving interpersonal transactions.
2 In professional or task-orientated relationships, trust can evolve over time from a rational transaction-based relationship to one involving more of a mutual identification of aims and intentions.
3 Situational circumstances and historical experience are important influences on the level and nature of trust.
4 Trust and distrust are fundamentally different concepts.
5 Employee perceptions of trust in the behaviour of management will be influenced by the consistency of behaviour, integrity of behaviour, sharing and delegation of control, communication and the demonstration of concern.

Sources include: Lewicki *et al.* (1998); Whitener *et al.* (1998); Lewicki and Wiethoff (2000).

In essence, there have been two leading lines of distinct, though compatible, research into the notion of trust. The first approach involves studies of individuals or representatives working together in teams or task forces to build up trust over time. The general thrust of much of this work is that an initial basis of trust is provided by the establishment of a pattern of interpersonal behaviour involving predictability, consistency and reliability, which can then be built on by increased openness and information-sharing that embraces a shared sense of similarity of identity, aims and objectives (Observation 2 in Box 7.1). The second approach is concerned with identifying the key determinants of trustworthy behaviour by management (as perceived by employees), both within and between organisational settings. A helpful summary of this line of research is provided by Whitener *et al.* (1998) (see Observation 5 in Box 7.1). These differing perspectives have informed much of the discussion in this chapter, and will be returned to in our final section, which draws out some practical implications of our work.

For present purposes we would argue that in the context of the process of joint consultation, trust needs to exist at all three of the following levels or points:

(i)   between constituents and their representatives;
(ii)   between the representatives engaged directly in the consultation process; and
(iii) between the representatives and what we term here 'the larger organisational context'.

In this chapter our concentration is very much on points (ii) and (iii), although some of our discussion and illustrative examples will certainly touch on point (i). While all three levels of trust are important for the process of joint consultation, we particularly highlight the potential importance of point (iii) here, for two main reasons. First, in our experience it is from this level that damage to the operation of joint consultative arrangements so often derives in practice. Second, much of the academic work on trust has been done in the area of conflict resolution, where a fairly standard definition of trust is: 'an individual's belief in, and willingness to act on the basis of, the words, actions and decisions of another' (Lewicki *et al.* 1998: 440). Implicit in such a definition is that the trust relationship is overwhelmingly a function of (for good or ill) individuals directly dealt with across the table. In the context of joint consultation, we argue that such a perspective on trust is an important part of the story, but far from the full story. Indeed, we would argue that point (iii) above is of increasing importance in view of the fact that, in the contemporary environment, the larger organisational context of many organisations is changing rapidly, and at the same time becoming increasingly complex in nature, so that the capacity to develop trust with particular individuals across the table is becoming more difficult. In short, what we are emphasising is analogous to the distinction drawn by Alan Fox (1985) between vertical and horizontal trust, where horizontal trust corresponds to colleagues at the same level in the organisation and vertical trust corresponds to hierarchical relationships between employees and line managers/senior management.

The organisational response: seeking to shape the consultation process

In the light of the implementation of the Information Disclosure and Consult-ation Directive in April 2005 (see Box 7.2), what lessons or insights might an organisation that is contemplating the establishment of a new or revised set of joint consultation draw upon from UK experience? In our view, they could obtain at least two major insights. First, on the basis of a longer historical perspective, they would realise that voluntary joint consultation arrangements have always played 'second fiddle' to the role of collective bargaining; this is reflected in the fact that joint consultative committees were not all that widespread, many did not stand the test of time, and many had a relatively loosely connected agenda of numerous, but rather trivial (relative to collective bargaining coverage), items. Second, they would note that in the relatively few statutory-based cases of joint consultation in the UK (for example, collective redundancies; TUPE transfer) the process was conducted within very tight deadlines in which strong emotions and time pressures were present, caused by the 'crisis' nature of the problem they were seeking to deal with (for example, proposed plant closure and subsequent job losses).

Box 7.2   Guidelines on the joint consultation process

1   The employer must consult the information and consultation represen-
    tatives on:

    • the situation, structure and probable development of employment within
      the undertaking and on any anticipatory measures envisaged, in particular,
      where there is a threat to employment within the undertaking; and
    • decisions likely to lead to substantial changes in work organisation or
      in contractual arrangements.

2   The employer must ensure that the consultation is conducted:

    • in such a way as to ensure that the timing, method and content of the
      consultation are appropriate;
    • on the basis of the information supplied by the employer to the inform-
      ation and consultation representatives and on any opinion which those
      representatives express to the employer;
    • in such a way as to enable the information and consultation represent-
      atives to meet the employer at the relevant level of management,
      depending on the subject under discussion, and to obtain a reasoned
      response from the employer to any such opinion; and
    • in relation to decisions likely to lead to substantive changes in work
      organisation or in contractual relations, with a view to reaching
      agreement in decisions within the scope of the employers' powers.

Source: Summary of relevant sections of Draft Regulations, August 2004.

On the basis of this experience, it is likely that the management of our organisation
might seek to establish a joint consultation process that was something of a mid-point
between the two extremes of:

(i)   dealing with a one-off crisis event; or
(ii) having a very routinised agenda of rather loosely connected 'small beer'
      items.

The search for this middle ground is certainly something we have observed in a
number of our current case studies. Indeed, in one of our ongoing case studies we
are working with an organisation that has experienced both ends of the spectrum in
less than three years. In this non-union electronics manufacturing establishment,
the elected members' council was involved centrally in dealing with the first-ever
collective redundancy in the organisation, which involved some one in three of the
workforce losing their jobs. Since all the drama, tension and hard decisions that were
involved then, the meetings of the members' council have become, at least in the
view of the senior HR person, 'little more than question and answer sessions'. That
is, the six elected employee representatives hold prior meetings with their constituents,

receive a list of questions about a variety of matters, and pass these questions on for answer to the two management representatives in the council meetings. In response to his view that the current process was 'a very tired one' the senior HR person arranged for an external facilitator to work with the council at one of their meetings to see to what extent his view was shared, and whether there was an agreed basis on which to move forward. This facilitated session was then followed by a special full-day meeting of the council. At the end of this full-day session it was agreed to introduce the following changes in the mode of operation of the council:

   (i)   the name of the body has been changed;

  (ii)   the chairing of the meeting will change at each meeting;

 (iii)   each meeting will consist of two sizeable agenda items. The previous meeting will choose these, and within the meeting they will be referred to two sub-groups (each comprising three employee representatives and one management representative);

 (iv)   the two working groups will actively work to progress their items between meetings, with paid time off for this being given to the employee representatives;

  (v)   the aim is to develop a joint problem-solving orientation where the following outcomes could occur: (a) the senior HR person (on the body) can make a decision; (b) the matter is referred to the plant's managing director for a decision at an appropriate stage; or (c) more discussion, information and deliberation needs to take place within an agreed time frame;

 (vi)   beyond these two core agenda items a small element of question and answer will be retained in each meeting; and

(vii)   rather than the minutes of the body being emailed to all employees and placed on bulletin boards, the topics being addressed and the outcomes or state of progress will be included in the monthly business briefing provided by senior management to all employees, and a dedicated quarterly newsletter is being contemplated.

To help support these changes, the employee representatives have agreed to raise many of their traditional questions with line management, seeking a relatively speedy decision; any difficulties related to this are to be reported to the senior HR person. Furthermore, training sessions on both assertiveness skills and group facilitation skills have already been provided by an external trainer to all members of the new body, with the representatives being asked to identify any other perceived training needs.

Any proposed changes along such lines (and this is certainly not the only one of our cases hoping for such changes) immediately raise the issue of changing and managing trust in various forms: potential changes in the relationship between constituents and representatives, and between the employee and management representatives. It is to the trust theme we now turn more directly.

In our view, it is useful to consider the level and nature of trust as being shaped by at least three important set of influences or factors:

(i) the nature of the broader, historical relationship between employees (unions) and management ('historical baggage');

(ii) the degree of shared expectations and understanding between the employee (union) and management representatives across the table ('the ground rules') about how the process will, and should be, conducted; and

(iii) the degree of confidence the representatives (particularly on the employee side) have in the larger organisational context, particularly as this context changes and becomes more complex in nature.

These three sets of influences undoubtedly overlap to a very considerable extent, but we believe it is helpful to make such a distinction because it emphasises the potentially rather fragile nature of the joint consultation process, where positive trust relationships between the representatives across the table are important, but is certainly no guarantee that the consultation process will remain viable and meaningful over time. That is, it can be shaped or disrupted at levels beyond the reach of the consulters.

Historical baggage

By definition, the way in which historical circumstances shape current perceptions and expectations of the 'value' and 'effectiveness' of contemporary joint consultation arrangements will vary substantially between different organisations. However, what does not seem to be in doubt is the fact that contemporary perceptions and expectations will be shaped strongly by historical experience. This may derive from previous experience with consultative arrangements in some organisations, though even in organisations where there has been no prior consultative experience, the absence of experience may be an important influence. Moreover, historical-based perceptions of the larger employee–management relationship will be influential (albeit in different ways) in all organisations based on current perceptions of the worth of consultative arrangements.

To illustrate how no new (or reformed) contemporary consultative arrangements can start with a 'blank sheet' we shall discuss briefly three of our recent cases that indicate very different 'starting' points in terms of current employee and management expectations. In the electronics manufacturing plant, the members' council has been meeting monthly for the full life of the plant (over ten years). Only in the last year has the company established UK-wide joint consultative arrangements by setting up a body, to meet on a quarterly basis, that has employee representatives from its two non-manufacturing sites. Employee focus groups conducted in the two non-manufacturing sites point overwhelmingly to employee uncertainty regarding the potential value of the new consultative arrangements.

This is because their responses indicated a limited understanding of the nature of the consultative process, and considerable doubt as to whether such a process could be of any real value to them, either as individuals or as a group ('you will listen to us as representatives, but ultimately you can decided to ignore our views'). Further, there was concern that the agenda of the UK-wide body could be dominated ultimately by the agenda and experience of representatives from the relatively large manufacturing site. As a result, the non-manufacturing sites found it very difficult to put forward people willing to serve as representatives. Hence no employee representative elections were held in the two non-manufacturing sites, as the number of employees who were nominated to be representatives did not even reach the number of representatives required.

In marked contrast is the perceived (by management) relatively optimistic starting point among staff in a professional services firm. This organisation is planning to introduce, for the first time, team-briefing arrangements (for information disclosure purposes) and then employee representative arrangements based on their newly reorganised set of business units. As a background exercise, they had an external consultant conduct a series of group interviews with approximately 10 per cent of the workforce. This exercise revealed:

(i) a considerable lack of understanding among staff about the current performance and future business plans of the firm as a whole; and

(ii) a very considerable desire on the part of staff to contribute actively to the process of business improvement in the organisation.

It is the latter finding that management view as a relatively positive basis on which the new arrangements must seek to build.

Our third, and final, illustrative example in this section suggests that perceptions of the workforce, as shaped by historical experience (at least as the workforce sees it), suggest an essentially cynical attitude towards proposals for change in consultation arrangements. In this engineering firm, our questionnaire responses and focus group material revealed overwhelmingly that a sizeable majority of respondents believed that 'consultation has no effect because management has already made up their minds'. On the basis of this material we would expect relatively limited numbers of nominations for people willing to act as representatives, and constituents not strongly behind their representatives in the sense of being engaged actively and meaningfully in the process.

Establishing the ground rules

Beyond the reputations and stereotypes that emerge from historical experience (albeit perhaps selectively recalled) interpersonal experience, particularly over time, is important in shaping trust between the representatives around the consultation table. Typically, researchers (see, for example, Lewicki, and Wiethoff, 2000) have argued – at least in the context of conflict resolution – that creating trust in a relationship is:

(i)   initially a matter of building calculus-based trust (ensuring consistency of behaviour, with people doing what they say they will); and

(ii) moving on to the build up of identification-based trust, where there is an increasingly shared identification with the 'other sides' aims and objectives.

In helping to develop such a direction of movement it is important to try and ensure relatively clear understanding and expectations of the process of consultation. This is what we mean by establishing the ground rules.

As a starting point to the process, one can obtain some useful initial guidance from existing legal judgments concerning the notion of 'fair consultation' (Sargeant, 2001: 356) which has been viewed as having four basic pillars:

(i)   consultation when the management proposals are still at a 'formative' stage;

(ii)   'adequate' information is provided by management as a basis on which to respond;

(iii) 'adequate' time for the employee representatives to respond; and

(iv)   management must exhibit a 'conscientious consideration' of the employee representatives' response.

The words in inverted commas are key words upon which the management and employee representatives need to focus, flesh out in more detail, and adhere to in their consultation process. Two illustrative examples of how one might approach the task of providing the detailed content of these key terms are presented below. For example, at one of our public-sector cases, we conducted a series of focus group exercises with groups ranging from senior managers to shop stewards, with a view to seeing whether any consensus existed around the principles and practices underlying the notion of 'good effective consultation'. Box 7.3 indicates the leading results obtained.

A second way of seeking to help build up a set of ground rules concerning consultation occurred in another of our cases. In this drinks manufacturing organisation the approach adopted to date has had three elements:

(i)   management has sought to locate consultation in their larger 'philosophy' of organisational decision-making, and provided their list of what consultation is and is not;

(ii)   an external body has provided a training session for the employees and union representatives, in which the nature of the consultation process was central to the material provided; and

(iii) The employee representative recommendations based on this training material have been accepted by the management representatives as needing to be incorporated in the process.

Box 7.3   Perceptions of the principles of 'good, effective consultation'

The common themes that emerged from our five focus groups were:

1   It is easier to say what consultation is *not*:

- not a right of veto;
- not a one-way process; and
- not information disclosure.

2   Strongest emphasis: formal consultation processes will mirror the quality of the larger employee (union) – management relationship.
3   Major errors to avoid:

- unclear scope or coverage (Do we all agree just exactly what we are consulting about?); and
- no explanation is provided by management of the rationale for the decisions ultimately arrived at.

4   Value of the process: it should generate additional (beyond management's original list) options, which should then be narrowed down over time to result in a quality of final decisions that offsets the slowing down of the decision-making process that must inevitably accompany consultation.

Source: Fieldnotes from Focus Group Interviews, 2004.

The contents of Box 7.4 outline the summary of this process to date.

Box 7.4   Developing and defining the process of consultation

1   Management presentation to newly elected employee representatives:

- 'decisions will be taken by those best qualified to take them and influenced by those most affected by them' (overall view of decision-making);
- consultation is *not*: decision-making or negotiating; telling; local or individual issues and grievances; delegates from workgroups; running a business area; bureaucratic, fixed; and
- Consultation *is*: influencing decisions/taking views; two-way; good news/bad news; representative of business area; understanding business; flexible and responsible; evolving; confidential in part.

2   The key sessions/topics in the initial training programme were understanding and developing the role of the representative body, defining consultation and developing a consultation strategy. Group work was utilised extensively, and from the latter session emerged the recommendations listed below.

Box 7.4   (Continued)

3   Management should:

- adhere to the constitution by informing at the earliest opportunity;
- give reasons for planned actions. This should include background on the market place, business goals, impact on the employees, impact on the business, and timescales; and
- the representatives should give feedback, and management should listen and respond.

Trust in the larger organisational context

Our research suggests that representatives engaged in consultation can, at least in principle, experience two different sorts of trust difficulties within the larger organisational context:

(i)   'passive resistance', whereby their recommended options or views seem to get absorbed, lost or selectively interpreted at various rather vague decision points in the larger organisational hierarchy; and

(ii) the notion of a 'strategic shock', whereby a specific announcement or decision by senior management is held to be 'inconsistent' with the explicit or implicit ground rules of consultation, and indeed ultimately suggests the very limited reach and effectiveness of the consultation process.

In our experience, these sorts of upsets to the consultation process have been particularly powerful when the process is embedded in larger partnership working arrangements (Beaumont and Hunter 2003). In the next two sections we present two cases designed to flesh out and illustrate the two lines of argument listed above.

Employee consultation in an increasingly complex larger organisational environment: the notion of passive resistance

This case study is based in the public sector, where two key management themes in recent years have been, (strongly encouraged and supported by the present government):

(i)   the need to ensure that management decisions are not determined solely by supply-side interests, and hence the key importance of engaging in a wider stakeholder consultation process; and

(ii) the notion of joined-up government, which can be manifested tangibly in various ways – for example, the integration of service delivery across two independent organisations in order to reduce resource duplication and provide more effective delivery for end users.

As we seek to illustrate here, these two lines of development have the potential to reduce significantly employee representative perceptions of the worth of any employee consultation process, and hence can seriously damage the viability of such a process over time. In essence, what is reported here is a twofold phenomenon: namely, employee perceptions of a relatively positive process of interaction, but, operating in a context of uncertainty and concern over the likely outcome of their deliberations as their recommendations entered the larger organisational environment. Hence, the use of the term 'passive resistance'.

The case study was located in the context of the Joint Futures initiative (Scottish Office 1998; Joint Future Unit 2000) that seeks increasingly integrated aspects of service delivery between providers in the health service and social work. Specifically, we examined the activities of five working groups of occupational therapists (each comprising individuals from social work and health), who were given the task of producing a set of recommendations for change under certain specified terms of reference that would enhance the move to integrated service delivery. Their input represented one aspect of an extensive consultation process governed within the overall community care planning structure outlined in Figure 7.1. (The occupational therapy working groups discussed here are shown in the box at the lower right of the diagram).

Employee consultation within the working group setting centred around five themes (assessment; service framework; standards and quality; equipment and adaptations; and

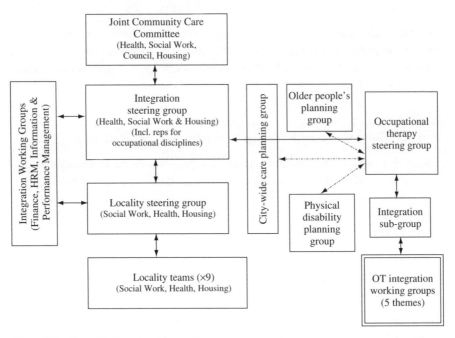

Figure 7.1 Consultation governance structure
Source: Documentation provide by case study organization, 2004.

development) and working groups were tasked with developing recommendations for service integration (health and social work) in relation to these themes.

On completion of this stage of consultation (a 6-month-long process), the working groups' recommendations for service integration were then subjected to a further cycle of consultation. Each of the planning groups identified in Figure 7.1 were given the opportunity to review the recommendations and to provide feedback. Stakeholder comments were then incorporated by the original working groups to provide a refined set of recommendations. Ultimately, the integration steering group (made up of senior managers) will ratify or veto individual recommendations. It is anticipated that the development and training recommendations will begin eight months after the feedback process, with other recommendations following after that time.

As background to our research work, the following points should be noticed:

- both Health and Social Work have a long history of consultation only with union representatives, and this process was continuing alongside that of the working group deliberations;
- this was the first experience that the vast majority of the occupational therapists had of being involved in such a consultation process;
- strictly speaking, there were no management representatives in the working groups, though all groups were facilitated by more senior people, one of whom was a member of the steering group for integrated services in occupational therapy; and
- alongside the five working groups were a variety of other joint future initiatives of a similar nature for other occupational groups.

Our research involved focus group discussions with all five working groups, together with the completion of short individual questionnaires by members of the groups. Both sets of information obtained (see Box 7.5) strongly pointed to very different views about the process of working together, and the outcomes of this working.

Box 7.5   Some key research findings from employee consultation

Illustrative quotes: '[we] mostly enjoyed [the process], found it educational, an eye-opener, and found it reassuring to see we shared views on the OT role'
'[I] felt the consultation and role in it was important but there's an element of symbolism in the process…we have done what we can but we're not sure how much will be taken on board'.

Employer: 59% of working group participants were employed by the National Health Service (NHS) and 41% by Social Work Services (SWS); 50% of them had worked in their current employment for more than ten years.

Involvement in the consultation process was voluntary for 63 per cent of working group participants. The remaining 37% were nominees; 73 per cent had not previously been involved in a process of this nature.

Participants felt that their main contribution to the working group discussions (expressed in terms such as knowledge of the client group, strategic understanding of the service) was their own personal experience of delivering occupational therapy services (see below). It is notable that only four participants had any managerial responsibility for implementation.

	Main contribution (number)	Secondary contribution (number)
Strategic knowledge about the service	7	5
Client group knowledge	6	11
Management responsibility for implementation	1	3
Extensive experience in clinical or social work practice	15	9
Experience of working in teams	6	7
Previous experience of service integration	2	2
Other (please specify)	3	1

Perceptions of the working group: the extent to which the work groups perceived themselves as teams differed considerably, with 39 per cent viewing themselves as a collection of individuals rather than a coherent team. In contrast, 27 per cent described their working group as having a 'shared bond and sense of identity'.

Although there was variance as to the extent to which they perceived themselves as a team, there did appear to be strong identification with the team (75 per cent identified closely with their working group) and high trust (97 per cent felt that there was a trust relationship between group members). Interestingly, 86 per cent felt their contribution to the group was of personal importance. This should be understood alongside the fact that 83 per cent agreed/strongly agreed that group contribution was important for career development purposes.

In summary, all five working groups appeared to gel relatively quickly, reported that they had enjoyed the process, had learned from it and were willing to repeat it. However, there was a very important attachment to the willingness to repeat the exercise – namely, their concern as to how their recommendations would be received by, and responded to, in the larger organisational context. In this regard, both uncertainty and scepticism were very much in evidence. That is, the relatively long time period between when they began their work (November 2003) and the earliest possible implementation date (April 2005) for any recommendations; the relatively long-drawn-out consultation process involving other relevant stakeholders; lack of knowledge of other working groups engaged in similar exercises outside occupational therapy; concerns that occupational therapy were not a high priority in the larger integration agenda; and, above all, concerns about the level of resources, funding and political and managerial will to underpin their recommendations all combined to produce the view that 'we have done what we can but we are not sure how much will be taken on board'.

The notion of a strategic shock

An illustrative example of this notion is provided by one of our ongoing cases. This foreign-owned organisation has a number of facilities in the UK. In recent years, UK management has in all its facilities sought to establish partnership-type working arrangements, in which the elements of consultation and trust are held to be absolutely central. However, a statement by an individual in corporate headquarters that a UK facility was to be closed, and the product transferred to a newly built facility in another country, was reported in the news media, and quickly reached the ears of union officers, shop stewards and employee representatives in the UK.

They made the point forcefully to UK management that the fact that this information was in the public domain before they were aware of it was unacceptable, for three major reasons:

(i)   it suggested that management did not trust them as individuals;
(ii) any such announcement was inconsistent with the organisation's rhetoric concerning partnership consultation, trust, and so on; and
(iii) it suggested that consultation on the issues that really matter to employees (that is, employment security) is a complete waste of time, with the final decisions having already been reached in venues outside the reach of the consultation process.

To try to offset this damage, senior managers from corporate headquarters have, in conjunction with UK management, spent a great deal of time in making presentations in the UK, and indeed in other EU member countries. The essence of these presentations has been:

(i) there has been something of an apology given in the sense of acknowledging a failure on the part of corporate headquarters to fully understand and appreciate all the details of this 'foreign' consultation process; and
(ii) a very detailed presentation of the business case that had been given to senior management and which provided the basis for the closure decision.

Beyond these short-term responses, corporate management has given the following commitments:

(iii) agreed that in the future any facility experiencing cost, productivity, quality and similar problems on a sufficient scale to raise doubts about their longer-term viability would be involved in a dialogue with headquarters that would make it clear just how much performance had to improve, and by when, in order to avoid such an outcome; and

(iv) employee representatives, stewards and union officers in all UK facilities were invited to meet, to produce an agreed list of best practice principles they would wish to see embodied in the consultation process where closures and sizeable job loss were involved. This list of principles would form the basis for discussions concerning their possible incorporation into company-wide business procedures for dealing with such situations.

In short, what we have here is an organisation beginning an attempt to recover and rebuild some of the trust among employee representatives that was substantially shaken, if not lost, by this particular 'strategic shock'.

Implications for joint working and consultation

We began this chapter with our contention that effective joint consultation 'all depends on trust'. As organisations move towards the increased use of joint consultation, creating and sustaining trust becomes increasingly important. We have suggested here that, as organisations move towards consultative arrangements, they need to concentrate not only on the specific mechanisms of electing representatives and chairing meetings, but that broader considerations also need to be taken into account. No organisational process is ahistorical. Some organisations may benefit from a positive starting position, where managers and employees are eager to work together; but others may not. In both settings, though, efforts will need to be made to clarify the nature of the consultation process, and to ensure that both management and employee expectations are realistic (regarding time-frames, agendas and the consultation process) so that there can be a shared understanding of one another's interests (identification-based trust). In other words, establishing the 'ground rules' is the crucial starting point.

These ground rules need to be developed within a broader organisational context that favours and supports consultation over the longer term to create an approach to consultation that seeks actively to overcome process-related problems such as 'passive resistance'. Here, emphasis needs to be placed on clarifying the range of organisational objectives on which the consultation has a bearing, and explaining related strategic priorities that will influence the development and implementation of those managerial policies that are the subject of consultation. Given potentially large numbers of individual and institutional stakeholders, particularly in the public sector, who are not only legitimately entitled to be consulted but with whom consultation may be mandatory, the organisational context for consultation is increasing in complexity. Clarifying organisational objectives in a multiple-stakeholder context will undoubtedly incur extensive discussion over a perhaps protracted period of time – a necessary phase if organisations are to move from a relationship of trust between individuals to one of a relationship of trust between representatives and the larger organisational context. In so doing, it is essential to ensure consistency between senior management behaviour and the ground rules of consultation, otherwise the potentially negative effects of 'strategic shock' may impede the effectiveness of consultation not only at the time of the occurrence, but also into the future.

There are therefore a number of issues for employees, managers and academics in relation to understanding the nature and dimensions of trust, and in terms of developing and sustaining trust in complex, and often relatively uncharted, organisational territories. We would argue that these issues present both a practitioner and research agenda which needs to be taken up as a matter of priority if public- and private-sector organisations are to make meaningful advances in the arena of joint working and consultation.

Some practical implications

By combining the insights from existing research (see Box 7.1 on page 90) and the practical lessons of our individual case studies, we believe that the establishment of a successful process of joint consultation, and its subsequent maintenance over time, requires: (i) mutual agreement as to what the process of consultation should essentially embody and involve; and (ii) seeking actively to ensure that potential organisational disruptions to this process are minimised over time.

In our view, the first step is essentially one of 'consulting about the nature of consultation'; that is, the designated employee and management representatives agree to sit down together to design and agree jointly the key elements of a 'good and effective' process of consultation, informed by the existing guidelines (see Box 7.2 on page 92). This first step is essential to both help to shape and to align the expectations of the two sides of the consultation table which are so important in producing the desired pattern of interpersonal and inter-role interaction that needs to be characterised by predictability, reliability and consistency. How two different organisations have gone about this initial first step is illustrated in Boxes 7.3 and 4 (see page 97). Although the two approaches differ, we want to emphasise, that both strongly reveal the importance of management providing clear-cut responses to employee-representative views, and a clear justification for the final decision when it is made.

As the management and employee representatives interact over time, on the basis of these initially-agreed ground rules, the likelihood of the initial basis of trust developing into one based on more of a shared identity and similarity of aims is nevertheless unlikely to occur if the larger organisational setting is a source of 'passive resistance' and/or 'strategic shocks'. Such perceived inconsistencies (by the employee representatives) are likely to raise concerns about managements' collective competence to organise and co-ordinate their own words and actions (Whitener *et al.* 1998: 16–17).

There is an analogy here with the 'no surprises' notion that is so prominent in current management thinking about how to conduct face-to-face performance appraisals and reviews. To eliminate all surprises completely in the rapidly changing context of so many organisations is a difficult (some would say impossible) task. However, what is clear is that the HR function has a major role to play in its inter- actions with other managerial colleagues – seeking to minimise such surprises by heightening the colleagues' awareness of just how sensitive a creature the joint consultation process is to such occurrences.

References

Beaumont, P. B. and Hunter, L. C. (2003) 'Collective bargaining and human resource managers in Britain: can partnership square the circle?', in Kochan, T. A. and Lipskey, D. B. (eds) *Negotiation and Change: From Workplace to Society*. Ithaca, NY: Cornell University Press, pp. 161–88.

Fox, A. (1985) *Man Mismanagement*, 2nd edn. London: Hutchinson.

Joint Future Unit (2000) *Report of the Joint Future Group*. Edinburgh: Scottish Executive.

Lewicki, R. J., Wiethoff, C. (2000) 'Trust, trust development and trust repair', in Deutsch, M. and Coleman, P. T. (eds) *The Handbook of Conflict Resolution: Theory and Practice*. San Francisco: Jossey Bass, pp. 86–107.

Lewicki, R. J., McAllister, D. J. and Bies, R. J. (1998) 'Trust and distrust: new relationships and realities', *Academy of Management Review* 23: 438–58.

Sargeant, M. (2001) *Employment Law*. London: Pearson.

Scottish Office (1998) *Modernising Community Care: An Action Plan*. Edinburgh: Scottish Executive.

Whitener, M., Brodt, S. E., Korsgaard, M. A. and Warner, J. M. (1998) 'Managers as initiators of trust: an exchange relationship framework for understanding managerial trustworthy behaviour', *Academy of Management Review* 23(3).

8

Consulting and informing employees in the public sector

Ian Kessler

One of the noteworthy features of discussion, deliberation and policy development on the Information and Consultation Directive in Britain has been the relative neglect of the public services. Indicative of this neglect is the way in which the government has chosen to shape and present the debate on the implementation of the Directive. The original Department of Trade and Industry (DTI) (2002) discussion paper on the Directive was keen to establish a link between informing and consulting employees and 'business productivity and competitiveness'. Clearly, this is a rationale that resonates in a much more direct and unproblematic way with the private sector, a point raised explicitly by the Employers' Organisation in Local Government (EO) in its response to the DTI document when it noted that 'The Consultation paper is very much oriented towards business rather than the public sector' (EO, 2002a). Indeed, their response progressed to express a 'hope that the voices of public sector employers will be listened to as we move towards the implementation of the legislation'.

In important respects these pleas for greater sensitivity to the public service context have gone unheeded. With the Regulations now in place, the overwhelming feeling among key union, management and employer stakeholders in the public services is one of some uncertainty, with a 'wait and see' mentality on the impact of the Directive on the sector very much to the fore. This chapter explores how, why and with what consequences a situation has been reached in which the application of the Directive and the Regulations to the public services remains at best opaque, and the stance taken by key actors essentially reactive.

In considering these questions, the chapter is divided into three main parts. The first looks at the coverage of the Regulations and highlights the ongoing doubts about their application to some parts of the public sector. The second sets out traditional and prevailing patterns of informing and consulting employees in the public services, and argues that the presence of an embedded and distinctive model of employee participation has important implications for how the Regulations have been perceived. Key actors have a vested interest in maintaining this model, and have therefore been keen to avoid precipitate action that might undermine it. Others may be tempted to challenge the model, but while uncertainty remains, they are cautious about the likely success of, or fallout from, any such challenge. In the context of these dilemmas, the third part of the chapter considers in greater detail how the key actors have responded to the Regulations. While caution and care characterise the positions taken by managers, employers, employees and their representative organisations, clearly they have had to confront the Regulations. This final section highlights their responses and the issues raised for them. The chapter is based on informal discussions with officials in a number of public service unions and employer organisations including those from Unison, Prospect, Public and Commercial Service (PCS), the Royal College of Nursing (RCN) and the Royal College of Midwives (RCM). The Local Government Employers' Organisation, NHS Confederation and the DTI.

The application of regulations: a basic uncertainty

The UK Regulations on informing and consulting employees explicitly cover public service organisations. Using the exact wording from the original EU Directive, the Regulations state that they apply to an 'undertaking', with 'undertaking' being defined as a 'private or public undertaking carrying out an economic activity, whether or not operating for gain'. It is a wording that appears to bring most of the 5.5 million workers employed in the four main parts of the sector – NHS trusts; local authorities; central government, including departments, executive agencies, non-governmental departmental bodies; and public corporations – clearly within the remit of the Regulations. However, a residual degree of doubt remains about the application of the Regulations to particular parts of the public services. The DTI, in its guidance on the Regulations (DTI 2004a), states that 'There is some uncertainty as to what extent public organisations fall within the scope of the legislation.' It is an uncertainty that revolves around the need for the undertaking to be involved in an 'economic activity'. The implication is that any public-sector undertaking not involved in such activity is (or may be) excluded.

This doubt about the exact coverage of the Regulations in the public services was raised by key actors at an early stage of the consultation process and highlighted repeatedly. The Local Government Employers' Organisation, in their initial response, stressed that 'at the very least the legislation and any associated guidance must clarify who it applies to' (EO, 2002a). One year later, when the Regulations were barely six months from implementation, the Employers' Organisation repeated its concerns: 'A critical issue for our sector is that there should be some early clarification on the application of the regulations to local authorities or, alternatively how the government intends to apply the principles of the Directive in the local government sector'(EO, 2003a).

Despite these calls, the government has continued to 'skirt around' this issue. The DTI Guidance on the Regulations flatters if not to deceive then certainly to provide little clarification. It holds out the promise of an inclusive definition of an 'undertaking', but one still heavily qualified by the economic test. As the Guidance states, an '"undertaking" may... include schools, colleges, universities, NHS Trusts and government bodies... if they carry out an "economic activity"' (DTI, 2004a). The use of the word 'may' rather than 'will' is particularly telling, and indeed the DTI guidance then moves on to question more explicitly whether certain parts of the public services will be covered. In short, it suggests that where a body is carrying out administrative or policy-making functions, it is 'unlikely to be viewed as an "undertaking"', but where the public-sector organisation is involved in some form of commercial activity, the Guidance notes the position is 'less clear'. It still, however, feels moved to cast doubt on the application of the Regulations where the commercial activity is ancillary to the primary function. The government has chosen not to clarify the position on the coverage of the Regulations to public service organisations, leaving it to others to adjudicate. As the DTI (2004a) Guidance concludes, 'Ultimately, it is for the courts to decide, with the Central Arbitration Committee in a position under the regulations to initially adjudicate.'

Such an approach is consistent with that taken by the government in relation to the Transfer of Undertakings (Protection of Employees) (TUPE) Regulations, 1981. These Regulations, implementing the EC Acquired Rights Directive, were couched in very similar terms to the Regulation for Informing and Consulting Employees, generating equivalent debate about their application to the public sector. In general terms, the TUPE Regulations sought to safeguard many of the employment rights of employees moving from one undertaking to another, with 'undertaking' being defined as 'a stable economic entity'. The judicial decisions seeking to clarify the application of this term to the public services in the context of TUPE have been drawn upon heavily by the DTI in its *Guidance on the Regulations for Informing and Consulting Employees.*

There have been a number of decisions made by the European Court of Justice (ECJ) that relate to TUPE and provide some possible indication of how the notion of 'an undertaking' might be interpreted in the context of the Information and Consultation Directive. A couple of ECJ decisions have suggested a relatively wide definition of an 'undertaking'. For example, the ECJ has ruled that it covers people providing healthcare services (*Porter* v *Queen's Medical Centre (Nottingham University Hospital)* (1993) IRLR 486) and assistance to drug addicts (*Dr Sophie Redmond Stitchting* v *Bartol* (1992) IRLR 366). However, it is the (*Henke* v *Gemeinla* (1996) IRLR 701 1996) decision that is seen as being particularly significant in setting some broad definitional principles, suggesting that organisations whose principal role is public administration or 'public authority' are not covered. Indeed, it is the emphasis the *Henke* decision gives to the 'dominant purpose' of an organisation that encourages the DTI to cast doubt on whether even public organisations involved partly but not principally in economic activities may be excluded. On this basis, 'The DTI view is that some civil servants and local authority employees would not be covered by the Information and Consultation Regulations' (DTI 2004a).

The unions have differed in their response to these judicial decisions and what they imply for the application of the Information and Consultation Regulations. The PCS (2004), for example, has been quite passive in this respect, accepting that quite a few of their civil service members are likely to be excluded. As their response to the most recent government consultation on the Regulations notes, 'The majority of PCS members work in the civil service or related bodies and the term undertaking would not cover most of those.' Other unions have been more challenging and critical of the DTI's interpretation. In responding to the same consultation exercise on the draft Regulations and Guidance, UNISON (undated: 3), in particular, rejected the interpretation in the DTI Guidance noting that '*Henke* only excludes a very narrow range of organisations from the definition of an undertaking'. Proposing a much more inclusive definition, the union suggests that if a public organisation can be contracted out and therefore be operated for profit it should surely be deemed as involved in an economic activity. 'The only consistent stance,' UNISON (undated) suggests, 'is to recognise that, in any case where the service is capable of being outsourced (at least in principle), the organisational entity providing it must be an undertaking for all purposes.' Very few public service organisations have been completely free from the shadow of outsourcing. Despite these debates and competing interpretations, the Regulations will be implemented with the uncertainties unresolved.

In summary, there is no doubt that the Directive and Regulations are explicitly designed to cover public-sector undertakings, but these undertakings have to be involved in economic activity. A residual degree of doubt remains about how some public-service organisations will be viewed in these terms. Judgments under TUPE suggest that some organisations that are principally involved in administrative work, may be excluded. However, the extent of this exclusion is contested and will only be resolved when tested in the courts. It is an uncertainty that makes it difficult for actors in the public services to move forward on the Regulations. The presence of a well-established model of employee participation in the sector has added to the difficulties in preparation and it is to this model that our attention now turns.

An established model of employee participation

The public sector has always had a distinctive model of employee participation and involvement, which in large part can be associated with specific characteristics of the employment relationship. While this pattern has varied in detail between different parts of the public services, it has proved to be a durable one with key elements essentially still in place. However, it is a model that has changed over recent years, with some core elements beginning to 'fray at the edges' and some newer components being introduced. The impact of the Information and Consultation Directive on the sector and the responses by stakeholders to it cannot be understood without a fuller appreciation of the present state of the model.

The current model of employee participation in the public sector can be seen to comprise a number of elements: a strong collective, representational dimension; a range of tiers; an underpinning style that combines adversarialism with partnership; and an element of direct employee involvement. Each of these components is considered in turn.

The collective dimension

The model of employee participation in the public sector continues to be heavily underpinned and driven by collective principles. This is reflected in the importance of independent, collective organisations in aggregating and articulating employee interests and in the extensive coverage of collective bargaining. In short, indirect forms of participation have been important, and enacted principally through a union channel of representation.

The strength of this collective dimension can be traced in large part to the government's role as employer or 'quasi-employer'. For much of the twentieth century there was a public policy consensus that, in a liberal pluralist society, trade union membership and collective bargaining should underpin the regulation of the employment relationship. Setting itself up as a 'model' or 'good' employer, it was only natural that the state should apply these principles to dealing with its own employees. This was apparent most clearly in central government (Parris 1973: 15–18), where the government was the direct employer. The recommendations of the Whitley Committee, which called for the establishment of joint committees, designed to provide a framework for the whole economy, were taken up most readily in the civil service with the establishment of the National Whitley Council in 1919. On the formation of the NHS, a General Whitley Council was set up in 1948 (Seifert 1992), while in local government, National Joint Councils for manual and while-collar staff also emerged on a stable and permanent basis (MacIntosh 1955). It was further indicative of this strong public policy commitment that a statutory obligation was placed on the major corporations established after the Second World War to enter into consultation with the appropriate unions to set up machinery for collective bargaining (Clegg 1953: 239).

The collective dimension of employee participation has been further strengthened by the nature of the workforce. Trade union recruitment in the public services has not always been straightforward. The wide dispersion of employees, particularly among the million or so local authority manual workers, required a major, resource-intensive process of recruitment among such unions as NUPE (the National Union of Public Employees), now part of UNISON.

However, the professional character of the workforce has encouraged employee membership of representative organisations variously described as professional association or professional unions (Burchill 1995). These organisations, particularly prevalent in the NHS, for example, in the form of the Royal College of Nursing and the Chartered Society of Physiotherapists, have attracted a high proportion of their respective professions into membership. This has enabled them to become key stakeholders in collective bargaining and the general regulation of the employment relationship, although there can be little doubt that their continued vibrancy and strength owes much to their role in supporting the professional development of members and in generally representing the profession (Kessler and Heron 2001).

The challenges to these collective principles and practices, particularly during the Thatcher years, most dramatically illustrated by the de-recognition of the civil unions at the Government's Communication Head Quarters, (GCHQ), have not undermined the model fundamentally in this sense. If anything, the 'New Labour' administrations have strengthened this collective dimension, albeit in qualified form (see p. 114). Indeed, the relative strength of collectivism is reflected in the fact that in the autumn of 2003, trade union density in the public sector stood at 59.1 per cent, while in the private sector it was just 18 per cent. Moreover, almost three-quarter of public service employees have their pay influenced by collective agreement, and most of the remainder are covered by Review Bodies. This compares to a figure of under a quarter (22 per cent) in the private sector (DTI 2004b).

The relative strength of union density and collective bargaining should not obscure the emerging fragility of this collective dimension. Union density is declining in the public sector. In the autumn of 1995, it stood at 61.5 per cent, indicating a fall of over 2 per cent in eight years. Interestingly, over this period, union membership in the public sector in fact increased, from 3.7 million to 3.8 million (DTI 2004b); for the unions, the problem is that clearly such increases are not keeping pace with the expansion in public sector employment. The coverage of collective bargaining has also narrowed, principally because a number of significant groups, such as nurses and teachers, formerly covered by this process now have their pay and conditions determined by Review Bodies.

A multi-tiered model

The second element of the public sector model relates to tiers of participation and, more specifically, is reflected in the fact that employee participation is fairly well developed at a number of different levels. Traditionally, certain aspects of employment relations in the public services have been highly centralised. National Joint Councils have largely determined pay and other terms conditions of employment. However, within the context of national bargaining, there has always been an institutional infrastructure that provided for a degree of employee involvement at lower levels. The original Whitley Reports called for consultation at different levels, and as instituted in the civil service, departmental Whitley committees have become an established part of the employment relations machinery in central governmental. Similarly in health and local government, such committees have operated for many years at the level of the former health authority and the local authority. Indeed, in the early 1980s and prior to a major restructuring of the sector, the Workplace Industrial Relations Survey indicated that almost two-thirds (62 per cent) of public service establishments were covered by a workplace committee or a high-level consultative committee. This compared with exactly a third of workplaces in private manufacturing, and just over a quarter (28 per cent) in the private services (Millward *et al.* 1992: 152).

In recent years, these lower tiers have increased in importance, and in large part this stems from the nature of public-sector restructuring. An integrated public service sector has become fragmented, with lower-level institutions becoming employing entities in their own right. In central government, the late 1980s saw many of the responsibilities associated with employment relations, including most importantly pay determination, being devolved from central government departments to over 200 executive agencies. Under the NHS and Community Care Act 1990, self-governing hospital trusts were created as independent employers. While most Trusts have continued to apply Whitley terms and conditions, they have assumed formal responsibility for the employment of their staff (IRS 1993; Bach and Winchester 1994). Alongside these structural changes, these lower-level joint bargaining and consultative tiers have assumed increased importance in the context of the broader process of public service modernisation, which in turn has generated a growing range of issues to be dealt with by them. This is illustrated most powerfully in local government and the health service. In local government, the Single Status Agreement in 1997 called on local authorities to undertake pay and grade reviews, in part to deal with equal pay concerns, but also in response to the need for authorities to develop pay structures that supported new approaches to service delivery. More recently, 'Agenda for Change' has sparked a similar process in the health service, with NHS Trusts being in the process of developing new pay structures within the context of a national framework.

There is considerable scope to question the capacity of local consultative structures and those union and management actors involved to respond to this expanding local agenda. In the case of workplace union organisation, there has been considerable debate as to whether or not this broadening and deepening of the employment relations agenda at local level constitutes an opportunity for 'trade union renewal'(Fairbrother 1994). Leaving aside such debates, it is clear that organisational change appears to be generating a wide range of employment relations issues for consideration by local consultative and bargaining machinery. Moreover, despite doubts over the robustness of this machinery, recent evidence suggests that it is still well embedded. The most recent Workplace Employment Relations survey (1998) indicated that 82 per cent of public-sector establishments were covered by a consultative committee. The contrast with the private sector is again stark, with only 43 per cent of establishments being covered by such a committee (Cully *et al.* 1999).

Adversarialism and partnership

The third component of the public-sector model of employee participation relates to the style and nature of employer and union relations. In the past, these relations might have been described as adversarial. However, the New Labour government rhetoric on partnership, while not being directed unambiguously towards union–management relations, has increasingly informed the development of public-sector industrial relations. Indeed, currently, employee participation in the sector might be seen to be underpinned by a sometimes uneasy combination of adversarialism and partnership. As the Local Government Employers' Organisation noted in its evidence to the Local Government Pay Commission, 'The Employers see the unions as partners and as adversaries' (EO 2003b, para. 10.5).

Over the years, public-sector employment relations have been characterised by considerable conflict and turmoil (Bach and Winchester 2003). Just as the government's role as a 'model employer' can lead to the adoption of 'progressive' industrial relations practices, so it can also encourage the disciplined and robust application of less palatable public policies such as those related to pay restraint. The 1960s and 1970s were littered with industrial disputes as public servants sought to resist or deal with the 'fallout' from successive government incomes policies, culminating most spectacularly in the 'winter of discontent' in 1978/9. The 1980s witnessed equally bitter industrial conflicts in the sector as unions, particularly in the nationalised industries, resisted plans for restructuring.

The period since the mid-1990s has not witnessed conflict on this scale, but contemporary industrial relations in the public sector are still characterised by a degree of antagonism. As the Local Government Employers' Organisation continued in its evidence to the Local Government Pay Commission, 'On the traditional bargaining agenda, the relationship remains one that is better described as an adversarial one'(EO 2003b, para. 10.5). The national strike in local government in 2002 is a testament to this observation, while the 2004 industrial action taken by the PCS in the a pay dispute with the Department of Work and Pensions similarly reflects this ongoing adversarialism. Indeed, in 2003, over half of the working days lost came from the public sector. Some 28 per cent of all working days lost were accounted for by ten disputes in public administration, and 26 per cent from fifteen stoppages in education (Monger 2004).

It is open to debate as to how far the development of a 'partnership rhetoric' has modified this adversarialism or affected practice at national and local levels. The term 'partnership' has been presented, interpreted and enacted in very different ways (Tailby and Winchester 2000). Most obviously 'partnership' has been used to restructure relations between public sector unions and employers. The initial moves toward this restructuring were reflected typically in a formal confirmation and endorsement of partnership principles at the national level. The application of these principles at workplace level, however, was much more uneven. In 2000, the civil service unions and the Cabinet Office signed a National Partnership Agreement. However, it was an extremely general statement unlikely to influence the character of employment relations at departmental or agency level. In the NHS, there was firmer evidence to suggest some moves at the local Trust level to review and reform patterns of union–management relations. Research has highlighted partnership agreements being reached at this level, leading to some restructuring of joint consultative and bargaining arrangements to provide more integrated systems and to extend union involvement in decision-making (Tailby *et al.* 2004). At the same time, this and other research (Bach 2004) has exposed the limits of these developments. In general, bargaining and consultative agendas have remained narrow, often confined to the routine formulation of policies, or heavily driven by managerial concerns, while the involvement of local union representatives has been significantly constrained by work pressures.

Arguably, this union-based form of partnership has been given some renewed impetus in recent years. The creation of the Public Service Forum in January 2003 involving the government and relevant unions was not only designed to facilitate top-level discussion on public service reform but also to encourage such a dialogue at local levels. The Forum commissioned a report, now published, providing details on ten case studies from the NHS, local and central, of 'good practice' in this area (Cabinet Office 2004) More tangibly, perhaps, partnership has been given a boost by major pay agreements in areas of health and local government. 'Agenda for Change', the 2004 agreement on a new pay system in the health service, commits itself to delivering this system through partnership working at national, and particularly at local levels. Similar principles underpin the three-year agreement reached by the National Joint Council for local authority staff in 2004, designed to encourage completion of local pay and grading reviews. Certainly, these developments restrict partnership to the traditional pay and grading arena. Moreover, the issues still remain concerning local capacity and managerial commitment when it comes to giving real meaning and effect to this approach. However, at the very least, they suggest an ongoing public policy and employer commitment to a partnership approach characterised by a strong trade union dimension to employee participation.

Partnership has also been taken forward through mechanisms designed to provide individual employees with a more direct involvement in aspects of work and employment. These direct forms of staff involvement constitute the final element of the public service model of employee participation.

Direct involvement

Direct forms of staff involvement embrace practices such as staff surveys, quality circles, team briefings and suggestion schemes, which tend to be centred more on work rather than on employment and power. The nature of public service work has always lent itself to this form of involvement. The exercise of work-related discretion and authority is one of the defining characteristics of a profession (Freidson 2001), and for doctors, nurses, teachers and social workers, a key part of their roles. Indeed, the professional character of much public-sector work is drawn upon to explain findings from a European study which found that direct forms of participation were more common in public-service than private-sector organisations across the EU (Hegewisch *et al.* 1998).

However, the use of direct forms of participation as a management tool, particularly in the context of organisational change in the public services, has grown in importance and by the mid-1990s appears to have been relatively well embedded. Data from the Workplace Employment Relation Survey, 1998 (Culley *et al.* 1999) indicated that almost a half (45 per cent) of public-sector work places had problem-solving groups. This compared with barely a third (35 per cent) in the private sector. Moreover, well over a half of organisations in the public sector (56 per cent) had recently conducted a staff survey. This was again considerably higher than the private sector, where the equivalent figure was 40 per cent (Cully *et al.* 1999: 68). Indeed, in some parts of the public services this form of involvement was extremely widespread. In public administration over two-thirds of establishments (68 per cent) had a suggestion scheme, and 75 per cent had recently been covered by a staff survey.

Again, more recently, these direct forms of employee participation have been given added impetus, being tied explicitly to 'New' Labour's modernisation agenda. As the government noted in its 'Modernising Government' paper (Cabinet Office 1999), 'We want staff at all levels to contribute to evaluating policies and services, and to put forward ideas about how they might be improved' (para. 17). There has been a degree of contrived ambiguity among policy-makers on how exactly these direct forms of staff involvement interact with the more traditional representational mechanisms. Often they have been presented under the umbrella of a union-based partnership approach. This type of involvement has been presented with some endorsement by the trade unions, and on the clear understanding that it is not designed to undermine union representation. Such an approach is most apparent in the health service (Munro 2002), where a range of health service unions co-operated with the NHS Confederation in endorsing a 'Resource Pack for Staff Involvement through Partnership Working'. In addition, a NHS Taskforce on Staff Involvement was set up with the Head of UNISON Health as a member (Department of Heath 1999).

There are, however, occasional instances of direct involvement being used as an alternative to, rather than as a complement to, representative forms of participation. Usually, this occurs where union membership falls to levels that seem to suggest the union 'voice' is no longer representative. The use of direct involvement appears to be associated less with conscious or strategic management attempts to weaken this union 'voice' (EO 2002b; Bach 2004). However, it is also difficult to deny that direct involvement, as an often unmediated form of contact between management and the employee, is likely to dilute the union–employee link.

In summary, there is a well-developed model of employee participation in the public sector. At its core is a strong collective dimension based on trade union involvement and joint machinery at different levels – national, organisational and workplace. Certainly, the scope of involvement has sometimes been limited to issues related to pay and conditions of employment, while the vibrancy of these institutions, particularly at local level, has been uneven and not always of the highest order. More profoundly, perhaps, it is a model that has changed in small but significant ways: union membership is not as pervasive, while forms of direct employee involvement are much more common. However, it is a model that remains deeply embedded and relatively widespread across the different parts of public services. It is a pattern of employee participation clearly very different from that found in the private sector, suggesting that the Information and Consultative Directive will present the public sector with a distinct set of issues.

The Information and Consultation Regulations: key issues affecting the public sector

General response

In broad terms, the response to the Information and Consultation Regulations from public sector unions and employers has been somewhat muted. Considerable attention has been drawn to the uncertainty surrounding the application of the Regulations to the sector, which may have tempered any response. But, equally, it could be argued that, given the nature and coverage of the prevailing model for informing and consulting employees, the Regulations present few challenges to the public sector, particularly relative to the private sector. The Local Government Employers' Organisation, for example, in raising some concerns about the absence of clarity on the application of the Directive to the public sector, noted, 'It is accepted that this may be because the public sector already tends to have processes which are more in keeping with the essence of the Directive and that therefore it is with the small and medium sized enterprises that the government feels it has the greatest work to do' (EO 2002a).

This generally muted response, however, should not detract from a level of activity and debate that is taking place within and between the employers and unions in the sector. Focusing initially on the employers, and drawing on the case of central government, there are moves afoot to cope with the uncertainty surrounding the application of the Regulations. It is likely that a code or statement of practice will be produced by the Cabinet Office which, it is widely assumed, will call for the principles of the Regulation to be applied to the civil service. The Council of Civil Service Unions has been holding meetings with the Cabinet Office to talk about such a code and, at the time of writing, publication is seen as being imminent. This is very much in line with the approach adopted by the government in dealing with the application of TUPE to central government. Public statements have stressed that, when it comes to TUPE, 'The Government's policy is that employees in public sector organisations should be treated no less favourably than in the private sector organisation when they are part of an "organised grouping" of resources that is transferred between employers'. It has given force to such an assertion in a Statement of Practice (Cabinet Office 2000) on Staff Transfers which adheres to the principles of TUPE and applies 'directly to central government departments and agencies and the NHS'. At the very least, it would seem somewhat anomalous if the forthcoming Cabinet Office code or statement on information and consultation with employees was not couched in similar terms.

As for local government employers, their representative body has been prepared to 'cut through' the general air of uncertainty by advising authorities to assume that the Regulations will apply. It is perhaps a bold assertion, in that a small shire district that had outsourced most of its frontline services, leaving it with a rump of largely administrative activities, might well be deemed to fall outside the definition of an 'undertaking' according to current case law. However, in advice, close to the position taken by UNISON on this issue, the EO (2003b) states 'Given that under the best value regime every area of local government activity seems capable of operation for the purposes of economic gain, it seems safest to assume that the whole of the authority is covered by the Regulations and we would recommend that authorities go forward on this basis.'

It is in the NHS that the national employer response has been at its most restrained. It is very difficult to find any expression of views or advice at the national level on this issue. This may be because the national employer role is in the process of finding a new 'home' as industrial relations responsibilities are transferred from the Department of Health to the NHS Confederation. It may be that the NHS is too preoccupied with other issues, in particular 'Agenda for Change', to devote much energy to the Regulations. It may well also be that, of all the parts of the public services, and for reasons to be discussed below, the NHS is the least challenged by the Regulations.

On the union side, the national response has also been varied. Certainly, in general, the public sector unions have given the Regulations a guarded welcome, but still approached them with some caution. Following years of contracting out and privatisation, most public sector unions now have members in both public and private sectors. Given the contrasting patterns of employee participation, they have therefore had to be sensitive to the very different implications of the Regulations for their members in the respective sectors. While in the private sector the Regulations lend some force to, and provide some means for, developing union-based forms of employee participation for the first time, in the public sector an established system needs to be preserved from the dangers that may be lurking in the Regulations. As UNISON notes in outlining the implications of the Regulations for its members, 'The effect may be very different depending on whether you are in an organised public sector workplace covered by a comprehensive set of agreement, or in a less well organisation private company' (UNISON 2004: 2).

Within this context, public sector unions have taken different approaches to the forthcoming Regulations, particularly in terms of how they have presented the resulting issues to officials, activists and members. UNISON has taken quite an assertive and active approach in drawing the attention of activists to the Regulations and providing detailed 'negotiating tips'. As UNISON (2004) notes in its advice, 'There is a quite a lot of technical detail around the scope of the directive and its mechanics. But the point to bear in mind is that it cannot and must not be ignored.' PCS (2004) has also sought to raises awareness, albeit on a lesser scale, providing a very short note on the implications that are mainly seen as relating to its members in the private sector. Other unions have chosen to keep a much lower profile on the issue. Mirroring the low-key employer response, NHS unions such as the Royal College of Midwives have provided a simple summary of the Regulations for their full-time officers, with no commentary or advice. The Royal College of Nursing appears to have provided little in the way of advice or even information. In the civil service union, Prospect, there has been some internal discussion between full-time national officers on the implications of Regulations but, beyond news reporting on their progress and content, no broader material has been produced for wider circulation.

From an uneven and varied set of general employer and union responses to the Regulations, it is still possible to identify a number of issues that have emerged with a degree of regularity as the basis for discussion and debate. Some of these issues have been of a detailed or technical kind. For example, in commenting formally on the Regulations, the public sector unions have consistently been critical of the fact that they will cover 'employees' rather than the broader category of 'workers'. In public-sector organisations, where, as noted, the provision of services by contractors has increased over the years, scope only for 'employees' to be informed and consulted about developments in the undertaking, which could have major implication for all who work there, has been a seen as significant limitation on the proposed rights. Detailed points aside, however, three main issues have dominated deliberations.

Pre-existing arrangements

The first relates to the formalities underpinning the current arrangements for informing and consulting employees. Under the Regulations, pre-existing agreements on information and consultation, if approved by the workforce, are acceptable under the Regulations. However, these agreements have to be in writing and must set out how the employer is to give information to the employees or their representatives and seek their views on such information. In the case of most NHS Trusts, this is unlikely to be a problem. The relatively recent establishments of such Trusts under the 1990 legislation, and even more recently the creation of Primary Care Trusts, has often been accompanied by the signing of a formal, written recognition agreement with the appropriate unions and professional associations (Bryson et al. 1995).

Such agreements have typically set out in detail the arrangements for information and consultation. A cursory review of such agreements reveals this to be the case. For example, the South Hams and West Devon Primary Care Trust's Recognition Agreement signed in 2001 provides details about the membership and role of a Joint Consultation Committee, while the Westminster Primary Care Trust Trade Union Recognitions Agreement, 2004, highlights the role of its Joint Staff Consultative Committee to 'provide a recognised and regular opportunity for exchange of information, consultation and discussion between accredited union representatives and management on matters affecting the interests of staff'. In fact, there are instances drawn from the NHS where the Directive clearly has affected the substance of these arrangements. A paper to the Board of the North East Ambulance Service NHS Trust in September 2004, on the revision of the Recognition Agreement, notes, 'When agreeing new arrangements the Trust needs to take account of the [Information and Consultation] Directive.'

Outside the NHS, however, there are some concerns about whether pre-existing agreements meet the regulatory requirements in this respect. In the civil service, executive agencies were not set up as employing organisations in the same statutory way as were NHS Trusts. Employment relations responsibilities were devolved in an incremental manner, and consultative arrangements tended to transfer from departments to executive agencies in an informal and internal way. There are some doubts whether, in all agencies, the details of these arrangements are set out in a formal written document.

This concern is raised even more explicitly in the case of local authorities. In an Advisory Bulletin, the EO (2003b) sets out the Directive's requirement for pre-existing arrangements and notes, 'We wonder how many authorities have information and consultation arrangements that are in a form that meets [these] requirements' (para. 36). It is an observation which prompts the EO to encourage authorities to review their consultative set-ups: 'This does seem to be an opportune time to revisit and revitalise our employee involvement and consultation mechanisms in order to ensure that they serve the purpose of helping us deliver high performance workplaces'(para. 36). In the absence of evidence, whether such a call has proved to be a stimulus for review must remain an open question. Clearly, there are some concerns that the existing arrangements in local government and the civil service are not formalised in ways that would protect organisations from the need to renegotiate them if challenged.

Channels of representation

The second issue raised by the Regulations relates very much to this concern about current institutional arrangements, and more specifically to the ongoing viability of a single, union channel of representation in the public sector. It is doubtful whether direct forms of information and consultation will meet the terms of the Directive, and provide a defence against employee attempts to trigger representative-based consultation arrangements (Hall 2004). However, the Directive and Regulations do leave open the possibility of information and consultation arrangements based on a non-union channel of representation.

The possibility of a non-union channel becomes a very real issue where levels of union density begin to fall below 50 per cent. Although employee support for the union is likely to extend well beyond membership figures, at this point the representativeness of the union begins to be questioned. As noted, aggregate figures suggest that union membership in the public sector remains well above half. However, it has been stressed equally that density is falling, and in some organisations may well have fallen below this figure. The Local Government Employers' Organisation highlighted their concerns in this respect in their evidence to the Local Government Pay Commission:

> The relative decline in union membership in the sector is becoming an issue. In whole swathes of southern and rural England, membership levels have fallen to a point at which it is difficult for councils to be confident that the unions speak for the workforce as a whole. Overall membership appears to have fallen below 40% of the local government service's workforce, to judge by the numbers balloted for the 2002 industrial action. (2003: para. 10.6)

There is little doubt that for the public sector unions this is where the major danger in the Regulations lies. It is a danger that takes different but equally unpalatable forms from their perspective. Where established joint machinery is in place with union involvement, an information and consultation system might be established through non-union channels of representation which then runs alongside, and in the longer term may even replace it. Various permutations can be envisaged. Where the joint union–management arrangements combine bargaining and consultation, the consultative element might be pulled out into a non-union forum; where separate union-based bargaining and consultative committees exists, the latter may shift to non-union forms of representation, restricting union involvement to bargaining; and where no machinery for information and consultation exists, it may simply be set up for the first time on a non-union basis. A 'worst case scenario' would be that employers used the Regulations as an excuse to shift all forms of joint involvement–bargaining, consultation and information – to a non-union channel. As UNISON (2004: 4) notes in summarising these possibilities and their consequences:

> The effect could be workers' councils springing up, either competing with long standing union–employer arrangements and confusing staff or, in the worst case – where representation is lower than ideal or employers actively hostile – unions being shut out by a different scheme of staff representation.

The UNISON (2004) advice to activists which naturally follows from this is that they should 'resist parallel bodies'. However, it is interesting to note that UNISON does suggest that local representatives might agree to consult with non-unionists over issues related to information and consultation. This is viewed as a way of pre-empting the need for parallel structures, and as an opportunity to recruit in new areas of the organisation. Indeed, more generally, the response of public service unions has been to use the threat of a non-union channel of representation as the basis for encouraging local activists to recruit more members. If alternatives are being considered because unions no longer represent of the majority, the 'best response' is to recruit more members to ensure that they do.

There are few indications that public-sector employers are intending to use the Regulations to undermine established bargaining and consultation arrangements. There are examples of attempts to set up forms of non-union representation, but at present these appear to be isolated instances. In local government, the Employers' Organisation is broadly supportive of the continuation of union-based arrangements. This is reflected in an awareness of the potential for the Regulations to 'disrupt established information and consultation mechanisms'. Indeed, the EO (2002a) called for legislation to be framed in such a way 'that approval of pre existing arrangements may be demonstrated more easily for employers and trade unions who jointly wish to preserve established arrangements that provide for consultation or employee representatives *who speak on behalf of the workforce*' (2002b; emphasis added). Clearly, however, this is a slightly barbed comment and suggests contingent support for established arrangements. It has been noted that the EO has drawn attention repeatedly to concerns among some local authorities as to how representative of the workforce are unions now. Indeed, there are suggestions that some authorities have sought to set-up non-union forms of representation. As the EO (2002a: 9) notes, 'Some authorities have found the need to supplement the traditional methods of adopting complementary mechanisms or a works council approach.'

In the health service, the heavy emphasis placed on 'partnership' in 'Agenda for Change' and the importance of ongoing developments in this area of pay reform at Trust level would suggest that attempts to undermine the union channel of representation are unlikely. It might be argued that in times of such major changes and the need to elicit employee support, trade unions, however flawed, are the 'best show in town'. Established arrangements may be notionally more vulnerable to the introduction of non-union channels of representation where they are dealing with non-pay issues which after all are the main focus on the Regulations. Bach (2004) has drawn attention to a consultative arrangement in a case study trust which dealt with clinical issues and involved nurses in a non-union representative capacity. More generally, it is not unusual for Trusts to have separate bodies for dealing with pay and non-pay issues, the former often being a negotiating forum and the latter a consultative one. For example, this is the case at the Green Park Healthcare Trust, the Cambridge and Peterborough Mental Health Partnership NHS Trust, and Westminster Primary Care Trust.

There are no indications that employers in the NHS are likely to use the Regulations to 'salami slice' consultative and bargaining arrangements, using non-union channels of representation for the former and union channels for the latter. However, there are indications in other parts of the public sector. Again, such instances are atypical but they can be found: for example, the Civil Aviation Authority (CAA) has recently established new joint arrangements that will continue to see trade unions as the sole channel of representation for pay bargaining purposes, but will allow for non-union representatives to sit on a new employee consultative forum. Management has suggested that the new Regulations did play a part in encouraging this revamping of the arrangements in the context of union membership, which had fallen to around 30 per cent of the CAA's main workforce.

The scope of information and consultation

The Regulations provide explicitly for an extension in the scope of information and scope to cover matters relating to the future development of the undertaking, and to employment and work organisation. In a sector where employee participation has concentrated heavily on issues of pay and conditions of employment, such an extension might be seen as presenting public sector unions and employers with some challenges. For the unions, in particular, this might be seen as an opportunity. In fact, this is an opportunity that does not appear to have figured prominently. Certainly, it has informed discussion in some unions such as Prospect; however, UNISON makes no mention of it in advice to members and activists.

This limited response may well reflect the fact that in the context of major change in public service organisations, pay and conditions issues are more difficult to disentangle from broader and related issues, suggesting that the scope for bargaining, consulting and informing may already have expanded. However, there may be more fundamental difficulties in extending the scope for information, and especially consultation, in some of the areas proposed in the Regulations. Given that public-sector organisations are driven by a political decision-making process, it can be problematic to have meaningful discussions on future developments and on employment relations fallout. The most obvious example of such a situation was where the Chancellor of the Exchequers announced major job losses in the civil service in his 2004 Budget. While employee representatives might be consulted about the processes for handling job losses, this was clearly a major public policy announcement on which the scope for discussion would always remain limited.

Summary and conclusion

The Regulations on informing and consulting employees are hovering 'off stage' as the established pattern of employee participation continues to play on in the public sector. The employment relations actors are more or less aware of them, and some have responded tentatively. However, it has been suggested that this 'off stage' role reflects particular features of the public sector and the way in which the Regulations interface with them.

Doubts about whether all public sector organisations are involved in economic activities continue to casts a shadow over the application of the Regulations. In practice, most organisations will be covered, particularly with a civil service code likely to assert that the principles underpinning the Regulations should be applied to central government. In such circumstances, any explanation for the low-key response might be seen to lie much more in the prevailing model of employee participation in the public sector. This is a model which suggests that both direct and indirect forms of participation are fairly well established and indeed have perhaps deepened in the context of change associated with the process of public service modernisation. The Regulations may present a distinctive set of challenges in this sector, given the very different patterns of employee participation it displays compared to other parts of the economy.

There has been a level of awareness and debate about the Regulations among key actors in the public services, and this has been more intense in some parts of the public services than others. It has become clear that the pace and nature of change in the health service has pushed consideration of the Regulations much further into the background than in central and local government. However, general issues of concern to various parties have been identified.

It has been suggested, for example, that the informality underpinning established arrangements for consulting and informing employees may well not be enough to resist employee challenges for the negotiation of a new set-up in some public service organisations. More significantly, concerns about the channel of representation haunt the unions as membership levels drop and non-union forms of involvement emerge as an option. While there is little to suggest that public sector employers are pursuing this option on a widespread or strategic basis, they are not beyond raising the spectre. For unions, the implications are clear and recognised: recruitment initiatives need to be strengthened to avoid any doubt that the union voice is representative of the whole workforce. The employers also need to consider the implications of any weakening in the union voice. It is extremely unlikely that a non-union channel will provide a more meaningful, efficient and effective voice than that presented by the unions. Rather than just pointing out this weakening in the union voice, the employers might more usefully consider how they can help the unions in addressing membership issues by adding their support and weight to union recruitment efforts.

References

Bach, S. (2004) 'Employee participation and union voice in the NHS', *Human Resource Management Journal* 14(2): 3–19.
Bach, S. and Winchester, D. (1994), 'Opting out of pay devolution? Prospects for local pay in UK public services', *British Journal of Industrial Relations* 32(2): 82–96.

Bach, S. and Winchester, D. (2003) 'Industrial relations in the public sector', in P. Edwards (ed.) *Industrial Relations: Theory and Practice*. Oxford: Basil Blackwell.

Bryson, C., Jackson, M. and Leopold, J. (1995) 'The impact of self governing trusts on trade unions and staff associations in the NHS', *Industrial Relations Journal* 26(2): 120–32.

Burchill, F. (1995) 'Professional unions in the NHS: issues and membership trends', *Review of Employment Topics* 3: 13–23.

Cabinet Office (1999) *Modernising Government*. London: HMSO.

Cabinet Office (2000) *Statement of Practice on Staff Transfers*. London: HMSO.

Cabinet Office (2004) *Trade Union and Employee Involvement in Public Service Reform*. London: HMSO.

Clegg, H. (1953) '239 employers', in Flanders, A. and Clegg, H. (eds) *The System of IR in Britain*. Oxford: Basil Blackwell.

Cully, M., Woodland, S., O'Reilly, A. and Dix, G. (1999) *Britain at Work*. London: Routledge.

Department of Health (1999) *Report of the NHS Taskforce on Staff Involvement*. London: DOH.

DTI (Department of Trade and Industry) (2002) *High Performance Workplaces*. London: DTI, July.

DTI (Department of Trade and Industry) (2004a) *Guidance on the Regulations for Informing and Consulting Employees*. London: DTI.

DTI (Department of Trade and Industry) (2004b) *Trade Union Membership*, London: DTI.

EO (Employers' Organisation in Local Government) (2002a) *Response to High Performance Workplace*. London: EO, 10 December.

EO (Employers' Organisation in Local Government) (2002b) *Enhancing Employee Involvement*. London: EO.

EO (Employers' Organisation in Local Government) (2003a) *Response to High Performance Workplace*. London: EO, 5 November.

EO (Employers' Organisation in Local Government) (2003b) *Evidence to the Pay Commission for Local Government Services' Staff*. London: EO.

Fairbrother, P. (1994) *Politics and the State as Employer*. London: Mansell.

Freidson, E. (2001) *Professionalism: The Third Logic*. Cambridge: Polity Press.

Hall, M. (2004) *EU Directive on Information and Consultation: How Will It Affect Employment Relations in the UK?* London: TUC.

Hegewisch, A., Kessler, I. and Van Ommeren, J. (1998) *Findings from the EPOC Survey: Direct Participation in the Social Public Services*. Dublin: European Foundation.

IRS Employment Trends (1993) 'Local Bargaining in the NHS', No. 537: 7–14.

Kessler, I. and Heron, P. (2001) 'Steward organisation in a professional union: the case of the royal college of nursing', *British Journal of Industrial Relations* 39(3): 367–91.

Local Government Employers' Organisation (2003) 'High performance workplaces: informing and consulting employees', *Advisory Bulletin No. 474*. London: EO.

MacIntosh, M. (1955) 'The negotiation of wages and conditions for local authority employees', *Public Administration* 23: 168–85.

Millward, N., Stevens, M., Smart, D., Hawes, W. (1992) *Workplace Industrial Relations Transition*. Aldershot: Dartmouth.

Monger, J. (2004) 'Labour disputes in 2003', *Labour Market Trends*, June: 235–46.

Munro, A. (2002) 'Working together – involving staff: partnership working in the NHS', *Employee Relations* 24(3): 277–89.

Parris, H. (1973) *Staff Relations in the Civil Services*. Oxford: George Allen & Unwin.

PCS (2004) *Informing and Consulting in the Workplace*, Factsheet No. 1, August. London: PCS.

Seifert, R. (1992) *Industrial Relations in the NHS*. London: Chapman & Hall.

Tailby, S. and Winchester, D. (2000) 'Management and trade unions: towards partnership', in Bach, S. and Sisson, K. (eds) *Personnel Management: A Comprehensive Guide to Theory and Practice*. Oxford: Basil Blackwell.

Tailby, S., Richardson, M., Stewart, P., Danford, A. and Upchurch, M. (2004) 'Partnership at work and worker participation: an NHS case study', *Industrial Relations Journal* 35(5): 403–18.

UNISON (undated) *UNISON's Response to the Government's Consultation Document 'High Performance Workplaces – Informing and Consulting Employees'*. London: UNISON.

UNISON (2004) *Fact Sheet: European Information and Consultation Directive*. London: UNISON.

9

Changing patterns of employee voice

Howard Gospel and Paul Willman

This chapter focuses on the mechanisms by which workers, unionised and non-unionised, are represented at work and through which they obtain varying degrees of voice in employer decision-making. In addition to collective bargaining by trade unions, it highlights the mechanisms of information sharing and joint consultation. One argument is that an understanding of the interaction of these representative mechanisms is important for an appreciation of the present and likely future patterns of worker representation in the UK. Specifically, it suggests that forms of representation other than collective bargaining may in future prove more popular voice mechanisms – with both employers and employees – than they have in the past.

The chapter's structure is as follows. The first section places the development of representative systems in Britain in a broad historical perspective. The second section then maps the current situation – it deals with what British workers get. This is compared broadly in the third section with arrangements in three other major countries – the focus here is on what workers in these countries get. The fourth then deals with what British workers say they want. Finally, in the light of recent European developments, we speculate about what British workers are likely to get.

What did British workers get in the past?

Historically, employers unilaterally made most decisions on work matters. In some instances, usually job-related issues, skilled or strategically placed workers could unilaterally regulate certain aspects of their working lives. From the late nineteenth century onwards, collective bargaining gradually developed. In some situations, to ward off collective bargaining, a minority of employers established joint consultative arrangements of various kinds (Gospel 1992: 79–84, 99). However, for the most part, unions were opposed to (or at least suspicious of) consultative committees, which they considered likely to undermine their appeal to workers and their ability to represent members.

During the First World War, both collective bargaining and joint consultation developed significantly at national and workplace levels. The Whitley Committee (1918) recommended that both should be further elaborated, with the former concentrated on pay and conditions, in particular outside the firm, and the latter on other matters, especially at the workplace. At the time, strong unions showed little interest in consultation; weaker unions accepted the proposals on multi-employer bargaining, but again showed little interest in joint consultation without collective bargaining. Equally, most employers were reluctant to accept workplace-level representation, either by shop stewards or by other worker representatives. It was in Germany that a system of combined collective bargaining and joint consultation was introduced by legislation (Feldman 1992). In Britain during the interwar depression, collective bargaining narrowed and formal joint consultation contracted. Subsequently, from the mid-1930s onwards and during the Second World War, with government support, both expanded (Milner 1995: 79–87; Gospel 2005). However, at the end of the war, again neither employers nor unions were sufficiently committed to sustain the joint production committees that had been established.

In the thirty years after the war, unions saw their membership and power grow and demanded collective bargaining in preference to joint consultation. As a result, in the private sector, joint consultation was overshadowed. This contrasted with the situation in continental Europe, where statutorily based employee consultation was firmly established in Germany, France and other countries, and operated alongside collective negotiations. In the late 1960s, the Donovan Royal Commission advocated exclusively collective bargaining for Britain: 'Collective bargaining is the most effective means of giving workers the right to representation in decisions affecting their working lives.' Approvingly, it quoted McCarthy as saying consultative committees 'cannot survive the development of effective shopfloor organization: either they must change their character and become essentially negotiating committees... or they will be boycotted by shop stewards and fall into disuse' (McCarthy 1967: 33; Donovan 1968: 27, 54). When, a decade later, the Bullock Royal Commission reported on industrial democracy, it recommended union-based representation on company boards alongside collective bargaining. Bullock briefly mentioned German works councils, only to dismiss them, even though arguably they were a more important part of the German system than board-level representation (Bullock 1977: 42–3, 48, 126). Union support for 'free' collective bargaining, hostility to joint consultation, and opposition to non-union channels of representation prevailed.

A number of conclusions may be drawn from this broad historical survey. First, the paradox of the UK's voluntaristic system of 'free' collective bargaining was that it relied heavily on a framework of legal immunities and state support. It provided neither much of a ceiling on union aspirations in favourable times, nor much of a floor in unfavourable ones. Second, in Wedderburn's terms, collective bargaining and joint consultation grew up in an interrelated and complex 'double helix' type relationship (1997: 30). At times they complemented each other; at other times one subsumed the other. Third, in retrospect, unions and employers missed a number of opportunities to build a system of employee representation based on interlocking collective bargaining and joint consultation. In the case of the unions, in the early 1970s they missed the opportunity to secure positive legal rights when they were strong. When, from the late 1970s onwards, the legal framework for the voluntaristic system eroded, the coverage of collective bargaining quickly shrank.

From the 1970s, a number of factors shaped representation in Britain. First, legal intervention steadily increased. Some of this was initially auxiliary to collective bargaining, such as the provisions for union recognition and for information disclosure introduced in the early 1970s. Some mandated forms of representation on specific issues, such as health and safety and, consequent on EU membership, collective redundancies and transfer of undertakings. These procedures initially gave legal priority to union representatives, but in their absence allowed for non-union representation (Gospel and Lockwood 1999). Second, the political and legal context that favoured unions changed with the election of the Thatcher government in 1979. Through the subsequent years, immunities were removed and restrictions were placed on unions and their collective bargaining activities. Third, union membership and the coverage of collective bargaining began to shrink. There were many factors, economic and social, that caused this decline, but undoubtedly in part this was the result of an increasingly hostile legal and political environment (Freeman and Pelletier 1990). Fourth, from the 1980s onwards, employers looked increasingly to alternative voice mechanisms, based in part on indirect representation via joint consultation, but more on direct communication and participation via direct workforce meetings, briefing groups and problem-solving circles (Forth and Millward 2002: 3–7). In these circumstances, unions faced a dilemma about acceptance of new forms of consultation established by employers or introduced under EU directives. Slowly and unevenly, they began to reconcile themselves to events-driven and multi-channel representation (TUC 1995). However, union conversion is still not complete.

The election of a Labour government in 1997 led to the reintroduction of law on union recognition and the reformulation of law deriving from European directives on representation in collective redundancies and transfer of undertakings. In the latter areas, priority in the choice of representatives is now vested in a descending order of, first, union stewards, followed by representatives of standing consultative committees, and finally by representatives chosen *ad hoc* for the specific purpose. In the case of multinational corporations, the government also implemented the European Works Councils Directive. This set two precedents. First, it established legally-based, standing, general consultative arrangements in Britain, albeit for a particular group of employees – those in transnational firms. Second, it treated representation as inclusive rather than exclusive, giving priority in the choice of representatives to the entire workforce and not to union members alone. Finally, from late 2001 the government has accepted the EU Directive on Information and Consultation rights in national level undertakings. This is considered below. Thus, in terms of the law and practice, Britain has moved decisively down a multi-channel road, but has been left with a fragmented system of information, consultation and representation (Gospel *et al.* 2002).

What do British workers get?

In this section, successive WIRS surveys are used for two purposes: first, to look at the state of employee representation in 1998, the date of the most recent survey; and second, to assess patterns of change over the period from 1980 to 1998. Overall, we identify the story of a reduction in coverage of indirect representation. However, the pattern of change is complex.

We turn first to the pattern in 1998. In that year unions were recognized in 42 per cent of all workplaces, with a presence (that is, membership but no recognition) in 11 per cent. In other words, around half of all workplaces had no union presence. In the private sector, unions were recognized in only 24 per cent of workplaces, and within this sector the highest proportions of workplaces with union recognition were in recently privatized industries, such as utilities, transport, and communications. Both organizational and workplace size are associated positively with union recognition (Cully *et al.* 1999: 92).

However, recognition is not representation. In 1998, 22 per cent of workplaces had union representatives, 10 per cent had non-union representatives, and 5 per cent had both. In the private sector, these figures were 15 per cent, 10 per cent and 2 per cent, respectively. On the whole, non-union representatives were slightly more likely to be found in workplaces where there was a union presence but no more recognition than in any other situation. Also, where they were found, there was a slightly higher number of non-union rather than union representatives per workplace (a mean of 4.7 as opposed to 3.7; Cully *et al.* 1999: 96). Of course, overall it should be kept in mind that a majority of workplaces had no representatives of any kind.

In 1998, the coverage of joint consultative committees was not very different from that of collective bargaining in that 29 per cent of all workplaces had a workplace-level consultative committee. In the private sector, this was 26 per cent of all workplaces. However, in both cases a slightly lower percentage had a functioning committee – that is, one which met at least three times a year (23 per cent and 20 per cent, respectively). The counterpart of this is that there was a decline in the scope of collective bargaining (Millward *et al.* 2000: 138–83). Consultative committees can exist at various levels. Thus, in the private sector, 16 per cent of workplaces had a committee at workplace level and 18 per cent at a higher level, but only 8 per cent had both. Size effects here are complicated. Workplace size is associated positively with the existence of a workplace committee, but negatively with the use of only a higher-level committee. Organizational size is associated negatively with workplace committees, but positively with higher level committees or a combination of the two (Cully *et al*. 1999: 99; Millward *et al*. 2000: 109).

Union recognition and consultative committees appear to be associated in each size band. Thus overall, 38 per cent of workplaces with a recognized union had a committee, compared to 20 per cent of those where there was no union presence. In the private sector, these figures are 32 per cent and 20 per cent, respectively. On the basis of this, Cully *et al*. (1999: 100) conclude that 'union representation and indirect employee participation go hand in hand rather than being substitutes'. However, they also suggest that, in non-recognised workplaces where there is union presence, consultative arrangements do not appear to be a springboard for recognition (Cully *et al*. 1999: 101).

Overall, the scope of joint regulation by any method is modest. Table 9.1, which covers both private and public sectors, shows the balance of negotiation, consultation and information-sharing by issue in the minority of workplaces where there is on-site representation. In workplaces where there are union representatives, bargaining is clearly dominated by pay and to a lesser extent by grievance handling. In these workplaces, aside from these two matters, consultation and information-sharing is the dominant joint process. The largest category overall is no joint regulation. In workplaces where there are non-union representatives and no union recognition, information and consultation are the dominant processes, but a surprising amount of negotiation is reported on health and safety and on pay and conditions. Again unilateral management regulation is a large category, but less so than workplaces where there are union representatives. The average number of issues over which negotiation occurred was similar at 1.1 for union representatives and 0.9 for non-union representatives. The average number of issues on which consultation occurred was 2.9 for union representatives and 3.7 for non-union representatives. Generally, the topics that score highest in terms of some sort of joint regulation are health and safety and grievance handling, both, of course, underpinned by statutory requirements (Cully *et al*. 1999: 104–5).

In the private sector at least, the main form of workplace communication and participation is of the direct kind. Thus 35 per cent of workplaces have problem-solving groups, 35 per cent regular workplace meetings, and 43 per cent team briefing groups. Taking these three practices (problem-solving groups, workforce meetings, briefing groups), 75 per cent of all workplaces and 72 per cent of private-sector workplaces had one or more of these; the average workplace had 1.2, and the average private-sector workplace had 1.1 (Cully *et al*. 1999: 64–9; Workplace Employment Relations Survey 98).

Turning to change in indirect representation over time, the main points to draw from Table 9.2 (p. 132) and from the survey of all the WIRS surveys (Millward *et al*. 2000) are as follows. First, there is a major decline in union density and presence, in particular

Table 9.1 The scope of negotiation, consultation and information provision by types of worker representatives, 1998

Issue	Cell percentages			
	Negotiates	Consults	Informs	None
Union representatives				
Pay or conditions of employment	38	13	17	32
Recruitment or selection	3	15	30	52
Training	5	29	24	42
Systems of payment	12	16	26	46
Handling grievances	18	54	13	15
Staffing or manpower planning	6	33	24	37
Equal opportunities	7	41	17	35
Health and safety	13	62	11	14
Performance appraisals	6	25	16	53
Non-union representatives – workplaces with no recognition				
Pay or conditions of employment	16	33	36	15
Recruitment or selection	2	33	32	33
Training	3	46	24	27
Systems of payment	4	20	48	28
Handling grievances	14	50	16	20
Staffing or manpower planning	3	36	40	21
Equal opportunities	10	45	23	22
Health and safety	18	62	19	1
Performance appraisals	2	48	19	31

Notes: All establishments with 25 or more employees. The figures for union representatives are weighted and based on responses from 923 managers in workplaces with 25 or more employees, union recognition and a union representative on site. The figures for non-union representatives are weighted and based on responses from 134 managers in workplaces with 25 or more employees and without union recognition, but with non-union representatives.
Source: Workplace Employee Relations Survey, 1998

in the private sector, where recognition also halves across the period. The proportion of workplaces where collective bargaining was the dominant form of pay determination fell overall from 60 per cent to 29 per cent between 1984 and 1998. In private manufacturing it fell from 50 per cent to 23 per cent, and in private services from 36 per cent to 14 per cent.

Second, the pattern of change in consultation is different. Overall, the decline is less marked than for the union-related variables. It is true that the relative proportion of workplaces with non-functioning consultative committees grows, but, as stated, there was also a 'hollowing out' of collective bargaining institutions. The overall and private-sector trends on consultation coverage are not as divergent as those on union variables; in fact, it will be noted that there is a rise in private-sector consultation coverage between 1990 and 1998. The percentage of private-sector workplaces with a union representative fell from 41 per cent to 17 per cent between

Table 9.2 Union presence, density and recognition, collective bargaining and joint consultative arrangements, 1980–98

	Cell percentages			
	1980	1984	1990	1998
Union presence – by workplace				
All	73	73	64	54
Private manufacturing	77	67	58	42
Private services	50	53	46	35
Union density – by employees				
All	65	58	47	36
Private	56	43	36	26
Union recognition – by workplace				
All	64	66	53	42
Private	50	48	38	25
Collective bargaining predominant form of pay determination – by workplace				
All		60	42	29
Private manufacturing		50	33	23
Private services		36	29	14
Consultation: incidence of joint consultative committee – by workplace				
All – any consultative committee	34	34	29	29
Private	26	24	18	26
Union recognition	37	36	34	30
No recognition	17	20	17	18
All – any functioning consultative committee	30	31	26	23

Source: Adapted from Millward *et al.* (2000): 85–7, 96, 109, 186–91, 197

1980 and 1998, whereas those with a non-union representative (but no union representative) increased from 21 per cent to 50 per cent. Both where there is union recognition and where there is presence, the incidence of union representatives has fallen, especially in the latter case. Non-union representative numbers have risen in all cases. However, overall, fewer workplaces had any form of employee representative in 1998 because the decline in union representation had not been fully offset by the increase in non-union representation (Millward *et al.* 2000: 115).

Third, we observe the growth of direct voice arrangements. Thus, regular meetings between senior managers and the workforce, problem-solving groups and briefing groups all increased significantly in the private sector. Between 1984 and 1998, the proportion of workplaces where there was union-only voice fell from 24 per cent to 9 per cent; the proportion where there was both indirect voice (union and non-union) and direct voice fell from 45 per cent to 39 per cent; but those where managers relied solely on direct arrangements rose, from 11 per cent to 30 per cent (Millward *et al.* 2000: 127). In the case of briefing groups, in 1998 the increase was confined to workplaces without a union and those without a consultative committee. In the case of regular meetings and problem-solving groups, these were more common where there was union representation and where there was joint consultation. Overall, according to Forth and Millward (2002: 22–3), direct communication practices do not seem to have been used to supplant indirect representation via trade unions, but there is some small evidence that they may be used to exclude unions.

Finally, on the survival rate of arrangements, 85 per cent of private-sector workplaces recognising unions in 1990 still had them in 1998. By contrast, the proportion of functioning committees to survive over the period was 63 per cent. The figure was a little lower for workplace-wide meetings (58 per cent), problem-solving groups (56 per cent) and briefing groups (42 per cent). Overall, therefore, despite its decline, union voice would seem to be more durable than non-union – but of course it has also been less likely to be established in new workplaces.

What do other workers get?

As part of the analysis of present and possible future UK patterns, it is useful to examine briefly forms of representation in three other major countries – the USA, Germany and France – chosen for the lessons they may have for Britain.

The USA provides a useful comparison, given a common inheritance of a reliance on collective bargaining as the key form of employee voice. Historically, US unions sought joint regulation with employers through collective bargaining, though with limited success. On the other hand, a leading set of large employers established employer-dominated unions and non-union representative committees (Jacoby 1985: 187–9; 1997: 20–34). With the New Deal, the 1935 Wagner Act outlawed the latter arrangements, and up to the time of writing indirect representation without unions risks illegality. As a result, employers have been constrained in operating consultative committees that are not union-based. Unions have sought exclusively to bargain and have not pushed for voluntary consultative committees or councils. The outcome is that collective bargaining coverage has shrunk and indirect forms of worker participation have not developed, while direct forms of employee involvement have grown.

Under the Clinton administration, the unions hoped to achieve changes in the legal framework that governs recognition for collective bargaining. Some of the research for the resulting Dunlop Commission touched on the possible desire on the part of US workers for joint consultative arrangements; however, proposals for legislative changes focused on the framework of recognition and collective bargaining law. As a counter, a group of employers promoted the so-called Team Bill, which would have promoted direct forms of participation. Neither set of proposals was passed into law. Thus US unions remain dependent on organizing for collective bargaining. Union density in the USA has fallen to 9 per cent of the private-sector labour force, and on one prediction could fall to 3 per cent by 2010 (Freeman 1995: 533).

Germany has provided a significant contrast with the UK for practioners and students of industrial relations. Unlike Britain, Germany went down the road of multi-channel representation – collective bargaining outside the firm, alongside legally-based joint consultation at the workplace and company levels, and representation on the supervisory board of companies. Our analysis of information disclosure and consultation in Germany (Gospel and Willman – Chapter 14 in this volume) shows that German unions have benefited from their relationship with works councils and vice versa. Works councillors tend to be union members, the union provides advice to the council, and this in turn gives the union influence. In law and practice, employees, through their works councils, receive more information and experience more consultation than their British counterparts. However, in recent years works councils have in some instances superseded unions, with more being discussed through the consultation process and with more deviations from nationally bargained agreements. For unions, this has presented the challenge and opportunity of developing new co-ordinating and servicing roles (Thelen 1991; Turner 1991; Mitbestimmung Kommission 1998; Frick and Lehmann 2001).

The German story is therefore usually seen as positive for union representation, where, on the whole, joint consultation and collective bargaining have complemented one another. Between 1980 and 2000 union membership fell from around 38 per cent in West Germany to around 29 per cent for the whole of Germany; the coverage and scope of collective bargaining and joint consultation remains high, though with some shift towards decentralised dealings with works councils.

By contrast, the French story of legally mandated Consultation may be seen as a more negative one for unions. Historically, France also went down the road of multi-channel representation, with legally-based joint consultation alongside collective bargaining. Periodically, French governments have intervened in industrial relations to support consultative arrangements. Since 1945, the law has mandated the election of a *comité d'entreprise*. As further amended by the Auroux legislation in the early 1980s, the purpose of the *comité d'entreprise* is to ensure expression of the views of employees and to allow their interests to be taken into account in decisions. French employers are legally obliged to inform and consult employees over a wide range of matters (Gospel and Willman – Chapter 14 in this volume).

However, periodically, French governments have needed to intervene to reinforce the system. In part, the more limited success of the French system is because *comité d'entreprise* have less extensive rights and are more employer-led than German works councils. In the main, it is because French unions are more fragmented, have less presence at the workplace, and consequently have been less able to use the law and institutions. Union membership fell from 18 per cent to 9 per cent between 1980 and 2000, and the scope of collective bargaining at workplace level is narrow. In France, it might be concluded that, on the one hand, there is evidence that joint consultation and collective bargaining have not complemented one another and the former has often come to substitute for the latter. On the other hand, French workers would undoubtedly obtain less in the absence of the *comité d'entreprise*, and arguably French unions have been able to maintain a foothold in many firms largely because of the role they play in these arrangements (Howell 1992: 100–2).

National systems are, of course, deeply embedded in national histories, and cannot easily be replicated. So, are there any lessons for British unions in these different national patterns? We would argue as follows. If British unions follow those in the USA, they may become ghettoised within the ever-shrinking perimeter of collective bargaining. On the other hand, there is a possibility that they could take advantage of works-council-type arrangements, as in Germany. However, the French case shows this is no automatic route to success if they are unable to take advantage of such arrangements. Drawing on Germany and France, an obvious question is whether European-style representational arrangements can be transferred successfully to the UK. We have seen that there have been changes in UK practice towards mixed systems; joint consultation is of some interest to employers and of increasing interest to unions. A key question is: would British workers be interested in a move towards joint consultative arrangements and mixed systems of representation on European lines?

What do British workers want?

There are substantial difficulties involved in ascertaining what representation workers want. Workers may say they want one thing in everyday circumstances, but something else in more exceptional circumstances when confronted with a major change in contractual arrangements or when there are major redundancies. Here we draw on the British Workplace Representation and Participation Survey survey, which on the whole is likely to reflect what workers want on an everyday basis.

As is often the case in such surveys, the majority of British workers report reasonably high levels of satisfaction in their jobs and in commitment to their employing organisation. However, they are often critical of management – more so than was suggested in a comparable US survey (Freeman and Rogers 1999) – and the majority desire more say in decisions about work tasks, pay levels and organisational governance. In total, 38 per cent identify current problems with unfair and arbitrary treatment in areas such as rewards and discipline, and report favouritism and bullying. Despite this, 50 per cent of all workers reported that they do not go to anyone for help with work difficulties. This fairly high flow of problems in British workplaces is confirmed by the rapid increase in recent years in enquiries to the Advisory Conciliation and Arbitration Service and to Citizens Advice Bureaux, and in cases to industrial tribunals.

There would thus appear to be a related representation gap. Table 9.3 suggests that most workers would prefer to deal with problems collectively rather than

Table 9.3 Preferences of employees for dealing with workplace issues

Would you prefer to deal with this problem on your own or with…	All employees	Union member	Non-union member	Only workplaces with union presence	Only workplaces with recognised unions	Only workplaces with WC or JCC	Both WC/JCC and union presence at workplace	Neither WC/JCC or union presence at workplace
				Cell percentages				
Sexual or racial discrimination at work								
Group of fellow workers	72	78	68	78	78	70	76	63
Union or staff association rep.	67	84	58	72	77	56	83	54
Negotiating salary								
Group of fellow workers	65	81	56	73	74	60	82	44
Union or staff association rep.	53	80	38	73	77	38	72	31
Negotiating hours and conditions								
Group of fellow workers	71	81	65	73	75	67	80	62
Union or staff association rep.	52	76	38	69	73	39	68	34
Promotion issues								
Group of fellow workers	46	50	43	39	37	54	50	38
Union or staff association rep.	27	36	23	34	35	21	33	20
Workplace bullying								
Group of fellow workers	69	72	68	70	71	74	74	60
Union or staff association rep.	58	80	46	65	69	46	75	41
Training and skill development								
Group of fellow workers	67	73	65	66	63	73	71	59
Union or staff association rep.	30	36	26	40	41	28	30	23

Notes: The sample was divided at random into two variants. One variant asked if the respondents preferred to solve specific problems on their own or with the help of a group of colleagues or fellow workers. The other variant asked if respondents preferred to solve problems on their own or with the help of a trade union or staff association representative. Each respondent could only choose either an individual or a collective solution.

Source: British Workplace Representation and Participation Survey, 2001, Q35

individually. The only area where there is a clear preference for individual dealings is promotion. However, in most cases the preference is for remedies via a group of fellow workers rather than a trade union or staff association representative. Perhaps not surprisingly, union members show a stronger preference for collective solutions and prefer union representation rather than working through a group of fellow workers. The exceptions are again on matters of promotion and training, where union members would look more to a group of fellow workers. Non-union employees prefer fellow workers to unions as the method of collective action on all issues. It is notable that workers in situations where there is a recognized union and where there is both a union presence and a consultative committee would seem to have the highest preference for collective solutions.

Table 9.4 explores this further and shows that the majority (72 per cent) of employees think their workplaces would be better with some form of collective representation. This breaks down as 92 per cent of union members and 61 per cent of non-union members. However, in the case of union members it is striking that only 11 per cent favour a union on its own, whereas 74 per cent favour both a union and a joint consultative committee/works council. Non-members' wishes are more dispersed: 34 per cent want no form of representation, 29 per cent favour a joint consultative committee on its own, 27 per cent favour a joint consultative committee and a trade union, and only 5 per cent favour a union on its own. Workers in situations where there is already a union and a consultative committee are the group most in favour of dual-channel representation (72 per cent), but it is also striking that workers in situations where there is a recognized union or a union presence are also well disposed to dual representation. There is little preference for a consultative committee on its own, except where this already exists. All this suggests that many union and non-union members see the various institutions as potentially complementary.

The survey also shows that 82 per cent of workers would be in favour of legislation that required management to meet with employee representatives. Overall, union members are more favourably inclined to statutory works councils than are non-members (89 as opposed to 77 per cent). However, the belief in legislation is strongest (92 per cent) where there are already dual channels. In addition, there is a strong feeling that works councils should be elected by workers (72 per cent), have legal protection from possible discrimination by employers (75 per cent), and meet on a regular basis and not just at management's discretion (89 per cent). However, the proportion favouring confidential information for employee representatives is relatively low (40 per cent in the case of union members and 33 per cent in the case of non-members).

Joint representation by a trade union and a consultative committee/works council would seem to have some pay-off in terms of satisfaction with information disclosure. Table 9.5 suggests that most workers feel very or quite well informed, with the lowest levels of satisfaction about future employment and staffing plans. There is no clear difference between union and non-union members, except that the

Table 9.4 Employees' perceptions of the effects of having trade unions and works councils in their workplace

Do you think your workplace would be better off with…	All employees	Union member	Non-union member	Cell percentages				
				Only workplaces with union presence	Only workplaces with recognized unions	Only workplaces with WC or JCC	Both WC/JCC and union presence at workplace	Neither WC/JCC or union presence at workplace
Trade union on its own	7	11	5	14	16	2	9	6
Works council on its own	21	6	29	11	10	40	9	27
Works council and trade union	44	74	27	60	63	24	72	20
Neither	24	5	34	11	8	31	9	43
Don't know	4	3	5	3	3	3	2	4

Source: British Workplace Representation and Participation Survey, 2001, Q51

Table 9.5 Employees' perceptions of how well they are informed on key workplace matters

				Cell percentages				
	All employees	Union member	Non-union member	Only workplaces with union presence	Only workplaces with recognized unions	Only workplaces with WC or JCC	Both WC/JCC and union presence at workplace	Neither WC/JCC or union presence at workplace
Future employment or staffing plans for your workplace								
Very/quite well informed	63	58	65	49	48	72	66	61
Not very well/not at all	37	42	35	51	52	28	34	39
What other people doing your job are earning								
Very/quite well informed	62	71	56	61	64	60	72	52
Not very well/not at all	38	29	44	39	36	40	28	48
The financial performance of your employer								
Very/quite well informed	68	68	67	63	62	75	72	61
Not very well/not at all	32	32	33	37	38	25	28	39
Your job prospects with your employer								
Very/quite well informed	75	71	77	63	61	82	78	72
Not very well/not at all	25	29	23	37	39	18	22	28
The training you need to advance your career								
Very/quite well informed	74	76	73	69	69	84	81	63
Not very well/not at all	26	24	27	31	31	16	19	37

Source: British Workplace Representation and Participation Survey, 2001, Q51

former have an advantage in knowing what other people doing similar jobs are earning, reflecting the union role in wage bargaining. Generally, workers in a situation where there was only a consultative committee/works council felt the best informed. This was followed closely by situations where there was both a consultative committee/works council and a trade union. Workers felt least well informed where there were no representative arrangements, but close to this were situations where there was exclusively a trade union. Of course, there may be good reasons why union members may feel they receive less information – they may have higher aspirations that are unmet; management may feel more constrained towards giving information; and union representatives may not pass on information to members. However, it is significant that where there is both a union and a consultative committee/works council there is a high level of satisfaction with information disclosure.

In summary, there is a demand for more indirect representation and voice among British workers. However, among both non-members and members, there is not a strong demand for union voice alone. Consultative committees/works councils, especially legally-based, are clearly very attractive to both non-members and members, and are viewed as being complementary to trade unions.

What are British workers likely to get – a new era in employment relations?

Finally, we turn to what representation British workers are likely to get. On union recognition, the record to date (Wood *et al.* 2003) suggests that the present legal procedures will have a small direct effect and a somewhat larger indirect effect. However, the overall impact will be limited. On union membership, over the last few years there has been some increase in numbers but no increase in density, and it will be an uphill struggle for unions to maintain or increase momentum in recruitment. Even if recognition and density were to stabilise or increase, there seems little likelihood that the decline in the coverage of collective bargaining will be reversed in the short term, especially in the private sector, where employers' and employees' preferences are for forms of representation and participation other than collective bargaining (Millward *et al.* 2000: 197–9). By contrast, on recent trends, direct forms of information sharing and employee participation are likely to continue to increase.

So, what of indirect representation via joint consultation and its intersection with collective bargaining? Here, the passage of the EU Directive on Information and Consultation (2002/14/EC) and its transposition into UK law via the Information and Consultation Regulations is likely to play an important part in shaping future developments.

The Directive will affect large enterprises (over 150 employees) by early 2005, and will eventually cover all undertakings with more than 50 employees by 2008. This means it will cover three-quarters of the UK labour force. Undoubtedly the Directive will start to have an immediate impact, as management and unions plan for its implementation. In the Directive and Regulations, consultation is defined as an 'exchange of views and the establishment of dialogue' (Article 2) – implying an ongoing process. Article 4(2) of the Directive outlines the substantive areas: (i) there is an obligation to provide information on the general business situation of the undertaking; (ii) there is an obligation to inform and consult on the likely development of employment and on 'anticipatory measures' that might threaten employment; and (iii) there is an enhanced obligation to inform and consult on decisions likely to lead to substantial changes in work organisation or in contractual relations. These are minimum mandatory topics, but other topics are permitted to be covered. Consultation must take place at an 'appropriate' time, to enable employee representatives to study the information and prepare for consultation. It must also be 'at the relevant level of management and representation depending on the subject under discussion' – implying that there should be different levels of representation and consultation within an undertaking. On item (iii), the consultation will be 'with a view to reaching an agreement' (Article 4) – implying an ongoing process of give-and-take. In all cases, management is obliged to provide a reasoned response to representatives' opinions. Representatives are also to be given adequate 'protection and guarantees' to enable them to perform their duties (Article 7). On matters of confidentiality, the employer may withhold information that it is considered would seriously damage the undertaking, and representatives and 'any experts who assist them' may be made subject to an obligation of confidentiality. Sanctions for failure to comply will be 'effective, proportionate, and dissuasive' (Article 8). Employers and employee representatives may negotiate different arrangements before and after transposition, but these would have to respect the principles of the Directive (Article 5).

The transposition of the Directive into UK law will depend on political circumstances, and the debate will be along a spectrum of what Wedderburn has described as 'soft' and 'strong' rights (Wedderburn 1997: 34). Some outcomes are reasonably predictable; others are more uncertain. For example, forms of direct participation will not qualify unless the employer and all employees desire this. Equally, *ad hoc* and issue-specific arrangements will not qualify, given that the Directive talks about a 'permanent' and 'general' system of consultation (Article 10). Where challenged, many existing systems of consultation will not qualify, such as where representatives are appointed by management. Trade union collective bargaining will qualify, subject to non-members not being disenfranchised. Moreover, from the wording, it seems likely that arrangements will have to be created at multiple levels within enterprises. Other chapters in this volume speculate about possible outcomes. As with all EU-derived law, the transposition will be subject to interpretation by the European Court of Justice, which in the past in areas such as representation, sex discrimination and working time has rendered Directives far-reaching. Above all, however, the implementation of the Directive will depend on the preferences of employees, and capabilities and actions of employers and unions.

On the basis of the foregoing, what can we speculate about this? On the part of employers, their advantage lies in the fact that for some time they have controlled employee relations and in many cases have introduced more sophisticated human resource policies. On the other hand, in addition to the new law, there are other constraints. Employees would seem to want more representative voice at work, and employers now confront rather more confident unions than they have for many years. Undoubtedly, some employers will seek to avoid new arrangements, arguing either that they already have adequate mechanisms or that their employees do not want arrangements on these lines. This strategy clearly has dangers in that it may be challenged by unions in all or in parts of an enterprise. For other employers, there is an opportunity to establish arrangements, either wholly or partially new, with or without trade unions.

On the part of unions, they fear that employers may use the Directive to exclude or eject them, and that they have neither the leverage nor the capability to mobilize workers to achieve and operate new information and consultation arrangements. However, there is evidence that employees desire more voice at work, many work-places already have a union presence that can be built on, and unions now have legal supports that they can potentially turn to their advantage. At one end of the spectrum, where unions already have a high level of membership and bargaining coverage, they may eschew new arrangements but use the law to capitalize on what they already have, and expand the scope and level of consultation and bargaining. At the other end of the spectrum, where unions have no presence, unions will have little choice but to accept what employers may put into place. Here, unions will have mixed motivations as to whether they wish to see such arrangements succeed. Where arrangements are successful, this may mean permanent union exclusion; where they are less successful, this may mean new opportunities to intervene. It is in situations at the middle of the spectrum, where there is hollow recognition or a partial presence, at some levels or in some parts of an undertaking, that unions will confront challenges and have real opportunities to increase their membership and activities.

Conclusions

To conclude, the UK has a differentiated system of representing workers, where direct voice has been on the increase, indirect voice through joint consultation has held up, and voice through trade unions has shrunk considerably. In terms of indirect mechanisms, in both law and practice, the UK has already moved down the road of multi-channel representation and is likely to move further in this direction in the future. British workers clearly want more voice, but with a preference for joint consultative arrangements and based on multi-channel representation. The current situation presents a set of major challenges and opportunities for the industrial relations parties. In the light of the Directive and Regulations, the opportunity for government is to establish for the first time in the UK a permanent and effective general system of information and consultation at work. Some employers may see this as an opportunity to create weak voice mechanisms; for others, there is an opportunity to establish strong arrangements that may complement one another. The challenge for unions is to be able to build on these arrangements, and to maintain and expand their role within them.

References

Bullock Report (1977) *Report of the Committee of Inquiry on Industrial Democracy* (Chairman: Lord Bullock) Cmnd. 6702. London: HMSO.

Cully, M., Woodland, S., O'Reilly, A. and Dix, G. (1999) *Britain at Work: As Depicted by the 1998 Workplace Employee Relations Survey*. London: Routledge.

Diamond, W. and Freeman, R. (2000) *What Workers Want from Workplace Organizations: A Report to the TUC's Promoting Trade Unionism Task Group*. London: TUC.

Donovan Report (1968) *Report of the Royal Commission on Trade Unions and Employers' Associations 1965–1968* (Chairman: Lord Donovan) Cmnd 3623. London: HMSO.

Ewing, K. D. (1990) 'Trade union recognition – a framework for discussion', *Industrial Law Journal*, 19(4): 209–27.

Feldman, G. (1992) *Army, Industry, and Labour in Germany 1914–1918*. Leamington Spa: Berg.

Forth, J. and Millward, N. (2002) *The Growth of Direct Communication*. London: CIPD.

Freeman, R. (1995) 'The future of unions in decentralized collective bargaining systems: US and UK unionism in an age of crisis', *British Journal of Industrial Relations* 33(4): 519–36.

Freeman, R. and Pelletier, J. (1990) 'The impact of industrial relations legislation on British union density', *British Journal of Industrial Relations* 28(2): 141–64.

Freeman, R. and Rogers, J. (1999) *What Workers Want*. London: ILR Press.

Frick, B and Lehman, E (2004) 'Corporate Governance in Germany', in H. Gospel and A. Pendleton, *Corporate Governance and Labour Management*. Oxford: Oxford University Press.

Gospel, H. (1992) *Markets, Firms, and the Management of Labour in Modern Britain*. Cambridge University Press.

Gospel, H. (2005) 'Markets, firms, and unions: historical and institutionalist perspectives on the future of unions', in Fernie, S. and Metcalf, D. (eds) *Unions and Performance*. London: Routledge.

Gospel, H. and Lockwood, G. (1999) 'Disclosure of information for collective bargaining: the CAC approach revisited', *Industrial Law Journal*, 28(3): 233–48.

Gospel, H. and Willman, P. (2002a) 'Representing workers – information, consultation, and negotiation: dilemmas in workplace governance', in Gospel, H. and Wood, S. (eds) *Representing Workers: Trade Union Recognition and Membership in Britain*. London: Routledge.

Gospel, H. and Willman, P. (2002b) 'The right to know: disclosure of information for collective bargaining and joint consultation in Germany, France, and Great Britain', Working Paper No. 1178, Centre for Economic Performance, London School of Economics.

Gospel, H., Lockwood, G. and Willman, P. (2002) 'A British dilemma: disclosure of information for collective bargaining or joint consultation?', *Comparative Labor Law and Policy Journal*, 22(2): 101–3

Howell, C. (1992) *Regulating labor: The State and Industrial Relations Reform in Postwar France*. Princeton, NJ: Princeton University Press.

Jacoby, S. (1985) *Employing Bureaucracy: Managers, Unions, and the Transformation of Work in American Industry, 1900–1945*. New York: Columbia University Press.

Jacoby, S. (1997) *Modern Manners: Welfare Capitalism since the New Deal*. Princeton, NJ: Princeton University Press.

McCarthy, W. (1967) *The Role of Shop Stewards in Industrial Relations*, Research Paper No. 1, Donovan Royal Commission. London: HMSO.

McCarthy, W. (2000) 'Representative consultations with specified employees – or the future of rung two', in Collins, H., Davies, P. and Rideout, R. (eds) *Legal Regulation of the Employment Relation*. London: Kluwer.

Millward, N., Bryson, A. and Forth, J. (2000) *All Change at Work? British Employment Relations 1980–1998, as Portrayed by the Workplace Industrial Relations Survey Series*. London: Routledge.

Milner, S. (1995) 'The coverage of collective pay setting institutions: 1895–1990', *British Journal of Industrial Relations*, 33(1): 69–91.

Mitbestimmung Kommission (1998). *Mitbestimmung and neue Unternetmeaskulturen – Bilanz and Perspective*. Gütersloh, Bertelsmann Stiffung.

Thelen, K. (1991) *Union of Parts: Labor Politics in Postwar Germany*. Ithaca: Cornell University Press.

Trades Union Congress (1995) *Your Voice at Work: TUC Proposals for Rights to Representation at Work*. London: TUC.

Turner, L. (1991) *Democracy of Work: Changing World Markets and the Future of Unions*. Ithaca: Cornell University Press.

Wedderburn, W. (1997) 'Consultation and collective bargaining in Europe: success or ideology?', *Industrial Law Journal*, 26(1): 1–34.

Whitley Committee (1918) *Ministry of Reconstruction, Interim Report of the Committee on Relations between Employers and Employed* (Cd. 8606, 1917–18) and *Final Report* (Cd. 9153) London: HMSO.

Wood, S., Moore, S. and Ewing, K. (2003) 'The impact of the trade union recognition procedures under the Employment Relations Act, 2000–2', in Gospel, H. and Wood, S. (eds) *Representing Workers: Union Recognition and Membership in Britain*. London: Routledge.

10

Information and consultation in small and medium-sized enterprises

*Susan Marlow and Colin Gray**

The contribution of small and medium-sized enterprises (SMEs) to British competitiveness has grown substantially since the late 1970s (Carter and Jones-Evans 2000; Curran and Blackburn 2001). In this chapter SMEs are defined in accordance with European Union (EU) parameters as being independently owned businesses with fewer than 249 employees. Since the late 1970s, both Conservative and Labour governments have invested considerable resources in encouraging the growth and sustainability of the sector, in the hope that such enterprises would foster entrepreneurial innovation and hence create wealth and new employment opportunities. Such ambitions have not yet been realised; for example, Stanworth and Purdy (2003) argue that while individual self-employment grew during the 1980s, the number of SMEs within the economy has changed relatively little since the middle of that decade. Moreover, given the high level of churning (new start-ups versus failures) within the sector, and the propensity for a very few smaller firms to grow into large enterprises, the case for wealth and new job creation is not yet proven. As Curran (1997: 34) observes, 'small businesses, on any realistic assessment of their role in the UK economy are not likely to transform it by themselves into a major player in the global economy though they will play a part in that process'.

However, while it would appear that SMEs are, on the whole, unlikely to be the much vaunted entrepreneurial agents of change within contemporary society, they still have an important role to fulfil, as Department of Trade and Industry (DTI)

* The authors gratefully acknowledge the assistance of Alan Ryan, De Montfort University, in the preparation of this chapter.

statistics indicate. Within the private sector in 2003, SMEs constituted 99.8 per cent of Britain's 4 million enterprises, and accounted for 58 per cent of employment and 52 per cent of turnover, though the vast bulk of these (71 per cent) operate as sole traders (DTI 2004b). The sector may not have performed in the dynamic fashion aspired to by successive governments since the 1980s but it still makes a significant contribution to national prosperity. Consequently, changes to the operational environment that affects the performance of such enterprises are of great interest and importance. This chapter considers the potential impact of forthcoming employment legislation, the Information and Consultation of Employees (ICE) Act, on these firms. As has been noted in earlier chapters, the ICE Act comes into force on 6 April 2005 for undertakings with at least 150 employees and will apply to all firms with more than fifty employees by April 2008. Although this will exclude small and micro firms, the 26,000 SMEs with 50–249 employees still account for 12 per cent of the labour force (Stanworth and Purdy 2003). The Directive itself (Article 19) indicates application to establishments with more than twenty employees. Given that small firms experience proportionately greater compliance costs (Edwards *et al.* 2003), the UK has chosen to apply these regulations to undertakings with fifty or more employees. However, there could be shifts in the future to include smaller firms. As it stands at the time of writing, however, as Ryan (2004: 307) notes, 'the inclusion of organisations employing as few as 50 people will extend the ambit of the legislation in this area to a greater number of firms than previously envisaged and represents a further challenge to traditional labour relationships in many smaller firms'. To explore the affect of the ICE regulations on SMEs, this chapter will start by establishing the context with a short overview of the literature on employment relationships within smaller firms. This will then be drawn on to indicate why full and comprehensive compliance with the ICE regulations will be challenging even for the medium-sized firms with fifty or more employees. Finally, comments and conclusions will be presented to draw these arguments together.

Managing labour in SMEs

In a recent critical appraisal of the literature exploring the employment relationship in smaller firms, Ram and Edwards (2003: 719) argue that within the study of work and organisations, this activity is 'a key exemplar of analytical advance (where) research has made empirical and analytical progress'. This observation was based on the growing sophistication of contemporary debate regarding labour management in SMEs. This has advanced substantially from the traditional harmony thesis, which persisted until the late 1980s. The perception that smallness – in terms of employment – was a foundation for industrial harmony was based on the absence of overt, collective conflict and dispute in smaller organisations noted by the Bolton Report (1971). Towards the end of the 1980s, this argument was challenged. Seminal work by Rainnie (1989) argued that labour management practices in the sector were in fact defined by autocratic owner prerogative and highly exploitative employment relations. This critique was based on a Marxist analysis of the markets within which smaller firms operated, where, it was argued, the domination of large firms within the economy ensured that SMEs, as either subcontractors or niche market operators, had little autonomy regarding the manner in which they managed labour. For the subcontracting firms, the pressure to meet cost constraints and quality standards dictated by larger companies within the supply chain denied firm owners any choice in employment management strategies, while those left within niches were so constrained by their limited markets that again cost containment was critical. Survival pressures ensured that most firm owners adopted directive or even exploitative management practices. Marlow (2004: 3) notes: 'this analysis broadened the debate to locate smaller firms within the wider market environment, arguing that centralised and fragmented capital have a symbiotic relationship, if asymmetrical in terms of power … [as such] large firms dominate markets so as to dictate the employment relationship in both their smaller suppliers and those confined to niche markets'.

This approach moved the debate forward but has been criticised for being overly deterministic regarding the market imperative, and failing to recognise heterogeneity within the sector where many different approaches to employment relations exist (Goss, 1991; Ram, 1994). During the 1990s, a growing case study literature emerged to illustrate the manner in which market constraints interact with the social relations of production, leading to highly complex employment relations where differing elements of negotiation between owners and employees emerge (Moule 1998; Ram 1999). These in depth and detailed studies of life within the smaller firm illustrated the dynamic interplay between negotiation, toleration and the exertion of employer prerogative. The study by Moule (1998) of a factory, where the researcher worked as an employee, is an illuminating example of such interplay; the physical proximity of the owner, management team and employees led to the intrusion of social relationships into the working environment. This led to a high degree of toleration of quite subversive behaviour from certain valued employees as long as they fulfilled their tasks, but was periodically interspersed with occasional outbursts of managerial prerogative. This served to remind employees where authority lay, so establishing a complex relationship of control and consent within the organisation. It was noted that employees without valued skills or close relationships with the directors were not permitted to behave in such a fashion. This reflects strongly earlier studies that highlighted the complexity of social relationships inside small firms embedded in their communities, because of the influence of external social relations and ties (Curran and Stanworth 1986). Such findings were echoed in other case study material that also noted the influence of family ownership on management approaches in SMEs (Holliday 1995) and issues such as the interplay of firm size, owner ethnicity and employee gender on the employment relationship (Ram 1994). Employment relationships within smaller enterprises cannot easily be defined by either harmony or market constraint. Rather, they reflect a myriad of social and economic influences bounded by a context of employer/employee proximity in an environment of smallness.

So, while it has become apparent that heterogeneity and complexity within the sector are evident, one theme that has emerged from surveys, interviews and case study material regarding labour management in SMEs is a preference for informality (Scott *et al.* 1989; Wynarczyk *et al.* 1993; Matlay 1999). This is reflected in a preference by firm owners either to manage employment issues themselves or to delegate this task to a general manager. Wynarczyk *et al.* (1993), in their study of managerial labour markets in SMEs, noted that as a firm grew, a personnel professional was usually the last member of the management team to be appointed. This finding was reflected in an analysis of the impact of the 1999 Employment Act on smaller firms by Marlow (2003), who found a distinct absence of professional HR policy and practice in the majority of her sample firms. Indeed, an OUBS study that compared HR policies and practices between large firms and SMEs found that formal policies in the latter were a feature of the minority of these firms, which in fact had explicit growth plans linked to their HR strategies (Thomson and Gray 1999). Consequently, employment relations policies and practices in smaller enterprises are more likely to reflect the idiosyncrasies and priorities of owners rather than a professionally informed approach. Indeed, data from the DTI (2003) supports this assertion in finding that some 20 per cent of firms with fewer than 200 employees had either no, or extremely inadequate, statutory discipline, grievance or dismissal procedures, relying instead on informal managerial prerogative to deal with such issues.

It would appear that such informality is preferred, as the close proximity between employer, management team and employee creates an environment where the utilisation of formal policy and practice intrudes into the fluid and negotiated social relations of production. Moreover, when individuals are working closely together, there is an element of irrationality in resorting to formality when grievances, discipline issues and information can just be exchanged or dealt with face to face and immediately. This may be why a recent quarterly survey of SMEs conducted by the OUBS-based Small Enterprise Research Team (2003), found that less than 5 per cent of microfirms with fewer than ten employees reported that staff dispute procedures caused them any problems, compared with 22 per cent of small firms and 39 per cent of medium-sized firms.

However, caution should be applied in subscribing to a dichotomy of formality and informality within large firms and SMEs, respectively. There are persistent elements of informality evident in large enterprises, usually expressed as custom and practice issues (Rose, 2003) or where line managers have the autonomy to interpret HR policy and practice. Equally, Cully *et al.* (1999) were able to identify some sophisticated utilisation of HR management (HRM) strategies within SMEs; so, as Ram *et al.* (2001: 846) note 'informality...is therefore, a matter of degree not kind'. While accepting these reservations it would nevertheless appear that the larger the organisation, the more likely it is to adopt a formally agreed HR policy and practices managed professionally by dedicated personnel staff. Such firms might tolerate the presence of custom and practice activities and line manager discretion, but they usually have formal boundaries established through agreed policies and procedures and so have a professional 'fall back' position to assert company rules if and when required. Smaller firms are less likely to have in-house professional HR managers or clearly established policies and procedures. Generally, they lack such a 'fall back' support mechanism to assert authority, and even those who contract their HR function to external agencies appear reluctant to use them for addressing day-to-day employment issues. This leads to problems, particularly regarding the development and application of fair, objective and clear employment rules and regulations. Where individual managerial prerogative dominates, there is obvious scope for spontaneous and subjective action. Indeed, this is evident in the statistics on employment tribunal applications, where smaller firms dominate in cases of unfair dismissal and those relating to redundancy (DTI, 2002). Such preferences for owner/management prerogative are also less likely to be challenged by employees within SMEs, given the lack of appropriate channels for either collective or individual voice in opposition to managerial decisions (Dundon *et al.* 1999). From the evidence available regarding unfair dismissal cases, it would appear that the preferred option for employees to voice their dissent is to leave the firm (Earnshaw *et al.* 1998) and protest through a tribunal appeal after exit.

Such preferences for informal labour management in SMEs also have critical implications for the manner in which contemporary employment regulation is incorporated into HR policy and practice. Successive Labour governments elected since 1997 have introduced a raft of domestic and European regulation to strengthen individual rights at work, and to a lesser extent to support trade union recognition. This has been evident by the enactment of two Employment Acts (1999 and 2002), a National Minimum Wage and the adoption of EU Directives – albeit, in a minimal fashion (McKay 2001). Evidence suggests that smaller organisations are likely to depend on differing degrees of informality in their labour management practices, therefore adopting and incorporating formal employment regulation into this approach will be problematic, and compliance will be challenging. Contemporary research which has considered employment regulation compliance in smaller organisations has, to date, found a less severe impact on their performance than had been prophesised by representative pressure groups (Federation of Small Business [FSB] 2000) or media commentators (Oldfield 1999). Blackburn and Hart (2001) found pessimistic predictions regarding deteriorating performance to be unfounded; it appears that the perception of potential problems does not seem to have been borne out in reality. The Small Enterprise Research team survey of the first quarter of 2003 found that two-thirds of SMEs reported that they were unaffected by the introduction of the National Minimum Wage (indeed, only 7 per cent reported that they had previously paid workers below the minimum rate). However, Marlow (2003) and to some degree Gilman *et al.* (2002) noted that this might be because of a tendency to ignore such regulations, particularly in the smallest firms in the sector, rather than being a case of unproblematic compliance.

To summarise this brief overview, while it is noted that the SME sector is heterogeneous, contemporary analyses of the employment relationship within such firms would suggest that, while differing in form and degree, there is a preference for an informal approach to labour management. Such informality can offer positive social relations of production and foster close team working, and facilitate rapid and direct communication channels. However, it also offers the potential for subjective, ill-informed, idiosyncratic managerial approaches; the outcome of such being detrimental to both firm performance and employee rights. It was believed that the increasing raft of national and EU employment regulation adopted by successive Labour governments since 1997 might assist in discouraging such informality, but it would appear (Hart 2004; Ram *et al.* 2001) that while it is perhaps subject to some minor amendments and shifts, informality persists. The latest enactment – the ICE Regulations – will represent a further challenge to such informality, as it combines a requirement to indicate compliance through formal information dissemination and consultation channels while also offering employees overt opportunities for voice. Drawing on the evidence presented above, if firms do comply with the regulation, this will represent a considerable shift from traditional unitary management approaches. Firm owners and managers must accept that all employees have rights to knowledge regarding firm performance, and that information must be delivered in an objective and formal framework; also that there is an owner/management obligation to consult with all employees about such an issue. So, again, from the evidence presented above regarding the extent and degree of compliance indicated within the sector to date, it would appear that the adoption of the ICE Regulations is likely to be patchy at best. And reflecting extant findings such as Wynarczyk *et al.* (1993) it is likely that the closer the firm is to the upper size limit within the SME sector (249 employees), the more probable that compliance will occur. This has serious implications for those employees in the smaller size bands, while clearly those in small and micro firms (fewer than forty-nine and nine employees, respectively) are excluded, although they do have a right to information regarding the number of people working in the business. Should there be any discrepancy in terms of an enterprises eligibility for the ICE, this will be decided by the Central Arbitration Committee.

Information and consultation in SMEs

As noted in earlier chapters, the ICE imposes a number of specific demands on the organisation; broadly outlined, these fall into the following categories, with further details available from DTI (2004) and ACAS (2004):

- the identification of employee representatives for consultation purposes and as conduits for information dissemination;
- consultation regarding changes to terms and conditions of employment; and
- information regarding terms and conditions of employment, firm performance and prospects.

As, at the time of writing, the Directive has yet to be properly implemented, evaluating the potential impact is a hypothetical exercise, but drawing on the extant evidence outlined briefly above, informed arguments can feasibly be developed. Overall, it is apparent that for those firms that favour an informal approach to managing labour, compliance with employment regulation *per se*, including the ICE, will be challenging. It has already been established that the social relations of production in smaller enterprises are influenced by the proximity between owner and employees, where interaction is usually face to face and on a daily basis. Hence, it might be argued that engaging with an elected employee representative will be relatively unproblematic, given such proximity and familiarity with the team – even where there are 249 employees it is not unreasonable to suppose that management and labour would have quite a strong degree of mutual familiarity. Conversely, however, such proximity does offer some scope to sponsor employee representatives who are the most sympathetic to the owner's and managerial team's perspective even in a secret ballot situation. Indeed, in firms that already have some form of staff consultation and representation, the ICE allows employees to be balloted regarding their wish to retain existing arrangements or adopt a system based on ICE guidelines. The representatives role in articulating any opposition to owner/management tactics and practices within the auspices of a small organisation, without the intermediary of a professional HR team and where the owner is always present, also generates concerns regarding how objectively the views of the representative might be perceived. The advantages of employee representation are lauded by ACAS (2004: 7) who suggest that: 'Having representatives also means that employees are likely to feel more confident about being able to voice their views frankly and freely ... employees may be reluctant to express their true opinions directly for fear that their comments might be interpreted as criticism and held against the person making them.'

In the context of the SME, however, there would be some question regarding how frank the representative may want to be with the firm's owner, who is also the direct employer. Moreover, in an environment where there is a small group of employees working in close proximity to management, some doubt must be expressed regarding the ease of maintaining the anonymity of employees who express dissatisfaction. A further facet of this proximity issue is also that the owner/management team would have to ensure that, contrary to the likely previous custom of sharing preferred information in an idiosyncratic manner, this practice must now focus solely upon the agreed employee representative with regular, formal meetings. Based on the evidence to date, the likelihood of this occurring is quite improbable.

The whole element of consultation and information is daunting for SMEs. It has already been established that opportunities for formal voice within such firms are generally limited because of an absence of a union presence and associated representatives combined with a lack of formally administered HR policy and practice. Accordingly, the mechanisms to facilitate consultation and information are often missing in the first instance. Added to this, however, is a wider structural issue related to market uncertainty; it has been recognised for some time (Storey *et al.*

1987; Storey 1994; Deakins 2002) that smaller organisations experience greater volatility within markets regarding their competitive sustainability and performance. This is associated with a variety of issues. To name just a few: they are likely to be younger, so less established; have a smaller market share; have higher levels of gearing; and have fewer professional managerial competencies in place than their larger counterparts. So challenges such as the loss of one key customer, temporary market downturns, a few bad debts or late payments are just a few examples of incidents that can be a serious threat to the future of the firm. However, within SMEs, such events are often part and parcel of the operating environment, with owners and management teams dealing with these threats as a key element of the management task. Yet, if firms were to comply fully with the ICE (ACAS 2004), they would have to inform employees of, for example, the perceived state of the market; current levels of investment and sales; income and expenditure; profit and loss; cash flow; and assets and liabilities. The degree of volatility over time that this information might reveal within an SME could foster insecurity and encourage key employees to seek alternative employment. In smaller enterprises, the owner might fear that, if such information were to be brought to the attention of suppliers and customers it might be very detrimental to business durability. However, there are provisions to protect confidential information, and to protect employees who exercise their rights.

The potential problems surrounding this issue are illustrated in a paper by Marlow and Patton (2002); this study of the impact of employment regulation on smaller firms explored specifically the notion of information sharing and consultation. One noticeable theme that emerged was a belief by owners that their employees would not understand financial information or performance cycles. By having access to such information, employees would either demand unrealistic pay increases if there had been a buoyant period or, in the case of certain staff, be tempted to seek alternative employment during downturns, even if this was a temporary situation. It was also argued that employees would share this information with competitors should they join another firm. When it was suggested that large enterprises, who have to reveal this type of information, also had to face such issues, it was felt that these companies were better able to present such information through formal, professional channels that were better able to obscure unpalatable facts. Moreover, the greater robustness of large companies ensured that employees were less likely to be concerned with problems in the short term, given the organisational resources available to withstand market shifts. Hence, it was argued that what might be a temporary problem regarding businesses durability in a smaller firm could be affected enough to threaten survival should the SME owner be compelled to reveal such information.

This point, regarding the presentation of information, is interesting in that, once again, the influence of informality is evident. By adopting informality where employees, owners and managers work closely together, the notion of a team or family environment is promoted (the firm as a family where the owner/management team acts as a figurehead working for the good of all is frequently cited by owners of small firms as justification for owner prerogative (Scase 2004). This enables the owner to justify the withholding of information on the basis that sharing might cause unwarranted concern for employees, and this then strengthens a reluctance to engage in meaningful consultation, to protect the business from 'ignorant' employee interference. This argument also reflects another longstanding assertion regarding the relationship between firm owners and their businesses. Gibb and Scott (1985) argued that the degree of emotional, social and financial capital invested by SME owners in their enterprises ensured that they had a deep-seated psychological attachment to the firm to the degree that it was almost an extension of their personalities. Consequently, external interference, regulation and advice is strongly resisted, not only because it challenges preferred personal styles but also because it is an affront to the owner's personal abilities and degree of investment in the business. While this observation might be made regarding any degree of regulation that demands compliance, the auspices of the ICE, which in themselves create specific channels for employee voice and potential criticism or owner/management tactics are particularly pertinent to this argument.

To date, this consideration of the impact of the ICE has rather presumed upon the notion of informality within an environment of relative owner/management benevolence. The research evidence (Rainnie 1989; Dundon *et al.* 1999) does, however, indicate that autocratic unitarism is not uncommon in SMEs, given the absence of formal employee representation, owner/employee proximity, the lack of formally administered HR policy and market constraints noted by Rainnie (1989). In such instances, the ICE is unlikely to be complied with in the spirit intended, as it will be perceived to be offering opportunities to challenge overtly owner prerogative. So, while limited channels of information and consultation may be initiated, these are not likely to offer employees real opportunities for greater influence on their terms and conditions of employment or information regarding the future of the business.

The notion of non-compliance is an issue in relation to all regulation; clearly, in the case of tax, value added tax (VAT) and national insurance payments the penalties are such that, for most, compliance is the rational course of action. However, in the case of employment regulations, enforcement is more challenging, particularly regarding SMEs. It would appear that, in specific instances – the National Minimum Wage, for example – this has been widely adopted, largely because of the high profile afforded by government, the media, trade unions and employers groups. However, again, the evidence (Hart 2004 and Marlow 2002) would suggest that, across the wider spectrum of employment regulation, compliance has been patchy. In the absence of any formal policing of regulatory compliance by government, trade unions or employers' groups, this appears to arise for three broad, interrelated reasons – avoidance, ignorance and lack of employee pressure – so, if a firm owner decides against compliance or is, indeed, ignorant of the regulation, pressure for change has to come from employees. Of course, SME owners and managers do have access to information pertaining to shifting regulatory requirements and frequently are targeted by support, information and pressure groups such as Chambers of Commerce,

Business Links, the FSB and private consultants. Yet again, however, available evidence (Storey 1994: Marlow 1998; Carter and Jones-Evans 2000) indicates that most SME owners and managers are averse to seeking external, formal sources of advice and assistance, and when they do, this is usually activated by some unforeseen event or crisis. This then leaves a scenario of employees acting collectively to ensure the introduction of a new regulation, while a hypothetical argument but drawing upon the evidence, within a small organisation this is highly unlikely. Alternatively, if employees use exit rather than voice strategies, they can move their case to a tribunal, but this is a time-consuming and often complex process, with relatively limited sanctions on the organisation and limited compensation for the complainant.

Moving away from this rather pessimistic scenario of presumed non-compliance, given the heterogeneity of the sector, a proportion of firms, particularly those towards the larger end of the spectrum, will aim to comply with the new legislation. For the reasons outlined above, (informality, limited access to HR professionals and a preference for personal management, a context of relative smallness, lack of knowledge and so on) even where firms are keen to introduce the ICE, this will be challenging. Referring to the detailed requirements of the ICE Regulations outlined by the DTI (2004), many of these are quite alien to the general SME context. For example, the election by secret ballot of employee representatives, formally agreed meetings, consulting to share specific performance and market related information, outlining detailed and formal details of terms and conditions of employment require a considerable degree of competence in a range of HR and general management skills net usually present in smaller enterprises. While some flexibility is incorporated into the forthcoming legislation to accommodate different organisational needs, it is rather clear that a substantial element of knowledge to implement such provisions is essential. ACAS (2004: 27) states that to fully comprehend and adopt the ICE successfully requires professional knowledge of the substantive elements as well as dedicated preparation: 'Both employee representatives and managers need an understanding of the concepts, processes and mechanisms of information and consultation along with training in such basic behavioural skills as public speaking, making presentations, brainstorming and diplomacy.' The quite detailed and extensive body of evidence pertaining to training and development in SMEs (see Westhead and Storey, 1997 for an overview) suggests that where both owner/manager and employee training is concerned, there is a clear preference for informal learning, experience is valued over qualifications, and formal training initiatives are not pursued enthusiastically. If dedicated training support is required to adopt the ICE legislation, the SME sector would not appear to be likely to embrace such an approach.

Conclusions

Drawing on these reflections on how the information and consultation law might affect SMEs in general, a number of themes emerge. Primarily, the underpinning preference for informal labour management and the context of smallness that informs this preference largely mitigates against compliance, as does a preferred management stance which is suspicious of external advice, training, information and support sources. If the more volatile operating environment of the sector is also factored into this portrayal, it can be seen that adopting the Regulations might be considered to be a real risk to competitive performance in uncertain markets. Overall, it might be supposed that, reflecting the general propensity to adopt employment regulation in a context of limited policing and sanctions, compliance will again be patchy.

Second, the wide heterogeneity of the sector needs to be kept in mind at all times. There are significant industry and size differences. The bigger SMEs will comply, as they will have HR people on site. However, their efforts will still be undermined by other managers preferring either to relate directly to individuals or to resist revealing sensitive information. Indeed, in an environment where conflict has largely been absent, how will the firms deal with potential collective resistance? This may be exacerbated by a growing preference to contract-out the HR function to profes- sionals. However, even in this situation, SME owners will often only call in external HR people to handle contracts or the after-effects of discipline or grievance issues that get out of hand (Marlow 2003).

Third, the most important issue from a longer-term perspective of more harmonious and productive employment relations, is the effect on employees. Do these arguments mean that, once again, a considerable proportion of the labour force will at best have limited access to any voice regarding the conditions of their employment and the future of the organisation? This draws in issues concerned with fairness and social responsibility, on the one hand, and effective working practices and productivity on the other (not to mention the open and sharing environments considered to be important in supporting creativity and innovation). To a large extent, these issues refer back to the heterogeneity of the SME sector. Open systems that encourage the sharing of information and knowledge are a feature of many SMEs in the creative and high technology sectors. In these industries, it is common for very small firms, including those with fewer that twenty employees, to consult and share information with their staff (Davis and Scase 2000). In contrast, in industries where there is a lot of use of semi-skilled employees and high staff turnover – for example, some processing, construction, call centres and so on – SMEs will be more resistant to sharing. In fact, the ICE Regulations do recognise this in emphasising that consultation need only be with representatives of the staff rather than with the whole workforce.

The problems experienced by many SMEs in adopting and complying with regulations such as the ICE are reflected in their general approaches to management, business strategy and participation in other initiatives (for example, the Data Protection Act, Working Time Directive, environmental legislation and so on). This is not to suggest that they necessarily seek to avoid compliance, rather that they are likely to begin to comply only when it is viewed as being necessary or relevant (often, in order to avoid penalties, or through customer and peer pressure). Furthermore, compliance levels with ICE Regulators are even more likely to be poor given that representations from a proportion of the work force is necessary to 'trigger' implementation of the provisions at the Act. The prevailing environment of informality and proximity between owners, managers and employees will mutigate against this.

There are also serious issues concerning awareness and understanding of the requirements of regulations. Regulations are often written in dry, technical, even opaque, language. The HR departments of large firms have plenty of advance warning of the early stages of legislation, the enabling legislation itself and the details of the regulations. SMEs are rarely involved directly in the framing of legislation, and may not be aware of its existence until the regulations are promulgated. By then, it is often too late for SMEs, with their associated flexibility, their entrepreneurial or survival orientation, and their team/family employment policies, to point out that the content and format of the legislation is inappropriate for them. In fact, this is partly why small firms with fewer than fifty employees are excluded from the ICE Regulations in Britain. However, it would be wrong to conclude that this reflects SME owner intransigence or managerial incompetence. A more powerful justification for exempting SMEs from the imposition of the structured and hierarchical approach embedded in much employment regulation such as the ICE is that it mitigates against the flexibility that is the very essence of what makes SMEs successful. As it is this flexibility that makes the SME so attractive to policy-makers, because of it positive effects on innovation and productivity, there is a strong case for suggesting that as much effort and time that has gone into developing the ICE Regulations should be spent on developing appropriate and effective systems for ensuring that SMEs – taking into account their industry and size differences – are properly consulted and informed during the framing stages of such legislation.

References

ACAS (2004) 'Information and Consultation', www.acas.org/info_consut/consultation.html.

Blackburn, R. and Hart, M. (2001) 'Ignorance is bliss, knowledge is blight? Employment rights and small firms'. Paper presented at the 24th ISBA National Small Firms Conference, Leicester, November.

Bolton Committee Report (1971) 'Report of the Commission of Inquiry in small firms', Cmnd. 4811. London: HMSO.

Carter, S. and Jones Evans, D. (2000) Enterprise and Small Business. London: Prentice-Hall.

Cully, M., O'Reilly, A., Millward, N., Forth, J., Woodland, S., Dix, G. and Bryson, A. (1999) The 1998 Workplace Employee Relations Survey. London: Routledge.

Curran, J. (1997) The Role of the Small Firm in the UK Economy. Kingston, UK: Kingston University.

Curran, J. and Blackburn, R. (2001) Researching the Small Enterprise. London: Sage.

Curran, J. and Stanworth, J. (1986) 'Worker involvement and social relations in the small firm', in Curran, J., Stanworth, J. and Watkins, D. (eds) The Survival of the Small Firm, Vol. 2. Aldershot: Gower, pp. 25–41.

Davis, H. and Scase, R. (2000) *Managing Creativity: The Dynamics of Work and Organisations*. Milton Keynes: Open University Press.

Deakins, D. (2002) *Entrepreneurship and Small Firms*. London: McGraw-Hill.

DTI (Department of Trade and Industry) (2002) *Findings from the 1998 Survey of Employment Tribunal Applications*, Employment Relations Research Series No. 13. London: HMSO.

DTI (Department of Trade and Industry) (2003) *High Performance Workplaces – Informing and Consulting Employees: Consultator Document*. London: HMSO.

DTI (Department of Trade and Industry) (2004a) *Employment Information and Consultation Directive*. www.gov.uk/er/consultation/proposal.htm.

DTI (Department of Trade and Industry) (2004b) *SME Statistics for the UK 2003*, Small Business Service. www.sbs.gov.uk/content/statistics/stats2002.xls.

DTI (Department of Trade and Industry) (2004c) *Employment Market Analysis and Research: Trade Union Membership*. London: DTI, July.

Dundon, T., Grugulis, I. and Wilkinson, A. (1999) 'Looking out of the "Black Hole" non-union relations in an SME', *Employee Relations* 21(3): 251–66.

Earnshaw, J., Goodman, J., Harrison, R. and Marchington, M. (1998) 'Industrial tribunals, workplace disciplinary procedures and employment practice', *Employment Relations Research Series 2*. London: DTI.

Edwards, P., Ram, M. and Black, B. (2003) *The Impact of Employment Legislation on Small Firms: A Case Study Analysis*, Employment Research Series No. 20. London: DTI.

Federation of Small Business (2000) '*FSB Delivers Damning "Red Tape" Dossier to Government*', 23rd May. www.fsb.org.

Gibb, A. and Scott, M. (1985) 'Strategic awareness, personal commitment and the process of planning in small business', *Journal of Management Studies*, 22(6): 597–632.

Gilman, M., Edwards, P., Ram, M. and Arrowsmith, J. (2002) 'Pay determination in small firms in the UK: the case of the response to the National Minimum Wage', *Industrial Relations Journal* 33(1): 52–68.

Goss, D. (1991) *Small Business and Society*. London: Routledge.

Hart, M. (2004) 'Labour regulation and SMEs: a challenge to competitiveness and employability', in Marlow, S., Patton, D. and Ram, M. (eds) *Management Labour in Small Firms*. London: Routledge.

Holliday, R. (1995) *Investigating Small Firms, Nice Work?* London: Routledge.

McKay, S. (2001) 'Between flexibility and regulation: rights, protection and equality at work', *British Journal of Industrial Relations* 39(36): 285–303.

Marlow, S. and Patton, D. (2002) 'Minding the gap between employers and employees: the challenge for smaller manufacturing firm owners', *Employee Relations* 24(5): 523–539.

Marlow, S. (1998) 'So much opportunity; so little take up. The case of training in small firms', *Small Business and Enterprise Development Journal*, 5(1): 38–49.

Marlow, S. (2002) 'Regulating labour management in small firms', *Human Resource Management* 12(3): 25–43.

Marlow, S. (2003) 'Formality and informality in employment relations: the implications for regulatory compliance by smaller firms', *Government and Policy* 21: 531–47.

Marlow, S. (2004) 'Introduction: managing labour in small firms', in Marlow, S., Patton, D. and Ram, M. (eds) *Managing Labour in Small Firms*. London: Routledge.

Marlow, S. and Patton, D. (2002) 'Minding the gap: managing the employment relationship in small firms', *Employee Relations* 24(5): 523–39.

Marlow, S., Patton, D. and Ram, M. (2004) *Managing Labour in Small Firms*. London: Routledge.

Matlay, H. (1999) 'Employee relations in small firms: a micro-business perspective', *Employee Relations* 21(3): 285–95.

Moule, M. (1998) 'Regulation of work in small firms: a view from the inside', *Work, Employment and Society* 12(4): 635–53.

Oldfield, C. (1999) 'Red tape is strangling enterprise', *Sunday Times*, 31 October 1999, p. 7.

Rainnie, A. (1989) *Small Isn't Beautiful*. London: Routledge.

Ram, M. (1994) *Managing to Survive*. London: Routledge.

Ram, M. (1999) 'Managing autonomy: employment relations in small professional service', *International Small Business Journal* 17(2): 13–30.

Ram, M. and Edwards, P. (2003) 'Praising Caesar not burying him: what we know about employment relations in small firms', *Work, Employment and Society* 17(4): 719–30.

Ram, M., Edwards, P., Gilman, M. and Arrowsmith, J. (2001) 'The dynamics of informality: employment relations in small firms and the effects of regulatory change', *Work, Employment and Society* 15(4): 845–61.

Rose, E. (2001) *Employment Relations*. London: Prentice-Hall.

Ryan, A. (2004) 'Representation, consultation and the smaller firm', in Marlow, S., Patton, D. and Ram, M. (eds) *Managing Labour in Small Firms*. London: Routledge.

Scase, R. (2004) 'Managerial strategies in small firms', in Marlow, S., Patton, D. and Ram, M. (eds) *Managing Labour in Small Firms*. London: Routledge.

Scott, M., Roberts, I., Holroyd, G. and Sawbridge, G. (1989) *Management and Industrial Relations in Small Firms*, Research Paper No. 70. London: Dept of Employment.

Small Enterprise Research Team (2003) *NatWest Quarterly Survey of Small Business in Britain* 19(1 & 2).

Stanworth, J. and Purdy, D. (2003) *SME Facts and Figures*, Report to the All-Party Parliamentary Small Business Group, University of Westminster.

Storey, D. (1994) *Understanding the Small Business Sector* London: Routledge.

Storey, D., Keasey, K. and Wynarczyk, P. (1987) *The Performance of Small Firms*. London: Croom Helm.

Thomson, A. and Gray, C. (1999) 'Determinants of management development in small businesses', *Journal of Small Business and Enterprise Development* 6(2): 113–27.

Wynarczyk, P., Watson, R., Storey, D., Short, H. and Keasey, K. (1993) *Managerial Labour Markets in Small Firms*. London: Routledge.

11

What kind of financial literacy do employee representatives need?

Peter Walton

The EU Directive on Information and Consultation requires that an employer informs employee representatives about the 'economic situation' of the business. The draft statutory instrument published in July 2004 to implement this in the UK talks about providing information about the 'recent and probable development of the undertaking's activities and economic situation' as well as the 'situation, structure and probable development of employment within the undertaking'.

The implications for employee representatives are many, but the specific area of concern examined in this chapter is the need for representatives to understand aspects of financial reporting and related management information systems. Although this is an acutely expressed need, the current level of provision to meet it is minimal. The purpose of this chapter is to explore what might be done and to expose the associated considerations. It covers an analysis of how the economic situation of a business may be conveyed, discusses how the 'basics' of management reporting might be determined, and considers earlier examples of employee councils and their ways of tackling finance. The implications for the training of employee representatives in financial reporting is also considered.

Understanding the 'economic situation'

The Directive requires employers to provide employees with information about the 'economic situation' of the organisation. However, the wording of the Directive leaves a great deal of latitude to management as to what constitutes enough information to convey this. The UK draft statutory instrument goes further, but is still short on specificity. Indeed, arguably the first and the greatest need for financial literacy that the employee representatives will have could be in agreeing what kind of information should routinely be provided. In some businesses there are very straightforward indicators that provide a quick check on business health, such as the sales per square foot in a retail environment, or the value of the forward order book in a manufacturing environment. Normally, a reading of the situation requires an assessment of whether these indicators are increasing or decreasing, and at what rate. Another kind of economic indicator is the company's planned future investment in productive capacity. Employers might argue that these 'quick indicators' are sufficiently powerful indices on their own and that no further information is needed to gauge the forward implications for the workforce.

At the other end of the spectrum, the annual financial statements of a multinational group will probably run to a hundred pages and include information about the pension plan, the group's exposure to different business risks, its use of derivatives, its financial structure and so on. An investment analyst would want both the quick indicators and the full financials, but it is likely that the employee representative's needs fall somewhere between the two. Since the focus of the Directive is on the immediate workplace, and in any event it does not apply to those parts of the business that are outside the EU, employee representation in a large group is likely to be organised at the level of the individual plant, or the subsidiary company, providing information at a level comparable with that of smaller companies.

The fact that the intended purpose, and therefore the focus of the information, is essentially designed to offer insights into continuing employment, this also means that it is unlikely that the employee representatives will need to concern themselves with issues such as audit, internal control, the general financing of the company or pension funding (this is, of course, important for employees, but their information here should come from the trustees of the pension plan and is not covered by this Directive).

As regards the overall financing of the company, a subsidiary company in a big group may not be autonomous in this area in any case. Further, in any company, financing is often only a major problem after the company has been running unprofitably for a time. Consequently, this is information that an employee would not routinely need, but if the company starts to get into difficulties, the representative would need to monitor this closely.

The most useful information the employee representative will need to see probably relates to the monthly operating statements used by management to run the business, and this may well be what was envisaged by the draft statutory instrument's reference to 'recent and probable development of the undertaking's activities'. The traditional basic information package internal to a company is normally presented in a manner as shown in Table 11.1. For simplicity, only the current month's data are given, whereas in reality there would normally be a set of year-to-date figures as well.

Of course, the precise choice of reporting lines is determined by the nature of the business. For example, 'cost of sales' is usually a key figure in a manufacturing or retail

Table 11.1 Typical monthly operating statement

Current month	Actual (£000s)	Budget (£000s)	Variance (£000s)	Last year (£000s)
Sales				
Product A	856	900	(44)	820
Cost of sales	(300)	(315)	15	(295)
Gross margin	556	585	(29)	525
Product B	633	600	33	550
Cost of sales	(285)	(270)	(15)	(253)
Gross margin	348	330	18	297
Total contribution (A + B)	904	915	(11)	822
Expenses				
Advertising	50	50	–	46
Distribution	156	140	(16)	149
Depreciation	90	90	–	90
Salaries	324	300	(24)	310
Other costs	125	125	–	132
Total expenses	745	705	(40)	727
Profit before interest and tax	159	210	(51)	95

business, but not in most service industries. Crucially, in order to properly understand this sort of statement, the employee would need to know where the numbers came from, and how they are used in a budgetary reporting framework. In other words, understanding the performance of the business turns on two issues: (i) understanding the measurement of the numbers reported; and (ii) knowing what the particular reporting techniques are designed to achieve. As far as the measurement is concerned, while the report talks of 'actual' data, the figures may represent observed transactions (hard facts), but they might also be estimates or just an allocation of an annual figure (somewhat softer information). Every reporting technique (several are described below) tries to focus on particular management issues. This budget/actual system is based in comparing performance against a plan, and progress towards an annual target.

In the example shown in Table 11.1, we have 'actual' data (from both the current and previous years) supplied from the company's financial accounting system, and then the use of these against a budget, a technique usually known as a budgetary control system. The question is how far the employee representative needs to be able to understand and go beneath the surface of such management reports.

What are 'the basics'?

In normal management education, the idea of 'financial literacy' has had to be addressed in designing MBA and other business courses. But even in these traditional and well-trodden courses, the issue remains a very difficult problem. Should a manager be able to critically assess financial reports, or merely to understand the basics? The same question applies to employee representatives. If the answer is that it is normally sufficient to be able to understand the basics, then that poses the obvious next question: what are the basics? In the EU generally, a public accountant is expected to have a degree-level education and spend at least three years studying professional subjects. In the USA, a public accountant needs at least five years of university education in related subjects and three years' practical experience before being licensed. How can we gauge how much of this is essential for a normal manager or an employee representative?

Accounting measurements are central to the management process. While they are a way of representing an economic reality, they have limitations as to what aspects of the economic reality they can capture, but they focus attention on their version of reality. These measurements make some aspects of a business visible, while making other aspects invisible. To put this point another way, we encounter the adage, 'what gets measured, gets managed'. A simple example would be training costs: accounting can measure the cost, but not the benefit that derives from it. It is fairly useful, therefore, and some might say essential, to be able to see 'through' the figures, or at least see the figures in context.

While the public perception may be that accounting provides more-or-less precise measurements, the reality is rather far from this. A very large proportion of accounting numbers are a matter of opinion (albeit within a precise range of alternatives), and when an accountant provides operating reports for internal management use, their figures include many assumptions, estimates and allocations, based on judgement, convention and training – but inevitably capable also of reflecting the particular accountant's own biases.

In business, a key question is whether something – for example, a whole business, a product line, or a trading unit – is making a profit. This implies that we can measure the revenues earned and the costs associated with them accurately, but employee representatives need to know that this is not often the case, and always to question on what basis such figures have been arrived at. Usually, the revenues are reasonably clear. But even here there can be grey areas – for example, when a dealer sells a car with zero interest financing, or three years' free servicing, some of the invoice price must be allocated to the financing or future servicing costs. But in comparison, the costs side is much more problematic. This is the area that generally involves allocations and estimates of future outcomes.

This sort of issue can be seen in the monthly internal report shown in Table 11.1 above. The accountant is usually required to break down costs and allocate them as far as possible to individual products or activities. In the example given, the annual advertising spend has been budgeted at £600,000. In reality, this will probably not be used in equal monthly amounts, but conventionally is spread across each month for reporting purposes so that the individual months sum to the annual total. However, the accountant will in the early part of the year simply use the budget figure as the best estimate of what the annual charge will be, and divide by twelve for the monthly 'actual'. As the year progresses, a more accurate estimate of the yearly total will be possible, but the monthly figure will still be an allocation of this estimate and it will be the end of the year before the accountant can be sure what the real figure was. The user of the report needs to explore what elements of the 'actual' are allocations put in to give a more holistic picture, and what figures represent observed transactions: real income and expenditure.

The question of allocations and estimates becomes much more complex when narrowing down the focus (which usually implies making more allocations) and looking at issues such as the profitability of a particular product – a key problem for future employment prospects. If we take a simple example, a manufacturing line consists of five machines that are capable of producing a number of different products. Each machine cost £100,000 to install and is expected to be used for about ten years. This means that there is an initial investment of £500,000 which, because of depreciation, will be worth nothing in ten years' time. This disappearing asset has to be charged to the cost of operations, and would be done by making a 'depreciation' charge of £50,000 a year: this is the first allocation of cost, into annual chunks, and its validity depends upon the accuracy of the ten-year life estimate.

Suppose that in the current year the machines are used for 10 per cent of their time to produce Product A, and for 30 per cent of their time to make Product B, and the rest of the time they are idle, and the accountant therefore decides to charge the £50,000 to the two products in relation to their time use (1:3). In the year in question the company produces 100,000 units of Product A, whose other costs are raw materials £12,000 and labour £30,000. Product A sells for 50p a unit. The 100,000 units produced in the year are costed at:

	£
Raw materials	12,000
Labour	30,000
Depreciation (50,000×0.25)	12,500
Total	54,500
Sales revenue	50,000
Loss	4,500

Calculated this way, the management perception might be that Product A should be discontinued, as it is losing £4,500 a year before even looking at selling costs. However, the figure includes an allocation for depreciation of £12,500. In reality the production line is idle 60 per cent of its time, and this idle time is being absorbed into the costs of the products being sold, thereby penalising them. If Product A was charged only 10 per cent of the machine time (what it is in fact using), the figures would be:

	£
Raw materials	12,000
Labour	30,000
Depreciation (50,000×0.10)	5,000
Total	47,000
Sales revenue	50,000
Gross profit	3,000

The perception of profit or loss in this case includes two allocation decisions (that the machine will be used for ten years, and the annual charge will be allocated to reflect usage), and different allocations would give a different result. Of course, taken from the perspective of the whole company, the depreciation is part of the annual costs and the company must in the long run generate revenues to meet it, but looking at Product A, it is making a 'contribution' and should not be discontinued unless it is using machine time that could be used more profitably on a different product. Cost allocations of this kind are frequent, and generally the larger the company, the more allocations are involved in costing. Groups may have research and development costs that are incurred in one country and allocated to plant in other countries, for example.

Reporting techniques

The budget/actual technique illustrated above is by far the most commonly used internal reporting model for all types of business. It involves an annual budget exercise, where management work out targets for the coming year. From the perspective of an employee representative, the budget could in fact be more significant than the actual results, since the budget reflects what management hope will be the outcomes of the next year, and therefore the next year's employment prospects – an obvious way of getting to the 'probable development' referred to in the draft statutory instrument. However, the budgetary process is much abused, with some managements putting in 'stretch' figures designed to set high targets and encourage everyone to work harder, while others put in higher costs and lower sales than might be expected so that their variances are always positive. Frequently, senior management build in very low or even nil salary increases, to discourage pay claims. Other similar playing with the figures is not unusual.

This 'gaming' that the budget enables and arguably provokes has motivated people to use other performance measures. These might simply be to measure against the previous year (but conditions are not necessarily the same) or to compare with some best practice (usually known as 'benchmarking') provided sufficient information is available. Economic value added (EVA) and similar notions have been very popular since the 1990s. These involve measuring the extent to which each business makes a profit over and above the profit that might be expected, based on the value of the assets used and the level of risk. Another technique is known as the 'balanced score-card': this tries to measure more than just financial performance, and allows some comparisons with competitors.

Thus, to summarise, the question is whether employee representatives need to have training in all these areas, and if so, what depth of knowledge. Especially important is what knowledge of the different techniques associated with each area is it necessary for the employee representative to have in order for him or her to make a meaningful contribution. A complicating factor is that no two businesses are exactly alike, and that each typically focuses on one preferred method of internal reporting.

Employee councils

There have been some earlier examples of how to address these dilemmas. For example, the French government faced this problem in the late 1940s. During the postwar reconstruction it introduced the employee council concept. Since that time, any company with fifty or more employees has been required to create a committee of employees and to provide it with financial information, including regular accounts, about the company. If any reorganisation of the business is planned and this involves redundancies, the plans have to be submitted to the employee council and they have to have the opportunity to make a counter-proposal (famously, Marks & Spencer failed to do this when closing their French operations). This, of course, poses the question of the financial literacy of the employee representatives. The French solution was not to provide education but to provide the employees with their own accounting adviser: the company is obliged to pay for an independent accountant to help the employees. As a result of this, there are now quite large specialist independent accounting firms in France whose sole client base is employee councils and trade unions, and who offer economic analysis and some legal advice as well as accounting.

This is an effective solution, not least because it avoids making choices about what areas of expertise are necessary, and it works well where there is a consultative process between management and employees. The employee council does not sit down with the board and discuss the issues; it receives reports and can seek advice and discuss the reports before going back to management.

The idea that the technical issues are too complex to expect a non-accountant to address is also gaining ground in the USA, albeit in a different context. The Sarbanes–Oxley Act, the rigorous post-Enron governance legislation, has a similar requirement. Companies must provide their audit committees (consisting of non-executive directors) with any specialist independent advisers the committees want to help them understand and deal with issues arising from their work.

Training

Returning to a framework where the non-specialist wishes to receive training in financial issues, we are left with the problem of defining which areas are most useful, and to what depth the training should be delivered. One way of approaching the question might lie in the specifics of the organisation where the knowledge will be used. Not all companies use all available internal accounting techniques; different industry segments have different critical measures. Training could therefore be made more efficient by tailoring it to different kinds of company and different industry sectors. Training might in fact be better focused by looking at the environment in which the employee representative will operate and using that to identify the knowledge base required.

The logical outcome of that approach might be to have training provided by the companies in which the employee representative operates, in the sense of providing the tightest focus on the areas likely to be of use. Linked to that idea is the point, inherent in the way that accountants are trained, that experience is a necessary part of the training. This is likely to be true for non-specialists as well: several months of sitting in on management meetings in a particular company will develop an understanding of the issues that are important for that company, provided this is linked to a source of education to supply the background fundamentals that underlie the decision areas.

Another approach to defining the cognitive base would be to ask non-specialists what it is they do not understand. Of course, that is very risky, since if they do not understand, they cannot in all cases know that there is anything to understand in the first place. A more scientific approach would be to ask those who have experience of participating in management meetings and now consider themselves financially literate, what the key areas are, and what level of technique they think need. Equally, research could be done using surrogates, such as non-executive directors, as the research target. In any event, it ought to be possible to start from the end product and work backwards to identify the training need.

The third approach, and the one that is commonly used, is simply for accounting educators to use their judgement as to what degree of knowledge is required. Typically, educators start from the level of knowledge of the professional examinations, and strip out as much as they think is feasible. This results in different institutions and different textbooks offering vastly different collections of material, all intended to give a manager financial literacy. Academics have radically different views about what is necessary. Some insist, for example, on starting with double-entry bookkeeping, where others dispense with this entirely. Many accounting educators have never sat on a company management committee and therefore, while this 'top-down' approach should result in a knowledge base that is coherent, it is not necessarily efficient or well-adapted to the needs experienced in the field.

Making a non-specialist into a person who is financially literate is an extremely challenging task. It may be that consideration of the French idea of parallel technical advice should be given as a support service. However, the central issue outside that, is how to define what is the necessary knowledge base. This question arises both in terms of restricting the overall fields and in determining what level of detail within each field needs to be covered. As no two companies are exactly alike, the financial subjects covered could well be quite different depending upon the size of the company, the international nature of its operations, and the business sector concerned. Anything short of a full professional training must be selective, and what happens in the actual workplace is probably the best determinant of what to select.

References

Dix, Gill and Oxenbridge, Sarah (2003) *Information and Consultation at Work: From Challenges to Good Practice.* ACAS Research Paper 2003/07 (London).

Drury, Colin (2005) *Management Accounting for Business,* 3rd edn. London: Thomson Learning.

Freshfields, Bruckhaus, Deringer (2003) *Implementing the Information and Consultation Directive* (24-page solicitors' booklet). London: FBD October.

Gray, R., Owen, D. and Adams, C. (1996) *Accounting and Accountability: Changes and Challenges in Corporate Social and Environmental Reporting.* London: Prentice-Hall.

International comparisons

Part 5 contains three chapters. Their joint purpose is to set all the other chapters in this book in the context of comparative European practice.

In Chapter 12, John Geary and William Roche give details about the unfolding developments in information and consultation in Ireland. This country-level case analysis is important to the British reader because it is the only other European country that, until the arrival of the EU Directive, had no general legal requirement for information and consultation arrangements.

In Chapter 13, Andrea Broughton makes a broad-ranging comparison of practices across the EU Member States. Key features of each state are tabulated, and compared and contrasted. She suggests that it is unlikely that existing co-determination systems will spread beyond the countries where they already exist, though there is some possibility because of the European Company Statute. The worker involvement provisions accompanying this Statute may result in co-determination in certain circumstances, Broughton argues. She suggests that it is likely that the new information and consultation Directive will ensure a certain degree of harmony around the EU in terms of basic information and consultation provision. However, it is also likely that the existing variation in provision around the EU will also largely remain in place.

Finally, in Chapter 14, Howard Gospel and Paul Willman focus on the require- ments for statutory information disclosure for the purposes of consultation and bargaining. They discuss the importance of information disclosure and then make a three-way comparison between France, Germany and the UK. The rationale for the use of law derives from the tendency to information asymmetry. The three different patterns of legal requirement reflect the prevailing industrial relations patterns in the three countries studied. This does not, however, necessarily mean that the patterns are well suited or stable.

12

The future of employee information and consultation in Ireland

John F. Geary and William K. Roche

In 2005, the EU Directive on Information and Consultation was to be transposed into Irish legislation. By common consent, this Directive is likely to represent the single greatest innovation in Irish employment relations in recent times. It will introduce for the first time a comprehensive legal code whereby management will be compelled to inform and consult with employees before making decisions on key business issues. For many organisations, existing information exchange and consultation provisions will need to be evaluated against the requirements of the Directive and, if found wanting, will have to be recast and underpinned by a formal agreement. In others, where management has made no such provision in the past, information and consultation arrangements will have to be introduced for the first time. In yet other workplaces, where employers have relied on direct information and consultation procedures, the legality of such arrangements may be called into question.

We begin this chapter by outlining the legislative and institutional framework within which information exchange and consultation occurs in Ireland. We then examine various arrangements for involving employees and their representatives in decision-making. The effects of such arrangements on a range of outcomes relevant to organisations, employees and unions are considered next. A series of conclusions are advanced as a prelude to our examination of the transposition of the Directive into Irish law and its likely effects.

Information and consultation: current practice

Like the United Kingdom, Ireland is unusual when compared with other EU countries in not possessing a system of works councils, enshrined in statute or collective agreement, and providing rights to information and consultation in firms or workplaces. But Ireland has been distinctive in comparison with the UK in the degree of its various attempts to involve employees. Statutory provision for information and consultation has existed in Ireland with respect to some specific issues or areas. Companies have been required by law to consult with employee representatives in the event of planned collective redundancies. The 1997 Transfer of Undertaking Directive also introduced provision for informing employee representatives of the implications of such transfers, and sought to promote agreement between the parties. Irish Health and Safety legislation also provides for consultation and participation, involving employees or their representatives on health and safety issues. The European Works Council Directive has, of course, also applied. And since 1988 some forty Irish state-owned enterprises have been required to establish processes at sub-board level for the exchange of information. Legislation in 1977 and 1988 also established a system of worker directors in fourteen state companies, and mandated the introduction of worker directors in other state companies. Candidates for election as worker directors are nominated by trade unions but elected by all employees.

Collective agreements between employers and unions have also addressed the area of information and consultation from the mid-1990s under the more general rubric of partnership and involvement. Since 1987, employers, unions and the state have negotiated an unbroken series of triennial 'social pacts'. These so-called social partnership agreements have addressed a progressively widening agenda, encompassing pay, macroeconomic management, taxation, social policy, labour market reforms, training and a host of other areas of public policy and industrial relations. The 1997–2000 social partnership programme was the first to promote an extension of partnership to enterprises and workplaces through a national framework agreement. This outlined the objectives of 'enterprise partnership'. These were taken to include the enhancement of the prosperity and success of the enterprise, the engagement of all stakeholders' ideas, abilities and commitment, and the creation of a basis for arrangements for discussion of major decisions affecting the organisation's future, including its future economic security (Partnership 2000: 62).

Crucially, no unitary model or institutional arrangement was agreed or advocated for partnership in firms and workplaces. Rather, firms, employees and their representatives were encouraged to tailor partnership arrangements to the circumstances of their own firms and workplaces. In the same way, there was no attempt at prescription with respect to the areas that might be encompassed by partnership. Instead, a list of possible areas was identified that might provide a focus for the parties 'depending on the particular circumstances of the enterprise'. These included employee involvement in meeting the challenge of competition; training and development; equal opportunities; financial involvement; workforce composition; co-operation with change; problem-solving and conflict avoidance; adaptability, flexibility and innovation; and representational arrangements (including trade union representation and facilities (Partnership 2000: 63–4). Subsequent social partnership programmes have also followed this approach, all containing national framework agreements endorsing voluntary, non-prescriptive arrangements and broad indicative agendas for the promotion of partnership and involvement in firms and workplaces.

Arrangements, approaches and mechanisms in firms and workplaces

As discussed above, institutional support for information exchange and consultation has come mainly from national framework agreements supporting partnership and involvement in firms and workplaces. We begin this section, therefore, by examining the incidence of partnership and involvement arrangements and approaches to decision-making. We then focus specifically on practice with respect to information and consultation.

A series of surveys provide a profile of different arrangements for involving and consulting with employees and unions in Ireland. A study of a sample of organisations with at least fifty employees drawn from the top 2,000 trading firms (defined by turnover or assets) and non-trading bodies (defined in terms of numbers of employees) reported that joint consultative committees or works councils were present in 21 per cent of private-sector organisations and in 38 per cent of public-sector organisations (Gunnigle *et al.* 1997: 210). A more comprehensive survey of workplaces found that 13 per cent of workplaces reported the existence of joint consultative committees or works councils (Roche and Geary, 2000: 10).

The workplace survey conducted by Roche and Geary (2000) sought to assess the manner in which management had sought to handle change across a range of operational and strategic areas. Eight areas of operational change were examined, including changes to payment systems, working practices, plant and technology, involvement initiatives and promotional structures. Four areas of strategic change were also examined, including the introduction of new products, the setting of business targets for the workplace, and plans with respect to mergers, acquisitions and divestments. In workplaces affected by changes in any of these areas, managers were asked whether they had relied *mainly* on direct employee involvement, on partnership with unions, on managerial prerogative or on traditional arm's-length collective bargaining with trade unions. Reliance on direct involvement or partnership with unions could be viewed as an 'inclusionary' approach to handling change, while reliance on managerial prerogative or traditional arm's-length collective bargaining could be viewed, in contrast, as an 'exclusionary' approach. In the case of workplaces recognising unions, the survey revealed that exclusionary approaches were more common than inclusionary approaches with respect to the handling of change in nine out of the twelve areas examined. The incidence of exclusionary approaches often exceeded inclusionary approaches by a wide margin, especially with respect to the handling of changes of a strategic character. Within the inclusionary category, direct involvement was generally much more prevalent than indirect involvement based on partnership with unions.

In non-union workplaces, an exclusionary approach (here involving reliance on managerial prerogative) was more common than an inclusionary approach (here entailing direct involvement) in eight out of the twelve areas examined. Again, the margin between the percentages of workplaces adopting exclusionary and inclusionary approaches was often wide, especially in the case of change in strategic areas. Data on managers' intentions with respect to approaches to handling change in the future pointed toward inclusionary approaches becoming more prevalent, but higher percentages of workplaces seemed set to favour exclusionary approaches to the handling of change in three of the six areas examined, and this pattern was found in both non-union workplaces and workplaces that recognised unions.

The advent of framework agreements on partnership and involvement in the workplace from 1997 and support for workplace initiatives of this kind in EU funding programmes were associated with a rise in the incidence of partnership arrangements in unionised employments in the private sector. A review by J. O'Dowd, based on all available secondary sources, identified fewer than 150 partnerships in unionized firms in the year 2000. Moreover, the rate of formation of partnerships appeared to tail off towards the end of the 1990s, as the initial impetus provided by the first national framework agreement and the possibility of the availability of EU funds abated (O'Dowd ongoing). A number of these partnerships have since collapsed, including some that were regarded as being among the most advanced in making provision for union and employee involvement at multiple levels within organisations.

The framework agreements in the national social partnership programmes resulted in the introduction of partnership arrangements in the public services from the late 1990s. Extensive formal partnership arrangements were put in place; in particular, in the civil service, health and local government sectors. The advent of such arrangements represented the most significant change in voice processes in the public service in half a century. Reviews of partnerships in the public service have concluded that much effort has been devoted to aligning the new structures with existing decision-making and industrial relations arrangements (O'Dwyer *et al.* 2002; Roche 2002). The agendas of partnership arrangements appear for the most part to have been restricted to 'softer' areas such as communications, training, personal development and the codification of policies. Mainstream business has figured a great deal less in partnership agendas, while areas of major concern for trade unions and their members have continued to be handled through established industrial relations channels (Roche 2002). Public service partnership arrangements also showed signs of being either 'top-heavy', with joint effort concentrated on central committees and little effort at workplace level, or 'bottom-heavy', with joint effort focused on workplace-based projects and little central co-ordination or integration of these in line with any joint overall strategy (Roche 2002).

Successive public service pay agreements have sought to incentivise the establishment of partnerships and the handling of joint programmes of change on a partnership basis.

Under proposals contained in the 2003–5 social partnership agreement, *Sustaining Progress*, pay rises in the sector have been linked with co-operation with public service modernisation and the maintenance of stable industrial relations (Sustaining Progress, 2003). A 'performance verification process' has been established to ensure compliance with an agreed change agenda. Within this process, public service partnership committees are required to prepare action plans focused on the modernisation agenda, and these are subject to endorsement by performance verification groups for different parts of the public service. Other initiatives seeking to align partnership arrangements with the joint handling of change include a 'joint statement' concluded in 2004 by local authorities and trade unions seeking to facilitate the handling of significant changes through partnership. A parallel joint statement on the handling of significant changes in the health service has been concluded by the Interim Health Service Executive, a new body charged with the management of strategic change in the health service, and the key health services union, SIPTU. This envisages regular meetings focusing on information and consultation, trust building, and gaining agreement on the channelling of change issues into joint problem-solving forums or into established industrial relations processes.

Three large-scale surveys undertaken in 2003, co-designed by the authors, provide perhaps the most comprehensive picture of current practice with respect to partnership, involvement, information provision and consultation. A survey of private-sector employers revealed that only 4 per cent had implemented formal partnership agreements involving unions and employees. A further 19 per cent stated that they were party to informal partnership-style arrangements, involving employee representatives. Turning specifically to information provision and consultation, 62 per cent of private-sector employers claimed to engage in information exchange and consultation with staff on change. A second survey of public service organisations sought the views of public service employers on their responses to pressures for change. Over 90 per cent of these identified the improvement of information flows and consultation as being important or very important, both currently and in the near future. Only the development of service quality standards, and training and development, were seen to be comparably important among a series of human resource policies and work innovations examined (Williams *et al.* 2004: 102).

A third survey of 5,000 employees report the situation in these areas as experienced by people at work rather than by employers or managers. Of those working in private-sector workplaces where unions were recognised, 18 per cent reported that partnership arrangements involving management and unions were in place in their workplaces, compared with 45 per cent in the public sector (O'Connell *et al.* 2004: ch. 7). Arrangements for *direct* involvement were reported by 62 per cent of employers in the private-sector survey (Williams *et al.* 2004: 56); by 35 per cent of private-sector employees; and by 47 per cent of employees in the public sector (O'Connell *et al.* 2004: 99–100).

The picture of extensive information exchange and consultation derived from the survey of private sector employers and the strong relative emphasis on these areas that emerged in the public-service employer survey, has to be set beside the results that emerge from the survey of 5,000 employees. As can be seen from

Table 12.1, between 37 per cent and 58 per cent of private-sector employees say that they hardly ever receive information on areas such as the level of competition faced by their employers (41 per cent), the introduction of new products and services (37 per cent), the introduction of new technology (40 per cent), plans to reorganise the company (58 per cent), changes in work practices (42 per cent) and trends in sales and profits (52 per cent). These data suggest that, for significant numbers of employees, a wide gap exists between employer perceptions of information exchange and their own experiences (O'Connell *et al.* 2004: 88). Public-service employees appear better informed than their private-sector counterparts, but here too a gap is apparent between the emphasis of employers on the priority of information and consultation, and the experiences of sizeable numbers of employees. Between 29 per cent and 44 per cent say that they hardly ever receive information on such areas as budgets (44 per cent), plans to improve services (26 per cent), the introduction of new technology (29 per cent), plans to reorganise service delivery (36 per cent), and changes in work practices (33 per cent) (O'Connell *et al.* 2004: 89).

The survey questioned employees with respect to their experience of consultation at the level of their own work. As is apparent from Table 12.2, 28 per cent of private-sector employees and 26 per cent working in the public services replied that they were rarely or almost never consulted before decisions were taken that affected their work. A further 22 per cent of private-sector employees and 20 per cent working in the public services

Table 12.1   Levels of information experienced by employees

		Informed on a regular basis (%)	Informed occasionally (%)	Hardly ever informed (%)
A	**Workplaces in the private and commercial publicly-owned sectors**			
	Level of competition faced by employer	33.8	25.0	41.1
	Introduction of new products/ services	36.7	26.8	36.5
	Introduction of new technology	34.9	25.6	39.5
	Reorganisation of company	23.2	18.8	58.0
	Changes in work practices	31.3	26.5	42.2
	Sales, profits and market share	28.5	19.1	52.4
B	**Public service workplaces**			
	Budget of the organisation	30.1	25.6	44.3
	Improvement of services provided	42.5	31.8	25.7
	Introduction of new technology	40.5	30.4	29.1
	Reorganisation of service delivery	36.6	27.4	36.0
	Changes in work practices	36.5	30.7	32.7

Source: NCPP/ESRI dataset

stated that they were rarely or almost never given the reasons why changes had occurred to their work. Lower percentages of employees in both sectors felt that they could rarely or almost never voice opinions they knew to be different from those of their supervisors, but still 23 per cent of private-sector employees and 22 per cent working in the public services felt that attention was rarely or almost never paid to their views, even if they were consulted. At the other extreme of the spectrum, comparable or somewhat higher percentages reported that they were almost always consulted or had their views listened to in such circumstances. The authors of the employee survey highlight the conclusion that high proportions of employees feel themselves to be excluded from information exchange, consultation and decision-making in the workplace (O'Connell *et al.* 2004: 96).

A survey of 379 member companies of the Irish Business and Employers' Confederation, with 145,000 employees, also examined the areas covered by information and consultation. The results indicate that information provision is generally more common than consultation other than in such areas as new forms of work organisation, problem-solving and conflict avoidance (Coughlan 2004: 40).

Case-based studies round out the picture that emerges from surveys by providing accounts of the nature and dynamics of arrangements for information exchange and consultation in Irish firms and workplaces, and their association with partnership and involvement. Dundon *et al.* (2003) studied information and consultation

Table 12.2 Levels of consultation experienced by employees

	Almost Always %	Often %	Sometimes %	Rarely %	Almost Never %
Are you consulted before decisions are taken that affect your work?					
Private and commercial public sectors	26.7	21.5	23.5	14.6	13.8
Public services	27.4	19.6	27.2	14.6	11.2
If changes are made to your work how often are you given reasons?					
Private and commercial public sectors	35.1	21.3	21.4	12.6	9.5
Public services	39.2	17.6	23.4	11.4	8.4
If your opinion is different to your supervisor/manager, can you say so?					
Private and commercial public sectors	52.1	19.8	15.0	6.9	6.1
Public services	53.9	17.0	17.5	6.8	4.8
If consulted before decisions are taken, is attention paid to your views?					
Private and commercial public sectors	31.6	18.3	27.3	12.5	10.3
Public services	30.4	18.3	29.3	12.2	9.8

Source: NCPP/ESRI dataset

arrangements in fifteen organisations spanning the private and public sectors, unionised and non-union employers, and small, medium and large employer categories. A variety of mechanisms were used to inform and consult, commonly in combination, but methods for direct information provision and consultation appeared to predominate. Of direct methods, email, staff briefings, focus groups and appraisal practices were used as one-way or two-way communication mechanisms. Direct consultative techniques included workforce meetings and attitude surveys. Indirect information and consultative mechanisms included joint committees and works councils (Dundon *et al.* 2003: chs 5 and 6). Partnership agreements sometimes provided the rubric for information and consultation in unionised firms.

Managers frequently understood the process involved in exchanging information and consulting employees as aspects of 'internal communication', 'dialogue' and 'empowerment', sometimes preferring these terms to 'information and consultation'. Mirroring the survey findings discussed above, many representatives and employees interviewed seemed more sceptical as to the depth and extent of information and consultation than did managers (Dundon *et al.* 2003: ch. 6). The case organisations were portrayed as located in general somewhere between practising information exchange and practising consultation (Dundon *et al.* 2003: 52).

With regard to the role of information and consultation in the management of change, it was concluded that centrally-driven change programmes often left little scope for consultation at the local level. The more 'transformational' the change programme, the less likely that consultation would occur, although information was still generally disseminated to employees. More incremental changes seemed easier to align with consultative processes (Dundon *et al.* 2003: ch. 7). The study concludes that information and consultation practices were most effective, especially in managing change, where they were integrated; where direct and indirect methods were used in combination; where there was commitment from top management to such practices; and where extensive informal dialogue supported more formal arrangements (Dundon *et al.* 2003: ch. 8).

The National Centre for Partnership and Performance (NCPP), established and mandated under the framework agreements to foster workplace partnership, conducted a second study of information and consultation practices and arrangements (NCPP 2004a). This examined fourteen organisations (two of which had been included in the study already discussed), again spanning the private and public sectors, unionised and non-union, and large and small employments. This study concluded that there was evidence of the 'incremental emergence of a more forward-thinking approach to informing and consulting employees', based on the fact that many of the organisations examined had identified communicating, informing and engaging with staff as an integral part of their business and organisational strategies (NCPP 2004a). This type of 'pro-active engagement' was aligned, in particular, with business strategies based on higher value-added activities, and tapping into the experience and expertise of employees.

Direct mechanisms for information sharing, ranging from newsletters and hand-books, email and web-based conferencing to team briefings and breakfast/lunch meetings, were again found to be widely prevalent. Indirect information sharing was found to be prevalent in unionised companies and practised either through established industrial relations channels, through partnership-style arrangements, or through both sets of channels. Only one of the four non-union case companies examined was found to have arrangements in place for indirect information sharing (NCPP 2004a: ch. 4). Direct consultation was practised through such individual mechanisms as performance reviews, attitude surveys and one-to-one meetings, and through a series of group-based mechanisms, including permanent and temporary work groups and various types of meetings with groups of employees (NCPP 2004a: 33–4). Indirect consultation occurred through the same representative structures as were employed for indirect information provision, as well as through informal exchanges between management and unions. In the majority of cases both parties assessed information and consultation practices as 'positive and improving' (NCPP 2004a: 36).

Effects on organisations, employees and unions

Studies of partnership, involvement, information exchange and consultation in Ireland have generally assessed their effects in positive terms. Managers in O'Dowd's survey of partnerships and their effects in unionised companies identified a series of positive outcomes for organisations, including higher business performance and higher workforce productivity. Most of the managers surveyed were also of the view that partnership was associated with higher levels of job satisfaction, and better pay and conditions for employees, but less than half (46 per cent) attributed higher job security to partnership and only a minority (19 per cent) reported a positive association between partnership and staffing levels. Most managers (53 per cent) reported higher levels of union involvement on a day-to-day basis, and 76 per cent associated partnership with higher levels of union influence over management decision-making. The majority of managers reported positive general effects in such areas as levels of trust, the quality of communications and the incidence of disputes and industrial relations grievances. Based on the pattern of survey replies, O'Dowd concludes that the most positive outcomes are in the areas favourable to businesses (the quality of relationships and performance), with less pronounced benefits in areas favourable to unions (union influence and involvement in decision-making) and employees (satisfaction, pay and conditions and employment security) (O'Dowd ongoing).

The large-scale employee survey examined above also sought to assess the effects of arrangements for partnership and involvement, both as directly perceived by employees, and through patterns of association between partnership, involvement and employee attitudes. The majority of employees in unionised workplaces with partnership arrangements identify positive effects from partnership in the areas of job satisfaction (72 per cent), productivity and performance (67 per cent), pay and conditions (71 per cent), employment security (70 per cent), employees' willingness to embrace change (73 per cent), and the confidence with which employees co-operate with management (76 per cent) (O'Connell *et al.* 2004: 106). Few employees affected by partnership arrangements or direct involvement reported that these had negative effects (O'Connell *et al.* 2004: 106).

Case-based research again allows us to round out the picture obtained from surveys. Roche and Geary (2002) studied a radical partnership initiative in the Irish Airports' Authority, Aer Rianta, and found that partnership had allowed the company and its unions to respond to the major commercial challenge involved in the loss of profitable intra-EU duty-free sales and to arrive at a joint view of the company's future status and focus. Notwithstanding mutual gains such as these, most employees were negative with respect to the effects of partnership arrangements on such areas as information provision, the quality of decision-making, levels of trust and how well their interests were represented. Partnership and involvement were also found in this case to be unrelated to employees' perceptions of their work performance and productivity. This was attributed to the 'top-heavy' character of partnership in Aer Rianta, where joint effort had become focused heavily around company-level structures, addressing commercial challenges, and where relatively little progress had been made with respect to workplace-level partnership arrangements. Partnership and involvement were nevertheless found to have had some positive effects on employees' attitudes. The higher the level of work autonomy experienced by employees, the more positive their assessment of the climate of industrial relations and the higher their level of organisational commitment (Roche and Geary 2004).

Officials of some of the company's main unions also reported that partnership had increased their effectiveness in representing their members, although, for a time, the middle managers' union was opposed to the form of partnership in operation in the company. The depth of union members' engagement with partnership activities was also found to be associated positively with commitment to unions (Roche and Geary 2002). No evidence was found that union activists were 'displaced' as a consequence of senior officials' close engagement with the operation of partnership in the company (Geary and Roche 2003). The Aer Rianta partnership eventually unravelled because of a complex of factors. These included its uneven record in handling change and in addressing substantive staff concerns, unclear boundaries between partnership and industrial relations; inter-union and intra-union tensions surrounding change and restructuring, problems of succession involving key management and union supporters of partnership, and changes in the external conditions faced by the company and unions.

The two case-based studies of information and consultation arrangements, examined above, reported positive findings with respect to business outcomes and the handling of change. Managers reported tangible benefits from information and consultation mechanisms in improving organisational effectiveness, promoting a willingness to adapt to commercial pressures and a fostering a better climate of employment relations (Dundon *et al.* 2003: ch. 7). In the second study, both managers and employee representatives reported that information and consultation fostered a greater acceptance of organisational change (NCPP 2004a: 46). Tangible benefits were also reported in the areas of organisational performance (including competitiveness and customer service), the quality of decision-making, problem-solving, the climate of employment relations. Benefits were also identified in areas of direct importance for employees, including the capacity to exercise voice, work satisfaction and work autonomy (NCPP 2004a: 42–3). Both studies also suggest that the impact of information and consultation mechanisms on all these outcomes may be mediated by a series of influences, including degrees of top-level management support for a participatory climate and managers' degrees of openness towards information disclosure (Dundon *et al.* 2003: 60–1; NCPP 2004a: 47). Incremental change initiatives and circumstances where local managers enjoyed some discretion with respect to changes were also seen to allow more latitude for information and consultation to impact positively on outcomes of value to managers, employees and unions (Dundon *et al.* 2003: 54–5).

The following broad conclusions seem warranted by the research evidence, although it should be emphasised that the different focus of surveys (firms, work-places and employees) and their different definitions of terms such as partnership and involvement means that quantitative estimates in particular should be viewed with caution.

- Representative arrangements for involving unions or employees in decision-making are present in significant minorities of firms and workplaces in the private sector; representative involvement takes the form of partnership arrangements, works councils and joint consultative committees. These arrangements probably cover about 20 per cent of firms, and about the same proportion of private-sector employees report the prevalence of such arrangements in their workplaces. Representative arrangements, developed under the rubric of partnership, are substantially more prevalent in the public services, with nearly half of employees stating that such arrangements extended to their workplaces.
- The majority of firms in the private sector report that they operate arrangements for the direct involvement of staff in decision-making. About a third of private-sector employees report the existence of such arrangements in their workplaces, and about half of those working in the public services report the use of various forms of direct involvement.
- Survey data also provide an indication of how partnership and involvement may connect with the handling of change. In the private and commercial public sectors, significant minorities among workplaces appear to have handled change across most of a broad range of operational issues on an 'inclusionary

basis', with smaller minorities involving unions, employees, or both, in the handling of strategic change. In the public service sector, the main focus of partnership has been on issues of relatively peripheral concern for managers, employees and unions, but partnership has been coupled more directly with the handling of change in recent years.

- The majority of employers in the private and commercial public sectors claim to engage in information and consultation with their employees on change, and public service managers assign a high priority to these areas. Viewed from the perspective of employees, the picture looks different, with minorities saying that they experience regular information provision and consultation, and similar or larger numbers saying that information and consultation is rare or hardly ever practised. Case studies confirm such a gap in perception between managers and employees.

- Survey data and case studies indicate that information provision is more pronounced in organisations than consultation, and case studies suggest that this is the case also in organisations with formal partnership arrangements.

- Partnership involvement arrangements generally, as well as information provision and consultation specifically, are usually assessed in Irish research as having positive effects on organisations, employees and trade unions. However, the degree to which such effects are evident appears to be contingent on a series of influences internal and external to organisations, including management and trade union postures, firms' and workplaces' levels of discretion with respect to change programmes, and whether such programmes are incremental or transformational.

The transposition of the Information and Consultation Directive into Irish law

The Department of Enterprise Trade and Employment (DETE) initiated preliminary consultations with the social partners on the transposition of the Directive into Irish Law in late 2002, following which both the peak employers' association, Irish Business and Employers' Confederation (IBEC) and the Irish Congress of Trade Unions (ICTU) made written submissions to the DETE. Subsequently, the DETE published a consultation paper (DETE 2003) to canvass the views of a wider range of interested parties. The government was to have published an Information and Consultation of Employees Bill by the summer of 2004, but at the time of writing (November 2004), this still had not been published. In its absence our assessment of the likely consequences of the Directive in Ireland is obviously curtailed but none the less, some interesting observations can be made. These are derived from the DETE's consultation paper and from a series of in-depth interviews conducted with senior employers, trade union representatives and government officials. The former document sets out, albeit in a preliminary form, how the government intends to proceed with the drafting of the text of the legislation.[1]

We begin our analysis with a review of the DETE's consultation paper. A series of items are described in the document as policy guidelines which were to be used as a guide in the drafting of the legislation (DETE 2003: 2–3). These include:

- The encouragement and facilitation of employers and employees to determine their own arrangements, in line with the terms of the Directive, which best suit their own specific circumstances. Where an agreement is not possible, the legislation will provide for a fall-back position ('standard model').
- An improvement in the provision of information and consultation is identified as serving the dual function of enhancing organisational effectiveness and developing partnership at enterprise level.
- Employees have a right to information and consultation without prejudice to the responsibility of management to make decisions.
- The facilitation of workplace change and adaptation.
- Underscoring the tradition of voluntarism in Irish industrial relations.

Notwithstanding the DETE's stated intention of encouraging and facilitating local agreements, allowing for as much flexibility as possible, the consultation paper stipulates that certain key principles must be adhered to when employers and employees are putting information and consultation arrangements in place:

- (i) they must be effective;
- (ii) they must take into account the interests of both the enterprise and the employees;
- (iii) they must have due regard to the rights and obligations of both parties;
- (iv) they must be negotiated and operated in a spirit of co-operation;
- (v) where there is an agreement to facilitate direct interaction between an employer and employees, employees must be free at any later stage to exercise their right to information and consultation through representatives of their choosing.

The consultation paper envisages that pre-existing agreements are likely to be permitted to remain in place provided they comply with the terms of the legislation and, in particular, where the procedure for information and consultation applies to the whole workforce, and employees have agreed to continue the arrangements without change.

It is further expected that the legislation will make provision for a 'standard or fall-back model', which will come into force where the parties to negotiations fail to reach an agreement. The basis for this provision will be Article 4 of the Directive. In addition, the DETE proposes including in these rules the creation of an 'Employees' Forum'. While the competence, composition and functions of such a forum are not detailed in the consultation document, the intention to establish such a body is potentially a very significant development, to which we will return later in the chapter.

The consultation paper further stipulates the following rules that the legislation 'is liable to impose':

- Agreements must apply to the entire workforce and must be negotiated, and not imposed by an employer.
- Negotiations must be concluded within a deadline, probably 6 months, with a possibility of an extension by way of agreement.
- Agreements must be in writing, dated and available for inspection by either a person covered by it or, in the event of dispute, an independent arbitrator.
- Agreements must be signed by the employer and either by all the employee representatives who negotiated it, or supported by the employees [*sic*].
- There must be a clear statement of the subjects and conditions and methods for information and consultation.
- There must be provision for renegotiation of some or all of the terms of the agreement in the event of any substantial changes in the workplace.

Issues left open in the consultation paper, and on which the DETE sought interested parties' views, included

- the usefulness or otherwise of negotiating a national framework agreement;
- whether or not the legislation should provide for a so-called 'trigger mechanism' to determine whether one or other party – employer or employees – should be obliged to initiate discussions or open negotiations on the possible introduction of an information and consultation procedure;
- the minimal level of employee support needed to approve the terms of local agreements, including pre-existing agreements;
- at what point, in the event of a breakdown of negotiations, should an employer be obliged to establish an employees' forum;
- further elaborations in defining information and consultation;
- subject matters;
- number of meetings per year;
- whether the legislation should apply to undertakings (firms or enterprises) with fifty or more employees or establishments (workplaces) with twenty or more employees;[2]
- how employee representatives are to be selected; how the independence and fairness of the selection procedure might be ensured; how employee representatives' role is to be defined;
- what provision needs to be made where only a proportion of the workforce have union representation; and should employees be able to appoint someone to act as a representative who is not an employee of the enterprise; and
- how should the legislation make provision for the use of experts, and how might the costs associated with this be met.

Other open questions related to the handling of confidential information, compliance and enforcement, definition of employees, and the requirement for protections and facilities for employees and employee representatives.

The social partners' response: competing views on 'crunch' issues

The issues highlighted above, and which the DETE left open in its consultation paper, are in the main the principal issues of concern to employers and unions in Ireland. On most of these issues, their views differ substantially. Whether the Directive will be seen to advantage one party over the other will depend critically on how the government seeks to accommodate these competing interests and perspectives. We shall examine a number of these key issues in turn.

A national framework agreement?

The Irish model of social partnership is now widely regarded to be one of the most novel forms of political exchange in Europe, not only because of the number and type of participants and the emphasis placed on adopting a deliberative approach to policy-making (O'Donnell and Thomas 1998), but also because of its particular architecture, which Teague and Donaghey (2004) have likened to a 'hub' and 'spoke' model. The central 'hub' is concerned with pay negotiations, which in turn are augmented by a variety of 'spokes'. The latter are centrally concerned with social inclusion and cover such varied issues as rural development, local area partnerships and, of more immediate relevance to us here, enterprise partnership. Recent national agreements, as indicated above, have successfully garnered union and employer support for the inclusion of framework agreements to promote partnership at the level of the workplace. In this context, and given Ireland's now lengthy and rich experience of social partnership, one might have assumed a priori that the social partners would have come together to formulate a framework agreement for the transposition of the Directive into Irish legislation. This, however, has not occurred, at least not at the time of writing.

The DETE's consultation document did seek interested parties' views on the usefulness or otherwise of a nationally agreed framework, participants who might be invited to such discussions, and the shape such an agreement might assume. During talks that led to a new national agreement, *Sustaining Progress*, and again under the so-called 'mid-term' review talks in 2004, ICTU approached IBEC to examine the possibilities of formulating a national framework agreement. While the latter indicated that they were positively inclined to engage in such talks, it was with the precondition that any such agreement would apply solely to unionised companies and that it would be voluntary. ICTU saw little value in pursuing talks on this basis; to have so done so, in their eyes, would have foreclosed the possibility and hopes, which ICTU nurtured, of extending the reach of union membership and recognition into the non-union sector on the back of the Directive.

Notwithstanding IBEC's expressed willingness to enter talks on a national framework agreement, they remained fearful that the terms of any such agreement could, first, be overly detailed and prescriptive; and second, and more critically, that the provisions therein might subsequently be adopted by the DETE in designing the so-called 'standard or fall-back model'. Evidently, if this happened, and a legally binding standard model was established, it would, in IBEC's view, not only be incompatible with Ireland's voluntarist industrial relations tradition, but would also have a prescriptive effect inconsistent with the principles and values underpinning the human resource practices of many of its constituent members, particularly non-union companies. Thus, IBEC was not prepared to support a national framework agreement that would establish a standard model and that could then be enforced on employers who were unwilling or unable to reach a voluntary agreement with their workforce. But even if such a scenario were to be avoided and the government formulated a standard model by some other means, there remained the apprehension within IBEC that the provisions agreed within a national framework agreement might provide employees in non-union companies with a set of parameters or a benchmark against which their extant information and consultation arrangements might be compared.[3] And while IBEC did not revoke unilaterally the possibility of talks on a national framework agreement, it was very wary of proceeding with any such negotiations. Guided by these apprehensions, IBEC's preference was for entering direct bipartite consultations with the DETE to shape the legislation in a way that best met their requirements.

The key element of IBEC's response to the Directive was to impress upon the DETE the desirability of adopting a flexible and pragmatic approach to its transposition in order to accommodate the different approaches to employee involvement and consultation that already exist within its member companies. In this context, IBEC endorsed enthusiastically the DETE's proposal that the new legislative framework would encourage and facilitate employers and employees at the local level to determine their own specific arrangements. By thus preserving Ireland's voluntarist system of industrial relations, IBEC believed that the full range of employee involvement and employee representative practices in Irish industry might reasonably be accommodated.

Central to understanding IBEC's response to entering talks on a national framework agreement is the wide variety of positions and sharp differences of view across and within unionised and non-unionised firms as to how the Directive ought to be transposed into Irish legislation. Different perspectives on the Directive reflect the emergence of a highly differentiated system of employment relations in Ireland based on firms' diverse nationalities, business sectors and competitive strategies. This differentiated system involves different approaches to information and consultation arrangements and partnership more generally as outlined above. It also bears emphasis that the diversity of employer approaches predisposing IBEC against a national framework agreement that could have legal spin-offs was also evident in the dynamics that led to a highly general voluntary framework agreement on workplace partnership (encompassing information and consultation arrangements, as outlined above) in the social partnership programmes of the late 1990s and early 2000s.

The difficulties thus associated with the representation of a diverse and variegated constituency make it very difficult for IBEC to represent and turn specific member interests into general, shared positions and policy strategies. Thus IBEC's adoption of a minimalist posture that places emphasis on a flexible and pragmatic approach to the Directive's implementation so as to accommodate the wide variety of employment relations models and preferences, can hardly come as a surprise. Certainly, a shared solution reached on the basis of compromise *with a union position*, would probably have sparked challenges from a significant section of IBEC's membership.

Provision for a trigger mechanism

With regard to whether the legislation should provide for a trigger mechanism, IBEC's position is clear and unequivocal: first, the legislation should indeed provide for such a mechanism; second, it should stipulate that it puts the onus on employees to 'pull the trigger' – it is they who must indicate to management that they wish to open discussions on the introduction of an information and consultation procedure; and third, that the threshold to indicate that there is sufficient support for such a request should be set at 35 per cent of the workforce. IBEC further stipulates that in the event of the required proportion of employees not endorsing a call for the introduction of information and consultation arrangements, a period of three years should elapse before negotiations may be resumed. The threshold proposed by IBEC would, if accepted by the government, be significantly different from the provisions established by the information and consultation Regulations in the UK. In the UK the threshold is set at 10 per cent of an undertaking's workforce triggering negotiations, although 40 per cent of employees must agree to a request to change the information and consultation provisions of a pre-existing agreement. IBEC's submission to the DETE makes no such distinction. The same proportional threshold is called for in instances where a workforce may seek to trigger negotiations on the introduction of information and consultation arrangements *ab initio* and where employees call for a review to revisit the provisions of a prior agreement.

IBEC's position is unacceptable to ICTU. For ICTU, the requirement to inform and consult with employees should operate automatically. It is not, in their view, a question of opting in or opting out, or of establishing thresholds. Their position is that the Directive confers rights on all employees, with size of establishment/under-taking being the only qualification and, this apart, the Directive should, in their view, have universal coverage. As one senior national union officer put it to us: 'You cannot have a plebiscite on a right.'

However, if the government proceeds with making provision for a trigger mechanism, and if there is also a provision that would permit employees to forgo their rights under the legislation, ICTU has proposed that it would be imperative that any such choice would be made freely by the workforce and without any undue influence. In this context, ICTU calls on the DETE to make it illegal for employers to include in contracts of employment the requirement for employees to cede their rights to information and consultation.

We have no way of knowing at the present time how the government intends to respond to these very different positions. ICTU, for its part, has appealed to the DETE to adopt a positive approach to the Directive, to honour the spirit of its aims, which it sees as providing an opportunity to modernise employee relations by encouraging deeper levels of dialogue and partnership, and to avoid what was described to the DETE as a 'minimalist or niggardly approach... [so as] to appease the more reactionary sections of employers'. Within its own constituency, ICTU declared that it is hard-pressed to convince some individual unions and officers that the government's support for social partnership and, in particular, its advocacy for diffusing partnership arrangements from the national level to the workplace, is more than just exhortatory. One senior national union officer put it in stark terms: 'there is no middle ground on this. If the government tries to offend no one, the opportunity will have been missed. The detractors within the union movement who are anti-partnership will be armed, and they will make the claim that this is a clear manifestation that the government aren't interested in partnership.'

Employee representatives

It is often assumed by commentators, including legal and industrial relations scholars, that the Directive requires employers to deal with employee representatives who are genuinely independent of management and representative of employees. It is certainly the case that such a provision must be made by employers in certain instances, but whether such a provision will have to be made in all instances is far from clear. Certainly, the employers' group, IBEC, and non-union employers in Ireland are of the view that the Directive does provide the government with sufficient scope to allow them to use direct forms of information and consultation, and more-over that they can obtain employee agreement for such practices without informing or consulting indirectly with representatives of employees. A senior HR manager in a US multinational company (MNC) operating in the high-tech sector, which is well known for its union substitution strategies, told us that his company intends to engage in direct dialogue with its employees as to whether their proposed involvement and consultation practices comply with the Directive's requirements. If following these direct talks, the number of employees who object to the company's proposals is above the stipulated threshold – assuming such a threshold will be set down in the legislation – then the company will redesign its information and consultation procedures, but, he stressed, 'there would be no ballot, nor employee representatives involved'. Many other non-union companies, particularly with parent organisations in the USA, have lobbied the government, together with IBEC, for a provision that would allow them to pursue such direct participation strategies, and have pressed the view that such a provision would be made explicit in the legislation. In other cases, including those of unionised companies, IBEC are insistent that employees nominated to act as employee representatives should be employees of the company.

ICTU, for its part, is adamant, as indeed is SIPTU, Ireland's largest private-sector union, that employee representatives should be defined as *union* representatives in line with industrial relations practice generally in Ireland, and consistent with the approach adopted in other legislation.[4] ICTU further insists that this provision should extend to all employees who are union members, even in those instances where their employer has refused to grant union recognition. In other words, ICTU is insistent that the legislation should provide for trade union representation in all situations – irrespective of whether the company is unionised or not – where employees wish to be so represented for the purposes of information and consultation. These circumstances apart, ICTU has lobbied the DETE to ensure that employees have the right to nominate, from among the workforce, independent employee representatives through a free and fair process. Like IBEC, ICTU accepts that employee representatives should be employees, but in contrast to IBEC, it is eager to ensure that the legislation will permit representatives to call on external experts of their choice for advice and help, and that the cost of providing such assistance would be met by the employer.[5]

Thus the definition of 'employee representative' is a critical choice confronting the government. For many employers, a definition that allows companies to continue with, or adopt, direct mechanisms of information and consultation is imperative in supporting their preferred human resource management strategies. A requirement to facilitate the appointment of employee representatives, or to hold ballots for such a process, 'smacks', in the words of one senior employer representative, 'of an old industrial relations world with which many non-union MNCs are uncomfortable'. In the UK, the enabling legislation does allow employers to use direct forms of information and consultation, whether they are provided for in pre-existing agreements or in agreements negotiated via the legislation's statutory procedure. It would appear, however, that the legality of such a provision, and of the provision sought by IBEC, is open to some doubt. Eminent labour lawyers and industrial relations scholars have questioned its provenance (see Bercusson 2002; Hall *et al.* 2002; Davies 2004) and have raised the prospect that the long-term viability of direct methods could be threatened by a legal challenge in the future.

A standard model

The legal definition of a standard or fall-back model of information and consultation has been a key issue for the social partners. ICTU has argued that, in the absence of a collective agreement governing the provision information and consultation, legislation should stipulate that organisations are required to adopt a standard model. In addition to the provisions outlined in Article 4 of the Directive, ICTU proposes that a standard model should legislate for the following: information should be provided in written form, in good time, before any decisions are made, and in a manner that is acceptable to employees and their representatives: With respect to consultation, ICTU recommends that meetings take place on a quarterly basis, and that employees and their representatives would have the right to raise issues that might not be covered under the terms of the Directive but which are of concern to them. Critically, ICTU argues that employees should have the right to seek advice from union officials in preparatory meetings, and that they should be accompanied by their union officials where employees deem this to be necessary. The standard model should also stipulate, ICTU argues, that decisions taken by management, without prior information exchange and consultation, should be declared invalid and unlawful.

While IBEC accepts the need for a fall-back model, they stress that companies should be given as much support as possible to develop their own mechanisms for information and consultation and, echoing their fears that a standard model might provide workers with a negotiating template, IBEC stresses that it should not be determined or inferred that company agreements with different procedures or practices are inferior or of a lesser value. Such agreements, IBEC emphasises, are simply reflecting the different circumstances and cultures of individual organisations.

While IBEC accepts the requirement to engage in consultations with employees 'with a view to reaching an agreement', they have made the case to the DETE that such discussions cannot be expected to continue indefinitely, and propose that the standard model would adopt a thirty-day deadline. Thereafter, it insists that once management has acted in good faith by providing employees with the requisite information, by eliciting their views and by giving a reasoned and considered response, it should be entitled to proceed with making a decision.

Scope of the legislation

The Directive specifies three subject areas – present and probable economic circum-stances of the firm, employment levels, and work organisation and contractual arrangements – for information and consultation, but these are dealt with in general and broad terms in the Directive. This is not to underestimate their significance, however. Certainly, in the light of our review of the research evidence above, the provisions of the Directive would appear to go in significant measure beyond the prevailing practice of information and consultation arrangements in many enter-prises and workplaces. The DETE's consultation paper requests parties' views on possible subject matters to be included in an indicative list. In reply, ICTU has suggested that the items listed in the national framework agreement to promote 'enterprise partnership' under *Partnership 2000* (these are detailed in the earlier discussion above) could usefully provide such a list. Thereafter, ICTU would seem to be at one with IBEC in that it would not be desirable to predetermine a definitive list of items, but that this matter might be better resolved at company level. Conceivably, therefore, the legislation will avoid adopting a tightly prescriptive approach in deciding on subject matter for information and consultation.

The issue of confidentiality and compliance has been an area of much concern for employers. IBEC, for example, has requested the DETE to formalise obligations of confidentiality for employee representatives, and to lay down sanctions in the event of breaches of confidentiality. IBEC envisages instances where employers may not be able to share confidential information with employees, either because it is particularly sensitive on commercial grounds or because management itself, in the case of foreign-owned companies, has not been privy to corporate management decision-making. Citing *force majeure* as a justifiable defence, IBEC argues that local Irish management *may* not be in a position to follow information and consultation procedures; any subsequent consultations with employees under the Directive will then be based on the implementation and consequences of decisions made elsewhere.

Where such matters and others become subject to dispute, IBEC's and ICTU's proposals for dispute resolution differ significantly. The former is unequivocal, arguing that any appellant procedures should not be vested within existing industrial relations institutions, but instead the Minister should establish a panel of independent arbitrators comprising people with legal and financial expertise.

The principal motivation for advancing this alternative form of dispute resolution is the reluctance, particularly on the part of some foreign-owned companies, to become caught up in what was described to us as 'an industrial relations wrangle'. In other words, for some employers, the state's institutions for conflict resolution and mediation – the Labour Relations Commission and the Labour Court – have become overly associated with adversarial models of dispute resolution.

Both IBEC and ICTU are agreed that the Directive should apply to undertakings (enterprises or firms) with fifty or more employees. It is likely, therefore, that the legislation will apply to undertakings. It is also probable that employers and employees will be permitted considerable flexibility to decide whether information and consultation should also take place at the level of the establishment (workplace).

ICTU is also insistent that the legislation should apply to all businesses and institutions in the private and public sectors, irrespective of whether they are operating for private gain. This is consistent with the provisions of the Directive. However, ICTU is also of the view that the legislation should extend to include employees in government departments and public services, although it is far from clear whether the Directive's provisions apply to such employees. The Directive simply refers to undertakings 'carrying out an economic activity'. It remains to be seen whether the legislation will indeed include employees in such employments.

The likely effects of the Directive: an opportunity for whom?

It is difficult at the time of writing to be able to anticipate with certainty the implications of the Directive for Irish employment relations. Our task is made more complicated by the absence of the details of legislative provisions that the Irish Government intends to introduce. None the less, on the basis of the evidence presented, and the interviews with employer and union representatives, it is possible to outline some probable outcomes.

An opportunity for employees?

The key feature of the Directive, certainly in an Irish context, is that it will enshrine for the first time in law a requirement that employers inform and consult with employees on the economic circumstances of the company, on probable developments in employment, and with respect to changes to work organisation and contractual arrangements. There is the additional implication that, for the first time too, the information and consultation policies of employers will be subject to external scrutiny, and the significance of this, particularly for non-union employers, should not be underestimated. Thus the Directive bestows important statutory rights on employees, which in turn will be enforced by legal sanction. There is the further but disputed implication in the Directive, notwithstanding that its provisions are without prejudice to existing arrangements for informing and consulting with employees, that information and consultation arrangements require employee *representation*. There is, therefore, the distinct possibility that it might establish the principle of indirect employee representation and, while it is implicit rather than explicit in the Directive, the Directive further implies that a permanent body, such as a works council or joint consultative committee, would be established. In the context of the evidence presented, where significant variations in levels and degrees of information provision and particularly of consultation are found even among progressive employers, and where many Irish employees report that their employers do not engage routinely in information exchange or consultation, the potential benefits to employees could be very considerable.

The reality, however, might prove to be more problematic. There are two issues here. First, the Directive will impose a significant burden on many employers, particularly those with small and medium-sized companies, that often do not have a dedicated human resource management function. IBEC has argued this, and the DETE have acknowledged the difficulty. To ensure that the implementation of the Directive will lead to an increase in the number of employees with access to information and consultation provisions, the government and the employers' organisations will need to dedicate significant resources to helping such companies meet the requirements of the legislation.

Second, there is the issue of what position the government will take in respect of any trigger mechanism for initiating the introduction of information and consultation arrangements. This is critically important. Assuming the government does decide that management will not be required to 'pull the trigger', but that that obligation will fall to employees, the diffusion of information and consultation arrangements across Irish workplaces will be significantly slower and more variable than it might otherwise be. A number of obstacles are immediately identifiable

(Hayes 2003; Hall and Terry 2004). First, it is difficult to see management actively seeking to inform employees of their rights to information, consultation and representation, unless they believe there might be some particular advantage for them in doing so. Second, in the absence of trade unions, employees may remain ignorant of their rights. Third, the requisite level of employee support required to trigger negotiations with management to introduce procedures to comply with the Directive may pose a significant obstacle for employees. Fourth, in workplaces where there is no tradition of representation or trade union organisation – the vast bulk of Irish workplaces – it may be very difficult for individual employees to 'raise their hand' and orchestrate sufficient employee support to request that management opens negotiations on information and consultation procedures.

In this context, it is difficult to see large numbers of employers willingly taking the initiative to introduce or recast existing procedures to comply with the Directive. There is, however, one important additional consideration. If the government makes provision for a standard model to include an employee forum, as indicated in the DETE's consultation document, this may well provide employers with a sufficient incentive to reach pre-emptory agreements with their employees, to shape information and consultation arrangements in a way that is appropriate for their particular circumstances, while at the same time meeting the minimum requirements of the legislation. In other words, the prospect of having to negotiate with an employee forum might propel some employers, in particular non-union employers, to act with some haste. Thus, one potential implication of the Directive is that it might give rise to what Hall (2004) has termed a 'legislatively-prompted voluntarism': that is, the legislation – assuming it provides for a standard model – could drive the spread of organisation-specific information and consultation agreements.

The point is, therefore, that while the Directive, in theory, is of significant benefit to employees, information and consultation arrangements will not be produced spontaneously. Practical difficulties on the ground are likely to pose significant challenges for employees wishing to avail of their new rights. Employers' associations, trade unions and the DETE are likely to play a critical role in enabling workplace information and consultation to emerge. The law alone will not be sufficient.

An opportunity for trade unions?

For some observers, the Directive's provisions will not only guarantee Irish workers rights that many of their counterparts in continental Europe have enjoyed for many years (see Rogers and Streeck 1995; Hall *et al.* 2002), but they will also be a godsend for trade unions. The assumption is thus made that the rights bestowed on workers will become, by extension – in unionised workplaces at least – *union* rights. Thus the Directive offers the prospect of buttressing union influence as well as helping to guard against the erosion of union power in the event of hard times; and, of course, wily and self-confident employee (union) representatives might be able to use their formal powers to extend their influence in collective bargaining negotiations.

There is also the possibility, or at least the hope, among unions – and, by contrast, a fear among management in non-union companies – that the obligation to establish a general and statutory system of employee representation for the purposes of information and consultation will provide a stepping-stone for the unionisation of non-union workplaces.

Such beneficial outcomes for trade unions cannot be presumed a priori, however. The implications of the Directive are likely to prove something of a double-edged sword for unions. First, it is worth emphasising that while the Directive is without prejudice to existing arrangements and traditions for informing and consulting with employees, employee consultation is conceived as involving employee-based rather than union-based bodies. In practice, of course, the selection of employee representatives in unionised workplaces is likely to come through existing union structures. In many such workplaces, however, there are likely to be non-union employees, and in these circumstances, representative provision will have to be made for these segments of the workforce. The Directive is thus designed to enfranchise all sections of the workforce, unionised and non-unionised alike. Any de facto monopoly that unions might have formerly enjoyed in respect of information and consultation could thus be challenged. In this sense, the Directive opens the possibility of admitting a new channel of representation, in parallel to, and separate from, existing union-based channels, and in which non-union employees, including members of management, might hold elected positions.

In making a prediction as to which scenario is the more likely – one where union presence and power is enhanced, or one that impairs and marginalizes union influence – it may be that both are possible, and the issue of whether unions are advantaged or disadvantaged by the Directive will depend on a number of factors. In strongly unionised plants and where there is a long tradition of management working closely with unions, the former scenario is more likely. In other cases, there is the possibility for employers who wish to marginalise and reduce unions' influence to establish and control channels of information and consultation, and thereby challenge the status and authority of unions to act as employee representatives. We would expect this to be more evident in circumstances where unions are relatively weak, where large sections of the workforce are not union members, and where management seeks to use the Directive strategically in an effort to marginalise the union. The important point here is that the legislation permits management, where it is so inclined, to open or develop and extend an alternative employee voice channel to union structures. Moreover, management can justifiably claim that it is legally required to do so and that all workers must be enfranchised. Thus, in some circumstances, management might be emboldened sufficiently to use the legislation to marginalise union representation.

Consideration in this context might be given to the incidence and influence of works councils in Germany, arguably the *locus classicus* for legislatively-enshrined information and consultation provisions. Outside of large workplaces in traditional industries, the legal code would seem to exercise comparatively less consequence for the conduct of worker participation.[6] It would also seem that in small workplaces the presence of works councils depends largely on unions being able to 'persuade' employers to adopt them (Poole *et al.* 2001). In other sectors of the German economy – in, for example, large, foreign-owned firms in the fast food industry (Royle 1998) and in the 'new economy' (Hassel 2002: 311) – employers have been adroit in using a variety of 'avoidance strategies', both legal and illegal, to resist or substitute for the establishment of works councils.

The point is therefore that legislation is not a determining influence; depending on management's orientation towards trade unions, its preference for individual, direct participation practices, and on the unions' power and ability to 'capture' or 'colonise' employee representative positions, the Directive cannot be expected to have an automatic effect one way or the other.

An opportunity for employers?

The evidence reviewed earlier in the chapter revealed that sizeable minorities of Irish employees feel there is little scope for information and consultation in their work-places. As also outlined above, assessments of the consequences of information and consultation practices and partnership arrangements more generally in the Irish literature point to significant positive benefits for employers. The international literature also illustrates that such practices are associated positively with improvements in organisational performance, particularly when they are linked to other so-called 'high commitment management' practices (European Foundation 1997; Knell 1999; Cully *et al.* 2000; Guest and Peccei 2001; Rubinstein and Kochan 2001). For example, the evidence in respect of the scale of associations between the presence of such practices (including employee involvement in changes to the workplace) and employees' job satisfaction and organisational commitment in the UK's Workplace Employee Relations Survey (WERS) was found to be 'compelling' (Cully et al. 2000: 189). Given the generally positive assessment of information and consultation arrangements on business outcomes in the Irish and international literature, and the relatively modest incidence of such practices in Ireland, at least as reported by employees, it would seem that a large number of Irish employers may be failing to reap the substantial benefits that can flow from active engagement with information and consultation practices.

It must also be emphasised that the possible benefits from effective information and consultation are contingent on a series of factors including the structure of control within multi-establishment companies; the level of autonomy permitted to subsidiary management within multinational companies; the types of change programmes being pursued; the extent of union engagement and commitment from union officials; and the degree of top-level management support for developing a participatory climate.

The benefits to be gained from information and consultation must also be viewed in the context of costs and hazards, including, for example, the resources and expertise required to implement and operate information and consultation practices properly;

second, the provisions of the legislation, particularly where companies may be forced to adopt the 'standard model', are likely to be 'alien' to many organisations' HR practices and preference for direct participation measures; and finally, there is the possibility that such arrangements could strengthen union representation in a way that might be seen by some employers as potentially damaging in other respects.

Notwithstanding these contingent conditions, potential costs and risks that may in combination determine the degree to which gains might be achieved, the research evidence would indicate that significant net gains can accrue to many employers from active engagement with information and consultation, and with partnership and involvement more generally.

An opportunity for moving towards partnership?

One possible implication of the Directive, as identified by Sisson (2002) in the UK, is that it might provide a means for insulating the processes of information and consultation from the more adversarial tendencies associated with negotiation and collective bargaining. In an Irish context, too, it is envisaged that the Directive might provide a catalyst for the promotion of better working relationships between management and unions (NCPP 2004b). Under the terms of the Directive, the employer and employee representatives are required to 'work in a spirit of cooperation and with due regard for their reciprocal rights and obligations, taking into account the interests both of the undertaking or establishment and of the employees'. Similar legal provisions relate to the functioning of works councils in Germany, and it is this requirement to work co-operatively with management, together with the potential insulation of managerial relations from collective bargaining, that is often identified as a key factor in explaining the 'consensual' relations between employee representatives and management in German workplaces. By contrast, the fusion of these processes in Ireland and the UK is often seen as an important factor in promoting an 'adversarial' or 'antagonistic' climate of industrial relations. In this context, therefore, the Directive does present a unique opportunity for the development of a partnership-based approach to management–employee relations.[7] But the contingent nature of partnership arrangements is likely to remain, as with works councils (see Thelen 1991).

Conclusion

It is clear that Irish employment relations are about to enter 'unchartered waters' (Dobbins 2003). The absence of a general, permanent and statutory system of employee information and consultation has set Ireland, along with the UK, apart from other European countries. There is the prospect that this will now change, but by how much is difficult to estimate. Convergence with practice elsewhere in Europe is, however, unlikely, certainly if the bar is raised to the level of voice permitted to works council representatives in Germany and the Netherlands. It is very likely that the Irish government will pursue a minimalist approach. It is free to 'determine the practical arrangements for exercising the right to information and consultation' and the balance between Community and national law in this case lies more heavily in favour of the latter than the former (Davies 2004). As a consequence, companies will be permitted to develop, as under current agreements to promote voluntary partnership arrangements: that is, 'privatised' versions of employee voice. We might therefore expect the continuation of considerable variation in the type of information and consultation practices to emerge and, given the practical difficulties that are likely to confront employees where they seek to take up their rights, which we highlighted above, it is difficult to foresee a radical recasting of Irish employment relations. In other words, we would not expect the legislation to be transformative in any real sense. It is our view that robust forms of employee information and consultation such as are envisaged in the Directive are more likely to emerge in strongly unionised companies, but it should be emphasised that the preconditions for this outcome existed prior to the Directive. In the absence of such preconditions, it is difficult to see how the Directive alone might instigate the adoption and diffusion of strong forms of employee voice in significant numbers of Irish workplaces.

Acknowledgements

The authors would like to acknowledge the research assistance provided by Ilona Hunek in the preparation of this chapter. The help provided by Liam Berney, Tony Dobbins, Frances Gaynor, Mark Hall, Brendan McGinty, Niall Saul and Tom Wall is also greatly appreciated.

Notes

1 Note that the government's consultation paper states explicitly that any indication given in the paper of the formulation of the legislation or likely policy choices is subject to change following the consideration of written submissions and deliberations between ministers, lawyers and the views of the government.

2 While the Irish legislation will apply to either an undertaking (firm or enterprise) or an establishment (individual workplace), the consultation paper states that the law will not stipulate at what level the information and consultation procedure *must* operate. In other words, if the legislation applies to undertakings, it may still be possible for the parties to agree that information and consultation will also take place at the level of each workplace within that undertaking.

3 Whether or not spurred by this consideration, IBEC has prepared a set of guidelines and established a support service to guide and counsel member companies so that their information and consultation arrangements might comply with the Directive and the forthcoming legislation.

4 ICTU cites three other pieces of legislation to support their position regarding the way that employee representatives should be defined: the Protection of Young Persons (Employment) Act, 1996; the European Community's Safeguarding of Employees' Rights on Transfer of Undertakings (Amendment) Regulations (SI No. 487 of 2000); the Transnational Information and Consultation of Employees Act, 1996.

5 IBEC have argued that there should be no requirement to involve experts and it would insist that such a facility would not be prescribed for in legislation, but might instead by a subject for local agreement between employees and their employer.

6 The most recent data estimate that while the vast majority of large firms (that is, 500+ employees) have a works council (91.7 per cent), in smaller firms their presence is significantly less evident (30 per cent in companies with 21–50 employees and 9 per cent in workplaces with 5 to 20 employees). Overall, only 16.3 per cent of German workplaces have a works council, although the proportion of employees employed in firms with works councils is far greater, at 53 per cent (Addison *et al.* 2004). It also bears emphasis that the share of employees in the engineering industry covered by a works council declined by fifteen percentage points between 1984 and 1998 (Hassel 2002: 313).

7 Bercusson (2002: 220) has noted that this requirement to work in a spirit of co-operation could amount to a 'peace obligation' or 'no strike' clause and might be so interpreted by the courts; and similarly, might be likened to a status quo clause in a collective agreement, and might also be interpreted by the courts to preclude unilateral action by an employer.

References

Addison, T. J., Schaubel, C. and Wagner, J. (2004) 'The course of research into the economic consequences of German works councils'. *British Journal of Industrial Relations* 42(2): 255–81.

Bercusson, B. (2002) 'The European social model comes to Britain', *Industrial Law Journal* 31(3): 209–44.

Coughlan, A. (2004) *Human Resources Management Survey 2004*. Dublin: Irish Business and Employers' Confederation.

Cully, M., Woodland, S., O' Reilly, A. and Dix, G. (1999) *Britain at Work: As Depicted by the 1998 Workplace Employee Relations Survey*. London: Routledge.

Davies, P. (2004) 'Directives 2001/86/EC (The "SE Directive") and 2002/14/EC (The "General Framework Directive"): Contrasts and Assumptions'. Paper presented at the Law Society of Ireland, 21 October.

DETE (2003) 'National Information and Consultation Directive 2002/14/EC: Consultation Paper on Transposition into Irish Law'. Dublin: Department of Enterprise, Trade and Employment.

Dobbins, T. (2003) 'Government launches consultations on implementation of EU consultation Directive'. *European Industrial Relations Observatory.* http://www.eiro.eurofound.ie/2003/09/feature/ie0309204f.html.

Dundon, T., Curran, D., Maloney, M. and Ryan, P. (2003) *Organizational Change and Employee Information and Consultation*. Dublin: Department of Enterprise, Trade and Employment.

European Foundation (1997) *New Forms of Work Organisation. Can Europe Realise its Potential? Results of a Survey of Direct Employee Participation in Europe*. Luxembourg: Office for the Official Publications of the European Communities.

Geary, J. F. and Roche, W. K. (2001) 'Multinationals and human resource management practice in Ireland: a rejection of the "new conformance thesis"', *International Journal of Human Resource Management* 12(1): 109–27.

Geary, J. F. and Roche, W. K. (2003) 'Workplace partnership and the displaced activist thesis', *Industrial Relations Journal* 34(1): 32–51.

Guest, D. and Peccei, R. (2001) 'Partnership at work': mutuality and the balance of advantage', *British Journal of Industrial Relations* 39(2): 207–36.

Gunnigle, P., Morley, M., Clifford, N. and Turner, T. (1997) *Human Resource Management in Irish Organizations: Practice in Perspective*. Dublin: Oak Tree Press.

Hall, M. (2004) 'Anticipating the Information and Consultation Regulations: Evidence from Four Companies'. Paper presented at the British Universities Industrial Relations Association Annual Conference, Nottingham.

Hall, M. and Terry, M. (2004) 'The emerging system of statutory worker representation', in G. Healy, E. Heery, P. Taylor and W. Brown, *The Future of Worker Representation*. Basingstoke: Palgrave.

Hall, M., Broughton, A., Carley, M. and Sisson, K. (2002) 'Works councils for the UK? Assessing the impact of the EU Employee Consultation Directive', IRS/IRRU Report. London: Eclipse Group Ltd and Warwick: University of Warwick.

Hassel, A. (2002) 'The erosion continues: a reply', *British Journal of Industrial Relations* 40(2): 309–17.

Hayes, T. (2003) *Transposing the Information and Consultation Directive into Irish Law*. Brussels: EIRI Associates.

Knell, J. (1999) *Partnership at Work*, Employment Relations Research Series 7. London: Department of Trade and Industry.

NCPP (National Centre for Partnership and Performance) (2004a) *Information and Consultation: A Case Study Review of Current Practice*. Dublin: National Centre for Partnership and Performance.

NCPP (National Centre for Partnership and Performance) (2004b) *The EU Information and Consultation Directive: Everything You Need to Know*. Dublin: National Centre for Partnership and Performance.

O'Connell, P., Russell, H., Williams, J. and Blackwell, S. (2004) *The Changing Workplace: A Survey of Employees' Views and Experiences*. Dublin: National Centre for Partnership and Performance.

O'Donnell, R. and Thomas, D. (1998) 'Partnership and policy making', in Healy, S. and Reynolds, B. (eds) *Social Policy in Ireland: Principles, Practice and Problems*. Dublin: Oak Tree Press.

O'Dowd, J. (ongoing) Ph.D. research on partnership in Ireland. Dublin, Michael Smurfit Graduate School of Business.

O'Dwyer, J. J., O'Dowd, J., O'Halloran, J. and Cullinane, J. (2002) *A Formal Review of Partnership in the Civil Service*. Dublin: Department of An Taoiseach.

Partnership 2000 for Inclusion, Employment and Competitiveness. Dublin: Government of Ireland.

Poole, M., Lansbury, R. and Wailes, N. (2001) 'A comparative analysis of developments in industrial democracy', *Industrial Relations* 40(3): 490–525.

Roche, W. K. (2002) 'Whither partnership in the public sector?', *Administration* 50(3): 3–26.

Roche, W. K. and Geary, J. F. (2000) 'Collaborative production and the Irish boom: work organization, partnership and direct Involvement in Irish workplaces', *Economic and Social Review* 31(1): 1–36.

Roche, W. K. and Geary, J. F. (2002) 'Advocates, critics and union involvement in workplace partnership: Irish airports', *British Journal of Industrial Relations* 40(4): 659–88.

Roche, W. K. and Geary, J. F. (2004) 'Workplace partnership and the search for dual commitment', in Stuart, M. and Martinez-Lucio, M. (eds) *Partnership and the Modernization of Employment Relations*. London: Routledge.

Rogers, J. and Streeck, W. (eds) (1995) *Works Councils: Consultation, Representation and Co-operation in Industrial Relations*. Chicago: University of Chicago Press.

Royle, T. (1998) 'Avoidance strategies and the German system of co-determination', *The International Journal of Human Resource Management* 9(6): 1026–7.

Rubinstein, S. A. and Kochan, T. (2001) *Learning from Saturn*. Ithaca, NY: Cornell University Press.

Sisson, K. (2002) 'The Information and Consultation Directive: unnecessary "Regulation" or an opportunity to promote "partnership"?', Warwick Papers in Industrial Relations, No. 67, Coventry.

Teague, P. and Donaghey, J. (2004) 'The Irish experiment in social partnership', in Katz, H., Lee, W. and Lee, J. (eds) *The New Structure of Labour Relations: Tripartism and Decentralization*. Ithaca, NY: Cornell University Press.

Thelen, K. A. (1991) *Union of Parts. Labour Politics in Postwar Germany*. Ithaca, NY: Cornell University Press.

Williams, J., Blackwell, S., Gorby, S., O'Connell, P. and Russell, H. (2004) *The Changing Workplace: A Survey of Employers' Views and Experiences*. Dublin: National Centre for Partnership and Performance.

13

European comparative practice in information and consultation

Andrea Broughton

The practice of informing and consulting employee representatives varies widely across Europe, a reflection of the different histories, traditions, customs and practices of individual EU Member States. This chapter gives an overview of the different systems and practices in place, examines the statutory framework governing rights to information and consultation (and co-determination rights, where they exist) and assesses the degree of actual compliance with the systems in place.

The statutory framework

Most 'old' EU Member states (the fifteen Member States (EU15) before the enlargement of the EU that took place on 1 May 2004) have a legislative framework that regulates, to a greater or lesser extent, arrangements for informing and consulting employee representatives. Arrangements vary from comprehensive and explicit rights for works councils, including rights of co-determination over some issues (as in the case of Germany, Austria and the Netherlands) to a comprehensive framework for works councils, albeit without any co-determination rights (as in the case of France) and the voluntarist systems that operated in the UK and Ireland until they were reviewed in order to comply with the new information and consultation Directive – see below (EIRR 2001a).

Collective agreements rather than legislation are the primary regulators of information and consultation arrangements in some countries. These include Denmark and Belgium, even though there is a statutory framework in these countries. In Italy too, although a statutory framework exists, the detailed operation of works councils is contained in sector-level agreements. (EIRR 2001a)

In the case of the ten new EU Member States, four of these (the Czech Republic, Hungary, Slovenia and Slovakia) operate a statutory works council system, although the issue of information and consultation through works councils is also under discussion in Estonia and Poland (Carley 2004).

Impact of the information and consultation Directive

The new Directive (2002/14/EC) establishing a general framework for informing and consulting employees in the European Community required implementation in EU Member States by 23 March 2005, although there is a more gradual implementation period for countries with no general, permanent and statutory system of information and consultation of employees.

In consequence, EU Member States reassessed their legislation in this area to ensure that it complied with the provisions of the Directive. In general, most countries (in the former EU15) did not need to change their legislation in any major way, although a debate is under way in Belgium about how to comply with the Directive (the threshold for works councils is currently 100 employees, whereas the Directive contains a threshold of fifty employees) (EIRR 2004). In Denmark, the Directive was incorporated into the trade union confederation (LO) and the employers' organisation's (DA) co-operation agreement in early 2004 (Jørgensen 2004). This will oblige company-level joint cooperation committees to inform and consult all employees in a business, not just those covered by an agreement between LO and DA. In the Netherlands, the government is changing its legislation on works councils (it submitted a Bill to this effect in December 2003 (van het Kaar 2004), making the operation of works councils more flexible and giving them influence over the appointment of members of company supervisory boards.

The exceptions are Ireland and the UK, both of which have been operating an essentially voluntarist system within some statutory parameters. These two Member States have therefore been consulting widely in a national context on how to implement the Directive. The UK's legislation came into force on 6 April 2005. The Irish legislation was published in draft form in July 2003 (Dobbins 2003) although no law was in place by the deadline of 23 March 2005.

Structures for informing and consulting employees

Information and consultation structures in many countries take the form of works councils, the setting up of which is underpinned by legislation. In many countries, such as Germany, Austria, the Netherlands, Portugal and Spain, these are employee-only bodies. By contrast, works councils in Belgium, Denmark and Luxembourg are joint employer/employee bodies, comprising elected employee representatives and nominated employer representatives. Works councils in France are also technically joint bodies, as they are chaired by the employer (EIRR 2001a).

There is considerable variation regarding the company size threshold above which a works council must be established or an employee representative appointed. For example, there is a five-employee threshold for employee representation in Austria and Germany (although the right to set up what could be termed a works council in Germany does not become effective until a company has a workforce of at least twenty-one employees, when three works councillors can be appointed). At the other end of the spectrum, there is a threshold of 100 employees in Belgium and 150 employees in Luxembourg, both of which are above the thresholds contained in the Directive and must be lowered in order to comply (EIRR 2001b).

Most countries allow works councils to expand in line with the size of the company. Further, some countries provide for the setting up of central or group-level works councils in larger businesses. This variety of practice is reflected in the Directive, which offers a choice between applying an undertaking-level workforce threshold of fifty employees, or an establishment-level threshold of twenty employees.

Provision of information and consultation

Each EU Member State is obliged to transpose into its national legislation a number of basic rights to information and consultation in particular situations or areas, as set out in these EU Directives:

- the collective redundancies Directive (98/59/EC). This Directive obliges employers to inform and consult their workforce if they are intending to make collective redundancies;
- the transfer of undertakings Directive (2001/23/EC), which requires employee representatives in both the acquiring and the transferred company to be informed and consulted before the transfer takes place;
- the European Works Councils (EWC) Directive (94/45/EC), which applies to companies of 1,000 or more employees with at least 150 employees in each of two Member States. It gives the EWC the right to be informed and consulted about transnational questions that affect workers' interests significantly. The Directive suggests that these could include: the situation and probable trend of employment, investments and substantial changes concerning the organisation; transfers of production, mergers, cut-backs or closures of undertakings, establishments or important parts thereof; and collective redundancies. The Directive also gives the EWC the right to

be informed about any exceptional circumstances, such as closures, relocations or collective redundancies; and

- a range of EU Directives in the field of health and safety, many of them emanating from the 1989 framework Directive (89/391/EEC).

All Member States must comply with the information and consultation provisions contained in these Directives, even if they do not have a system that provides for works councils or other permanent employee representatives bodies for the purposes of information and consultation. However, many countries go beyond these basic required information and consultation rights. An overview of statutory information and consultation rights around the EU is given below, relating to: financial matters concerning the business; the employment situation of the business; and foreseen structural changes to the business. Selected national examples are highlighted. Further details are provided in Table 13.1.

Informing and consulting on the financial situation of the business

Many countries give employee representatives the right to be *informed* about the current and predicted financial situation of the business, usually on an annual basis. In the case of the potential development of a company's activities, employee representatives are to be informed once a year in countries such as Germany, Belgium, Luxembourg, Greece and France. Information on the potential development of a company must be provided every six months in Finland, Luxembourg and the Netherlands, rising to four times a year in Spain and Belgium, and in the case of larger companies in Germany.

There is less evidence of an obligation to 'consult' on these issues. However, in Germany, the works council is to be consulted regarding any structural changes to the financial situation of the business. Consultation requirements also exist in countries such as Luxembourg, the Netherlands, Spain, France and Austria.

Informing and consulting on the employment situation

Employee representatives in many countries have a right to receive regular information on the situation and structure of employment in their company. This is an annual obligation in countries such as Germany, Belgium, the Netherlands and France. In addition, countries such as Germany, Belgium, Luxembourg, the Netherlands and France require the employer to provide regular information on the measures that can be taken to avoid redundancies, to promote employability measures, and to enhance training.

In terms of consulting on employment-related matters, the Netherlands obliges the employer to consult employee representatives on recruitment and to wait for their opinion before going ahead with any plans. Finland puts a similar obligation on employers in relation to employment and training plans. In Austria, the employer is obliged to consult employee representatives four times a year on the employment situation of the company.

Table 13.1 Features of information and consultation systems in individual European countries

Country	Type of structure	Workforce threshold	Information rights	Consultation rights	Co-determination rights	Protection	Resources
Austria	Elected works council (employee-only)	Five employees	Financial information, employment, including recruitment, changes to the business	Financial situation, four times a year on employment	Rest breaks; daily working time; payment systems; recruitment of temporary workers; social plan in redundancy situations; training and re-training measures. Matter to be referred to a conciliation board if no agreement can be reached	Dismissal only following a court ruling	Paid time off to carry out duties. Full-time works council members in companies of at least 150 employees. Three weeks of time off for training per four-year term. Provision of meeting space and stationery. Works council payment may be levied on employees (maximum of 0.5% of pay).
Belgium	Works council (employer and elected employee representatives)	100 employees	Financial data (basic dossier every four years, written report once a year plus up-to-date information four times a year) Employment situation, once a year plus quarterly updates. Planned changes to work organisation or the structure of the business	Personnel policy; employment policy; vocational training and re-training measures. Consultation on planned changes to work organisation; new technology; production transfers; mergers; closures; redundancies; and relocations	Formulation and change of employment conditions, planning of paid educational leave, management of day-care centres and canteens	Protection against dismissal beginning one month before and throughout term of office	Paid time off, training, premises and other facilities, paid expert assistance

Country	Body	Threshold	Information	Consultation	Negotiation	Protection	Facilities
Denmark	Joint co-operation committee	35 employees	Six times a year on financial situation and forecasts; employment situation; work organisation; new technologies; and changes to the structure of the business	Six times a year on employment situation; work organisation; and new technology. Consultation in advance of any decisions on changes to the structure of the business	None	Covered by general dismissal protection for shop stewards. Extra notice period for representatives who are not shop stewards	Employers to bear costs related to the co-operation committee. Meetings may be held in paid working time
Finland	Employee representatives	30 employees (20 in the event of collective redundancies)	Financial information twice a year and immediately if there are any proposed changes. Information on envisaged changes to employment and training	See 'co-determination'	Obligation for employers to negotiate with employee representatives on issues such as changes in activities that affect the workforce, or proposed job cuts. This effectively has a staying effect of up to six weeks, depending on the issue under discussion	Protection against dismissal	Paid time off to carry out representative duties. Many collective accords also oblige employers to provide facilities to enable representatives to function
France	Elected works council (chaired by the employer)	50 employees (works councils); 11 employees (employee representatives)	Basic information every two years, plus annual report on financial situation. Annual report on employment, and oral monthly analysis. Information four times a year on changes to production methods	Consultation on general financial management issues. Annual consultation on employment developments, health and safety and training. Prior consultation on decisions relating to structural changes	None	Protection against dismissal – employee representatives can only be dismissed following consultation with the works council and authorisation by the Labour Inspectorate	20 hours of paid time per year to carry out duties, which may be extended, plus time to attend meetings. Five-day training course in paid working time. Employer to provide facilities to allow the works council to carry out duties. Employers finance works councils with a payment of 0.2% of the gross wage bill. Works councils may make use of experts

Table 13.1 (Continued)

Country	Type of structure	Workforce threshold	Information rights	Consultation rights	Co-determination rights	Protection	Resources
Germany	Elected employee-only works council	Five employees	Financial information once a year, plus development reports four times a year. Immediate information in the case of changes. Annual information on employment plus regular updates. Consultation on structural changes that affect the workforce, including mergers, transfers, closures and relocations	Consultation in the event of financial changes and in the case of forecast changes to employment. Works council to be consulted and may make proposals in the areas of flexible working time; elimination of overtime; part-time working; phased early retirement; new forms of work; alternatives to contracting-out; and guidelines for redundancy selection	Co-determination in the operation of working time organisation, overtime, rest breaks, the administration of pay and benefit systems, health and safety, behaviour and performance monitoring, the introduction and operation of vocational training and the operation of teamworking	Dismissal only with the agreement of the works council. Protection continues for up to two years after expiry of mandate. Candidates for election to works councils also have protection for the following six months	Paid time off to carry out duties. Full-time officers in companies of at least 200 employees. Employer to provide facilities. Works council may make use of experts by agreement
Greece	Elected employee-only works council and employee representatives	50 employees (works council); 20 employees (employee representatives)	Annual information on economic and financial situation. Information on any anticipated changes to employment. Prior information on changes to work organisation and changes to the structure of the business, such as mergers, closures and relocations	Consultation on issues such as proposed changes to working hours and issues covered by EU Directives in areas such as collective redundancies; business transfers; and health and safety	None	Protection against dismissal or transfer during mandate and for one year afterwards	Employers to provide facilities and time off to enable works council to carry out duties. It should be noted that very few works councils operate in the private sector

	Representatives	Threshold	Information	Consultation	Co-determination	Protection	Facilities
Ireland*	Shop stewards	No threshold	Information is voluntary, with the exception of obligations under EU Directives on collective redundancies, business transfers and health and safety	Consultation is voluntary, with the exception of obligations under EU Directives on collective redundancies, business transfers and health and safety	None	Protection against dismissal on grounds of union activities	All provision of facilities by agreement
Italy	Elected/nominated trade union representative bodies (RSUs)	15 employees	Information on collective redundancies, business transfers; and health and safety. Other information rights contained in collective agreements at sectoral and company level	Consultation on collective redundancies; business transfers; and health and safety. Other consultation rights contained in collective agreements at sectoral and company level	None	Protection against dismissal. Trade union must agree to transfers	Time off to carry out duties. The employer must provide facilities
Luxembourg	Joint works committees (elected employee representatives and nominated employer representatives), workforce delegations	150 employees (joint works committees); 15 employees (workforce delegations)	Annual report and information on financial situation. Information once a year on employment and training developments. Prior information on any anticipated changes to the business or the economic situation of the company that will affect employment	Consultation twice a year on financial developments. Consultation once a year on employment and training developments. Prior consultation on all major planned changes, including redundancies; closures; transfers; and relocations	Co-determination on company policy on recruitment; promotion; transfer; and dismissal; employee appraisal; works rules; health and safety; and the use of equipment to monitor employee performance	Protection against dismissal for works council election candidates (three months after the election), during the mandate of a works councillor and for six months afterwards	Costs of works council to be borne by employer. Paid time off to carry out duties

Table 13.1 (Continued)

Country	Type of structure	Workforce threshold	Information rights	Consultation rights	Co-determination rights	Protection	Resources
Netherlands	Employee-only elected works council, personnel delegations	50 employees (works councils); 10 employees (personnel delegations)	Basic financial information every two years, plus annual economic report and twice-yearly report on financial developments. Annual information on employment. Prior information on changes that affect the workforce	Consultation on financial changes and on investment decisions. Prior consultation on changes to work organisation, the introduction of new technology and changes such as mergers, closures and relocations. Works council to give an opinion following consultation on investment decisions, recruitment and changes to the structure of the business, resulting in a one-month staying effect	Agreement of works council needed on recruitment; redundancy; promotion; training; evaluation procedures; pensions, savings or profit-sharing schemes; working time and holidays; registration; handling and protection of personal data of employees; dismissal policy and workforce consultation arrangements; and grievance procedures	Dismissal protection for works council candidates, those in office and former officers (for a total of two years)	Works councils may hold meetings in working hours, members may attend a minimum of five paid days of training a year. Costs associated with works council borne by employer. Works council may be assisted by experts
Norway	Joint work environment committee (elected employee representatives and nominated management representatives)	50 employees	Regular financial information plus monthly information on financial developments. Monthly information on employment; regular information on training, work organisation and new technology. Prior information in the event of collective redundancies and business reorganisation	Monthly consultation on employment issues and prior consultation on anticipated changes to the structure of the business, including transfers, mergers and changes involving redundancies	None	Protection against dismissal and right to maintain employment conditions throughout mandate	Paid time off to carry out duties plus time off for training. Employer to bear costs associated with running the committee

Country	Representative body	Threshold	Information	Consultation	Co-determination	Protection	Facilities
Portugal	Employee-only elected workers' committee	No threshold	Financial and economic information; employment information	Consultation on social measures such as working conditions; changes to working time and holidays; relocations; changes to job classification; and promotion systems. This consultation includes allowing the committee to formulate an opinion, which the employer must consider before acting	None	Protection against dismissal for workers' committee members, extending for five years after expiry of mandate	Members may carry out duties in working time. Employer must bear the costs of the operation of the workers' committee
Spain	Elected employee-only workers' committee. Workers' delegates	50 employees (workers' committee); 6 employees (workers' delegates)	Regular financial and economic information, plus information on development of financial and employment situation four times a year	Prior consultation on proposed financial changes, consultation on training plans and on all employment structural change likely to affect employees; 15 days to formulate an opinion	None	Protection against dismissal and discrimination on grounds of works council duties, during mandate and for one year afterwards	Duties may be carried out in working time. Employer to provide facilities for the operation of the works council
Sweden	Trade union representatives	No threshold	Regular information on financial and economic situation, and employment. Information in the event of changes to the structure of the business	See 'co-determination'	Obligation to negotiate on certain issues such as changes to the structure of the business and investments. This includes plans such as closures; mergers; and relocations. Employer decision is suspended during the negotiations. Matter referred to national-level social partners if no agreement reached	Trade union representatives enjoy protection against dismissal and priority for being retained during redundancy selection	Paid time off to carry out duties, provisions of facilities, Unions may also have recourse to experts

Table 13.1 (Continued)

Country	Type of structure	Workforce threshold	Information rights	Consultation rights	Co-determination rights	Protection	Resources
United Kingdom**	Trade union representatives. Draft law (ICE Regulations) providing for the establishment of employee information and consultation bodies at workplace level. Came into force in April 2005	Statutory right to trade union representation in companies of 21 or more workers if a majority of the workforce wishes. ICE regulations will introduce a threshold of 150 workers from 6 April 2005, falling to 100 by 6 April 2007 and 50 by 6 April 2008	Information rights in accordance with EU business transfers; collective redundancy; and health and safety EU Directives. Right to be informed on training issues. Other subjects by agreement. ICE Regulations introduced information requirements on the undertakings, activities and economic situation; the employment situation; and any decisions likely to lead to substantial changes in work organisation	Consultation rights in accordance with business transfers, collective redundancy and health and safety EU Directives. Right to be consulted on training issues. Other subjects by agreement. ICE Regulations introduced consultation requirements on the employment situation and any decisions likely to lead to substantial changes in work organisation	None	Dismissal on grounds of trade union membership or activities is unfair (not subject to usual one-year qualifying period for unfair dismissal). Prohibition of discrimination on grounds of union membership. ICE Regulations introduced protection against dismissal for information and consultation representatives	Union representatives have a statutory right to 'reasonable' paid time off to carry out their duties and to undergo relevant training. Operation of this is clarified in an ACAS code of conduct. ICE Regulations introduced entitlement to 'reasonable' paid time off to carry out their duties

Notes: * The Irish government published a consultation document in August 2003 on how to implement the information and consultation Directive, with a view to putting legislation into place by March 2005. This deadline was not met.

** In July 2004, the UK government issued revised Information and Consultation of Employees (ICE) Regulations, aimed at implementing the information and consultation Directive by 6 April 2005.

Source: European Commission; EIRO; EIRR; national sources

There is provision in France for the employer to consult employee representatives annually on a range of matters, including developments in employment and skills levels within the company, health and safety measures, and training measures and their implementation. In Germany, employee representatives have a right to be consulted in advance on any anticipated developments in employment, including training measures.

Structural changes to the business

Most countries require employers to provide employee representatives with full and immediate information relating to any planned changes to their business, particularly if they involve collective redundancies. This includes transfers of production, mergers, closures of all or parts of the business, and relocation plans.

In most Member States employers are obliged to consult with employee representatives before carrying out plans in this area, because they are required to inform and consult on planned collective redundancies and business transfers in accordance with the provisions of the EU collective redundancies and business transfers Directives.

In Germany and Austria, legislation requires employers to consult the works council prior to any plans to change the structure of the business, including mergers, closures and partial closures, relocations and production transfers. In Portugal, employers are required to consult with and obtain the opinion of employee representatives before they implement any measures likely to lead to a cut in the size of the workforce or to a deterioration in employment terms and conditions. In Spain, employers must consult the workforce before any changes to the business that are likely to have an effect on the workforce. Employee representatives subsequently have fifteen days in which to draw up an opinion on the employer's plans, although they do not have the power of veto.

Co-determination

In some EU Member States there is an obligation on employers to reach *agreement* with employee representatives on a range of issues before they can proceed with their plans. This means that, in certain areas, management cannot implement decisions on a unilateral basis. These areas tend to be workplace-level practices such as implementation at local level of pay systems, holidays, working time and overtime systems.

The most notable example of co-determination at workplace level is the German system, within which works councils have co-determination rights in a range of areas (for more details, see Table 13.1). Austria also has a well-developed system of co-determination, operating in much the same way as the German one.

In Belgium, the works council has some co-determination powers in a range of local areas, including changes to employment conditions, the planning of paid educational leave and the management of social institutions such as day-care centres and canteens. Similarly, in the Netherlands, the agreement of the works council has to be obtained by the employer if the company wants to introduce or change a policy across a range of local areas. Otherwise, employers must delay their action by one month.

In some Nordic countries, although employers may ultimately act unilaterally, there is an obligatory process of negotiation with employee representatives in many areas, which essentially has a staying effect on management decisions. This is the case in Finland, where employers are obliged to negotiate with employee representative on any major employment-related changes. A similar system operates in Sweden.

The situation in the new EU Member States

The enlargement of the EU on 1 May 2004 from fifteen to twenty-five countries has extended the scope of all EU legislation to its ten new Member States. Accordingly, these countries have been revising their legislation in all areas, including that of information and consultation, to bring it into line with EU provision. In general, more legislative amendment of existing provisions is needed in the central and eastern European countries than in the southern European new Member States of Cyprus and Malta. An overview of some of the key developments is given below.

In general terms, information and consultation channels in the new EU Member States can be divided into four types (Tóth and Ghellab 2003):

(i) countries with a single channel of employee interest representation: only trade unions are entitled to represent employees in terms of information and consultation;

(ii) countries with a single channel of representation (trade unions), but where the law also provides for the election of workers' representatives for non-unionised workers, alongside union representatives;

(iii) countries with a primary channel of representation (trade unions), but where the law allows election of a supplementary secondary channel of elected employee representatives to represent workers in non-unionised workplaces. These may be works councils or other forms of elected employee representatives, such as workers' trustees or employee representatives; and

(iv) countries with dual-channel representation: statutory works councils operate in parallel with trade unions.

For more detail, see Table 13.2.

In Estonia, work is under way to formulate a Social Dialogue Act, which would establish general principles for the information and consultation of employees. Estonia has a dual model of employee representation, with workers represented both by trade unions and elected 'workers' trustees' (Kallaste et al. 2004).

This dual approach is also taken in Latvia, where both works councils and trade unions operate. Similarly, in Hungary, works councils operate on the basis of the

Table 13.2 Information and consultation arrangements in the new EU Member States

Country	Dual channel	Single channel	Single channel with a complementary secondary channel for non-unionised workplaces		Information	Consultation	Codetermination
			Primary channel: trade union	Secondary channel: employee council			
Czech Republic					Yes	Yes	Yes
Cyprus	Trade union				Yes	Yes	
Estonia		Trade union and elected representatives of non-unionised employees			Yes	Yes	
Hungary	Works council and trade union				Yes	Yes	Yes
Latvia		Trade union and elected representatives of non-unionised employees			Yes	Yes	Yes
Lithuania		Trade union			Yes	Yes	
Malta		Trade union			Yes	Yes	
Poland		Trade union			Yes	Yes	Yes
Slovakia	Works council and trade union				Yes	Yes	
Slovenia	Works council and trade union				Yes	Yes	Yes

Source: Tóth and Ghellab (2003)

Labour Code (Act XXII of 1992), from a threshold of fifteen employees. However, these bodies are for information and consultation purposes only – trade unions fulfil a bargaining role (Ladó 2002).

In the Czech Republic, an amendment to the country's labour code in the year 2000 allows for the establishment of works councils in companies with at least twenty-five employees and where there is no trade union presence. These bodies are information and consultation channels only. In smaller companies, a workers' delegate may be elected, with identical rights to those of a works council. The existence of all of these structure is, however, dependent on the absence of trade unions at the workplace (Ladó 2002).

In the Slovak Republic, amendments to the Labour Code that came into force in July 2003 changes the legal framework governing information and consultation rights. Previously, trade unions had been the only bodies to enjoy rights to information, consultation and participation. The new Labour Code introduced the concept of elected works councils, in companies with fifty or more employees, or workers' trustees in organisations with more than five but fewer than fifty employees. These bodies have negotiation, information and inspection rights, but only in organisations where there is no trade union (Cziria 2004).

In Poland, trade unions are the main channels of employee representation, although some worker committees exist in state-owned enterprises. The Polish Ministry of Economy, Labour and Social Policy is preparing regulations introducing a new non-union institution to exercise employees' rights to information and consultation (Gardawski *et al.* 2004).

In Slovenia, existing legislation is deemed sufficient to meet the requirements of the EU information and consultation Directive. The legislation here dates from 1993 (Law on the Participation of Workers in Management) and 2002 (Law on Labour Relations). The legislative framework provides for the setting up of elected works councils or workers' trustees in smaller companies of fewer than twenty employees (Skledar 2004).

Compliance with statutory and agreed provisions

The level of compliance with statutory and agreed provisions governing employee representation around the EU varies significantly. The most notable example of non-compliance is Greece: this country has a comprehensive statutory framework which dates from the 1980s, providing for the setting up of works councils. However, hardly any works councils exist in practice, particularly in the private sector. The most recent survey on this dates from 1995 and was carried out by the Greek Ministry of Labour (Stamati 2003). It found that there were 6,441 companies covered by Greek works council legislation, but there were only 126 works councils in operation. It estimated that the percentage of companies where works councils could have been established, but which in fact had done so was only 2 per cent.

This low level of compliance is reported to be largely a result of trade union resistance to these bodies (EIRR 2001b, Stamati 2003). This opposition is based mainly on the fact that unions see works councils as a potential threat to workplace trade union representation. Works councils exist in a number of Greek public-sector companies, particularly in the telecommunications and utilities sectors. However, as these industries are undergoing a process of privatisation at the time of writing, these works councils are likely to disappear in the future.

In Germany, because the request to set up a works council must come from the employee side, the incidence of works councils is relatively low, particularly in small companies. The federal Employment Service's Institute for Employment Research (Institut für Arbeits- und Berufsforschung – IAB) (Dribbusch 2003) found that there were around 113,000 establishments in Germany with works councils in 2002. It also found that around 11 per cent of all establishments in the private sector covered by works council legislation had a works council. However, of all establishments with 501 and more employees, 95 per cent do in fact have a works council.

Similarly, the German government found in a survey in 1998 that just 4 per cent of the smallest companies eligible to set up employee representation arrangements (with a workforce of between five and twenty employees) in fact had arrangements in place. This percentage rose to 28 per cent in slightly larger companies, with twenty-one to 100 workers. This finding was one of the main drivers behind the German government's reform of German co-determination legislation in 2001 (EIRR 2001c).

A similar situation exists in France, where the smaller the company, the more likely it is not to have a works council in place. The French Ministry of Employment's Office for Research and Statistics (Direction de l'animation de la recherche, des études et des statistiques du Ministère de l'Emploi – DARES) published in 2001 the results of a survey of employee representative bodies and structures carried out in 1999, using a representative sample of 11,000 workplaces and 900 businesses with at least ten employees (Dufour 2003) It found that more than half of all workplaces with at least ten employees, accounting for one in five employees, were not covered by any representative structure. However, collective employee representation was usual in companies and establishments above the statutory threshold for setting up works councils (fifty employees): fewer than 7 per cent of workplaces with fifty employees or more had no representative body, while 98 per cent of those with over 250 employees had at least one form of representation.

Discussion

In summary, it is clear that structures providing for the information and consultation of workers and their representatives vary widely around the European Union, although there are many points of similarity. The majority of countries, certainly in the former EU15, have for many years operated a system that uses elected works-council-type structures. As we have seen, in most cases these are employee-only bodies, although in the case of Belgium, Denmark, Luxembourg and Norway, these are joint employer/employee bodies. The trend, aided by the information and consultation Directive, is towards more formal and harmonised structures, although the impact will be felt mainly by Ireland and the UK, which were the only EU15 Member States without a formal structure in place prior to the coming into force of the Directive. Both of these Member States have drawn up legislation providing for the setting up of information and consultation bodies at workplace level.

Company size thresholds for the establishment of information and consultation bodies vary considerably, an element the Directive takes into account. Thresholds range from five employees in Germany to 100 in Belgium, and 150 in Luxembourg, but many countries have a 50-employee threshold. This variety of practice is likely to remain, given that the Directive allows for the application of either an undertaking-level workforce threshold of fifty employees or an establishment-level threshold of twenty employees, although those countries with national thresholds above the Directive will need to amend them to comply.

In terms of information and consultation rights, there is already a certain degree of harmonisation in practice, as all EU Member States must comply with the information and consultation rights set out in existing Directives regulating collective redundancies, business transfers, European works councils, and health and safety in the workplace. However, many countries operate systems that provide for additional information and consultation rights and it is likely that, in practice, these differences will persist to a certain extent. While countries such as the UK and Ireland have needed to set out additional rights in new legislation, bringing their systems more into line with practice elsewhere in the EU, the countries that give employees enhanced rights to information, consultation – and in some cases, co-determination – will not alter their practice, even though there has been a recent debate in Germany about the merits of that country's unusual co-determination system.

Nevertheless, it is interesting to note that Germany's already extensive information and consultation framework was overhauled in the summer of 2001, giving works councils more power to delegate some everyday activities, increasing co-determination rights in some areas, and lowering the company size threshold at which employers are obliged to allow full-time works councillors (from 300 to 200 employees).

In general, however, it is unlikely that existing co-determination systems will spread beyond the countries where they already exist, although it is a possibility through the European Company Statute (Council Regulation (EC) No 2157/2001 of 8 October 2001). The worker involvement provisions accompanying this Statute (Directive 2001/86/EC) may result in co-determination in certain circumstances (EIRR 2002).

The state plays a key role in the establishment of information and consultation structures and practices in most Member States by devising the legislative framework within which systems operate. However, in some countries – such as Denmark – although there is a statutory framework, the operation of employee representative bodies is in fact governed by collective agreement at national level. The same can be said of practice in Belgium, where a national collective agreement has legal force. In Italy, the detailed operation of employee representative bodies is enshrined in sector-level collective agreements, despite the existence of legislation. The two countries that operated an essentially voluntarist model – the UK and Ireland – now operate within a statutory framework; albeit, certainly in the UK, one that encourages the voluntary conclusion of agreements on information and consultation structures at workplace level. In conclusion, it is likely that the new information and consultation Directive will ensure a certain degree of harmony around the EU in terms of basic information and consultation provision. However, it is also likely that the existing variation in provision around the EU will remain in place to a large extent.

Statutory instruments

Council Directive 89/391/EEC of 12 June 1989 on the introduction of measures to encourage improvements in the safety and health of workers at work. Official Journal L 183, 29/06/1989.
Council Directive 98/59/EC of 20 July 1998 on the approximation of the laws of the Member States relating to collective redundancies. Official Journal L 225, 12/08/1998.
Council Directive 2001/23/EC of 12 March 2001 on the approximation of the laws of the Member States relating to the safeguarding of employees' rights in the event of transfers of undertakings, businesses or parts of undertakings or businesses. Official Journal L 082, 22/03/2001.
Directive 2002/14/EC of the European Parliament and of the Council of 11 March 2002 establishing a general framework for informing and consulting employees in the European Community. Official Journal L 080, 23/03/2002.
The Information and Consultation of Employees Regulations 2004. Available from the UK Department of Trade and Industry, www.dti.gov.uk.
Consultation paper on transposition into Irish law of the information and consultation Directive, Irish Department of Enterprise, Trade and Employment, July 2003.

References

Carley, Mark (2004) 'Industrial relations trends and developments in Europe'. Paper delivered at European Foundation Workshop on Industrial Relations in the EU, Japan and the USA, October. (London: Spire Associates).
Cziria, Ludovít (2004) '2003 annual review for Slovakia', *European Industrial Relations Observatory* (EIRO), June. Dublin.
Dobbins, Tony (2003) 'Information and consultation Directive brings Irish IR into uncharted waters', *Industrial Relations News* 30, July. Dublin.
Dribbusch, Heiner (2003) 'Works councils and other workplace employee representation and participation structures (Germany)'. EIRO, September. Dublin.
Dufour, Christian (2003) 'Works councils and other workplace employee representation and participation structures (France)'. EIRO, September. Dublin.

EIRO (2004) *Annual Review 2003*, Dublin: European Foundation for the Improvement of Living and Working Conditions, Spring.

EIRR (European Industrial Relations Review) (2001a) 'Information and consultation of employees, Part 1'. EIRR 334, November. London: IRS.

EIRR (2001b) 'Information and consultation of employees: Part 2'. EIRR 335, December. London: IRS.

EIRR (2001c) 'Government outlines new codetermination rules'. EIRR 325, February. London: IRS.

EIRR (2002) 'European Company Statute adopted'. GRR 336, January. London: IRS.

EIRR (2004) 'Employee representation in SMEs'. EIRR 367, August. London: IRS.

EIRR (2002) 'Information and consultation of employees: Part 3'. EIRR 336, January. London: IRS.

Gardawski, Julisz, Czarzasty, Jan and Towalski, Rafal (2004) '2003 Annual Review for Poland'. EIRO June. Dublin.

IRS Employment Review (2004) 'DTI publishes draft guidance and Regulations on informing and consulting employees'. 805, August. London: Industrial Relations Services.

Jørgensen, Carsten (2004) 'EU consultation Directive incorporated in DA–LO cooperation agreement'. EIRO March. Dublin.

Jørgensen, Carsten and Navrbjerg, Steen E. (2001) 'The involvement of employees and collective bargaining in company restructuring'. EIRO July. Dublin.

Kallaste, Epp, Philips, Kaia and Eamets, Raul (2004) '2003 annual review for Estonia'. EIRO May. Dublin.

Kohl, Heribert and Platzer, Hans-Wolfgang (2004) 'Industrial Relations in Central and Eastern Europe' (trans. Pete Burgess). Brussels: European Trade Union Institute.

Ladó, Maria (2002) 'Industrial relations in the candidate countries'. EIRO July. Dublin.

Macaire, Simon and Rehfeldt, Udo (2002) 'Industrial relations aspects of mergers and takeovers'. EIRO June. Dublin.

Skledar, Stefan (2004) '2003 annual review for Slovenia'. EIRO, June. Dublin.

Stamati, Anda (2003) 'Works councils and other workplace employee representation and participation structures in Greece'. EIRO September. Dublin.

Tóth, Andras and Ghellab, Youcef (2003) 'The challenge of representation at the workplace in EU accession countries: does the creation of works councils offer a solution alongside trade unions?'. International Labour Office; Sub-regional Office for Central and Eastern Europe, Budapest.

van het Kaar, Robbert (2004) 'Changes ahead in employee involvement legislation'. EIRO July. Dublin.

14

Statutory information disclosure for consultation and bargaining in Germany, France and the UK

Howard Gospel and Paul Willman

Information is a basic resource in enterprise decision-making. It is also essential for joint consultation, collective bargaining, and other mechanisms that give employees voice and regulate employment. In practice, most information relevant to employee relations originates with the employer, and there is a pervasive asymmetry of information between employer and employees. Employees and their representatives will often seek information from the employer through consultation and bargaining. The employer's propensity to disclose information voluntarily depends in part on the perception of the balance of common goals against distributive interests (Kleiner and Bouillon 1988; Morishima 1989, 1991).

In most countries, company information is available publicly as a result of statute. Under company law, there are obligations on firms to disclose information in annual accounts and as part of reporting requirements. Such information is often made available voluntarily to employees, and used in wage bargaining by unions. However, it is usually highly aggregated and backward-looking. Under individual employment law, in most countries, there are statutory obligations on employers to provide individuals with information on contracts of employment, health and safety, and pensions (Clark and Hall 1992; Kenner 1999). This may also extend to a more general 'good faith' obligation to provide individuals with a reasonable amount of information as part of their contracts of employment (Brody 1998).

In some countries, notably the members of the European Union (EU), additional collective labour law addresses specifically the informational asymmetry between employers and employees by detailing obligations to provide information to trade unions for collective bargaining, or to works councils or other bodies for joint consultation. These arrangements are of two types, which we term *process-driven* and *event-driven*.

Where information disclosure is process-driven, the trigger for its use lies within a bargaining or consultation agenda. The legislative approach to this tends to be a set of general rules on disclosure within a specified process such as a consultative or bargaining forum. The central purpose of such a law is to enhance the operation of a process that itself may be either voluntary or mandated. By contrast, where information disclosure is event-driven, it is triggered by a specific employer-initiated event that affects employment contracts irrespective of the representative context – examples of this are changes of ownership, or redundancy. Here, the central purpose of the law is to create a temporary process around an employer-initiated event that has implication for terms of employment.

The concern of process-driven disclosure is with a set of interlinked issues, and with the vitality of the bargaining or consultative process, while the concern of event-driven disclosure is primarily procedural justice in a specific context, such as the termination of employment contracts. Process-driven disclosure assumes an ongoing relationship and may enable employee representatives to take proactive measures. Event-driven disclosure tends to operate more in a palliative rather than a preventative way, and need have no continuous impact on the relationship between employer and employees. However, from the employees' perspective, there is one major advantage of event-driven disclosure: it can exist in the absence of representation, which in most countries has tended to shrink in scope and coverage. In the EU, both types commonly co-exist within national legal frameworks.

Here we examine the character of three national sets of disclosure requirements in the EU. The purpose is to understand how they are framed, to assess their comparative effectiveness, and to consider the likely impact in different countries of EU Directives that seek to harmonise practices across Member States.

The structure of this chapter is as follows. In the next three sections, legal arrangements for information disclosure are considered in three countries – Germany, France and the UK – chosen because of their distinctive approaches, within a common EU context. In part the order reflects the historical timing of the development of law on disclosure in the three countries, but it also reflects the extent of the law, the coherence between different laws, and the complementarity between legal and institutional arrangements. In the final section, the three countries are considered comparatively and the impact of EU Directives is addressed.

Germany: a coherent system under new pressures

In Germany, company information is disclosed primarily to employee representatives in the works council and on the supervisory board of the company. Legislation on disclosure was first enacted in the 1920s. It was reintroduced in 1952 and since then there have been a number of further extensions of the law.

Works council representatives and their information rights

The Works Constitution Act (*Betriebsverfassungsgetz* or *BetrVG*) of 1952 (as amended in 1972, 1988 and 2001) established the works council (*Betriebsrat*), giving it important powers in social, personnel and economic matters. Under the law, at the workers' request, a works council must be established in any company with at least five full-time employees. Its duties are to represent employees, to see that their justified suggestions are implemented, and to ensure that laws and higher-level agreements are observed. In the absence of such laws or agreements, the *Betriebsrat* is entitled to conclude works agreements (*Betriebsvereinbarungen*) concerning various aspects of employment.

The *BetrVG* 87(1) lists the areas of competence of the *Betriebsrat*. These include *inter alia*: working hours, wages and benefits, leave arrangements, monitoring of employees, health and safety, social facilities, standards governing pay systems, and principles governing suggestion schemes. The works council must act 'in a spirit of mutual trust', whereby both sides agree 'to refrain from activities which disturb operations or peace in the establishment' (*BetrVG*, 2 and 74–2).

To carry out its functions, the works council has extensive access to information: it has to be kept 'fully and promptly' informed, and any documents it requires are to be made available 'on request at all times' (*BetrVG*, 80 (2)). Confidentiality is not an acceptable reason for failing to inform the council (Daeubler, 1995). To ensure that information is provided and can be used effectively, the Act and case law guarantee that access to information must be in good time, which is defined as 'sufficient time for suggestions and objections to be taken into account at the planning stage'(*BetrVG*, 106; 90). The frequency of information exchange with the employer is legally mandated as monthly for both the *Betriebsrat* and its Economic Committee, to which annual accounts must be submitted. At the request of the council, information flow and meetings may be more frequent. In addition, when the workforce exceeds 1,000, the employer must inform employees directly in writing at least once each quarter of the financial state and affairs of the undertaking (*BetrVG* 74 (1)).

To facilitate its activities, the works council has a number of privileges. Council members have the right to paid time off for training, and a number of works councillors can be released from normal duties. Operating expenses must be met by the employer, who must make available premises, equipment and secretarial support (*BetrVG* 37–38 and 40–41). To process information better and to avoid overload, the council is entitled to form special committees. The most influential of these is the Economic Committee, mandatory in all undertakings employing over 100 people. Interpretation of information is facilitated through the right of recourse to experts and for the outside union to attend council meetings in an advisory capacity. In the case of multi-plant and affiliated companies, where it is felt that the real information and decision-making centre is beyond the reach of any single works council, a central council may be established by the resolution of individual works councils.

The central council is composed of delegated members of the individual councils (*BetrVG* 28, 31, 80 (3), 106, and 108 (4) and (5)).

If it considers that there is obstruction to its rights, or where the parties cannot agree on the interpretation of information or a course of action, the council has recourse to a conciliation committee. This consists of an equal number of people representing each side and is usually chaired by a non-voting labour court judge. Employers prefer not to go to such a committee, in part because they pay for the proceedings, but more importantly because, in areas of co-determination, any decision is legally binding and supersedes all other agreements between the employer and the council (*BetrVG* 76 and 87(2)). There is thus strong pressure to reach an agreement. The council has significant access to information and the capability to process it. As will be described below, its links with the outside union are crucial to its capacity in this respect.

Through so-called *Mitbestimmung*, or co-determination, German workers also have representation on the supervisory board (*Aufsichtsrat*) of their companies, with proportions depending on type and size of company. Meeting at least twice a year, its main functions are to elect the members of the management board (*Vorstand*) and to supervise its activities. The legal rights of employee representatives are identical to shareholders' representatives, and they therefore have access to any information accessible to the *Aufsichtsrat*. At the very least this allows a direct monitoring of annual accounts and balance sheets. At least once a year, the management board must supply the *Aufsichtsrat* with comprehensive information on all basic issues concerning the management of the enterprise. In addition, at any time, any member of the *Aufsichtrat* can request additional information on affairs of importance for the enterprise. However, a duty of confidentiality applies to all members of the *Aufsichtsrat*. While the supervisory board in theory controls the management board, in practice the latter is often very strong, not least because of its control over the flow of information. Nevertheless, in practice, in most companies the works council is the more important employee voice mechanism.

Special event disclosure and the minimal impact of the EU

Below we shall see that EU Directives and special event disclosure have had some effect on developing law and practice on information disclosure in France, and an even greater effect in the UK. By contrast, they have had very little impact on German law and practice. For all three countries, we focus specifically on collective redundancies, transfer of undertakings, takeovers, and the impact of the European Works Council (EWC) – all areas of major importance where there have been EU Directives.

In the case of collective redundancies, the works council has always had a significant role. In firms with over twenty employees, the council has extended co-determination rights in the case of changes that may have 'serious disadvantages' for a substantial proportion of the workforce (*BetrVG* 111).

The labour court has specified that the works council must be consulted whenever redundancies affecting 10 per cent or more of the labour force are planned, and that a special works agreement must be concluded between the employer and the council, following 'socially acceptable' criteria for dismissals. Where the council has not been consulted or where no agreement has been reached, dismissals are without effect. In practice, while most redundancies are accepted, this process affects the numbers and terms of the redundancy (Standing and Tokman 1991).

Despite the low number of hostile takeovers, there has been growing concern about takeovers in Germany. However, there is no specific legislation in this area governing disclosure to employees. Yet, as described above, the legal rights of the works council and board representatives apply. In practice, as in other countries, it is difficult to reconcile the right to information and the confidentiality inherent in such situations. There are various problems – the secrecy rules imposed by national stock exchanges; the danger of adverse market reactions given the time needed to convene such a meeting; the content of the information to be provided; and the nature of any sanctions to be applied for non-disclosure.

While giving the possibility of creating EU-wide consultation institutions for German firms, the introduction of the EWC Directive has had a limited effect within Germany itself. During the negotiations on the Directive, the German unions tried to preserve the 'workers only' composition of EWCs. However, in the end, the Directive did not align with the German definition. German unions have been concerned about the possibility that use of EWCs may undermine the position of the domestic works council.

Trade unions and information disclosure

In Germany, there is no direct legal right for unions to receive company information for collective bargaining. This reflects the tradition that unions operate outside the enterprise and bargain at multi-employer level for a whole industry (or part of it). Under multi-employer bargaining, information on any single company is of less relevance, and the German legislature has never therefore seen fit to mandate information disclosure to unions. However, unions have an exclusive prerogative on collective bargaining matters, and works' agreements by the *Betriebsrat* cannot derogate from collective agreements negotiated by unions (*BetrVG* 77 (3)). Workplace union delegates (*Vertrauensleute*) may be invited to attend meetings with the employer, but have no information rights.

In practice, however, German unions play a major role in the receipt and processing of company information. First, they play an important role through the works council, and 79 per cent of works council members are also union members (Jacobi *et al.* 1992; Muller-Jentsch 2003). Moreover, at the request of members, the union has the legal right to be present at all council and Economic Committee meetings (*BetrVG* 2). In addition, the unions provide training and advice to *Betriebsrat* members. Second, German unions also play an important role via the supervisory board. Most board level representatives are also union members. Moreover, full-time union officials may sit on supervisory boards as employee representatives, and this allows them direct access to company information, subject to the confidentiality requirements.

In sum, German law requires that substantial information be provided in good time to worker representatives. The approach is largely process-driven and facilitates the development of an employee agenda. However, there are challenges. First, while EU requirements have not had a major impact on German practice, there has been fear that EU measures, for example EWCs, may undermine stronger German requirements. Second, there are new fears concerning takeovers, and some debate as to whether new legal requirements should be introduced to deal with these specific events. Third, in recent years, employers have criticised the 'straitjacket' of collective agreements at industry level, and settlements have allowed for specific works agreements (negotiated by the works council) that permit a measure of flexibility on matters such as hours and work organisation. These so-called opening clauses (*Öffnungsklausen*) constitute a new dynamic in the German system and allow for more devolution to works councils. As a result, some commentators speak of the German system as being 'in crisis' and speculate that works agreements may supplant collective bargaining with the union. If decoupling were then to take place, this would have major consequences for the German system of information provision, with its complementarity between works council consultation and union collective bargaining.

France: extensive law but blocked institutions

France has multiple mechanisms for information disclosure to employees. In this respect, the legislature has been inventive and the law has been built up in layers over time, reflecting critical political events. The French approach has involved both process- and event-driven elements.

The *comité d'entreprise* and its information rights

In successive amendments to the *Code du Travail* (*CdT*), since 1945, the law has established and extended the rights of the *comité d'entreprise*. Such committees are mandated in companies with fifty or more employees. As further amended in the early 1980s, the purpose of the committee is to ensure expression of employees' views, and to allow their interests to be taken into account in decisions concerning a wide range of work, employment and economic matters. To this end, the committee is to be informed and consulted on matters relevant to the organisation, management and general operation of the enterprise. This obligation requires the employer to provide written information in sufficient time to allow it to be considered. In turn, the committee may formulate comments and questions that must be answered by management (*CdT* 420-1–426-1, 431–432).

Under the statute and case law, the *comité d'entreprise* has a right to be informed and consulted on broad aspects of pay and conditions, personnel policy, working time, work organisation, health and safety, and levels of employment. It also has the right to be consulted on the wider social consequences of significant decisions: important alterations to the structure of the enterprise, its economic organisation, and its legal status; the evolution of R&D policy; mergers, acquisitions and sales of significant parts of the company; and restructuring of the broader group to which the establishment belongs (*CdT* 431-4, 432-4, 432-11).

To ensure that information is provided and can be processed effectively, the *comité d'entreprise* has legal supports similar to the German *Betriebsrat*. Thus the employer must make available facilities and allow time off for training and involvement. In order to carry out its duties, it is entitled to form special committees, such as health and safety committees (*CdT* 236). Consideration of information is facilitated by the right of recourse to experts and provision for the presence of union delegates (*delegués syndicaux*) in an advisory capacity. In the case of multi-plant enterprises and holding companies, where decisions are made higher up in the organisation, and where information received by any individual committee might be incomplete, a central committee may be established with related information rights.

The frequency of information exchange with the employer is legally mandated. Monthly, there should be a meeting of the *comité d'entreprise*, though extraordinary meetings may also be called in exceptional cases. Quarterly, it must receive information covering the changing composition of employment, the state of orders and production schedules, and planned changes in plant, equipment and production methods. Annually, the employer must provide a written report covering the following: the composition of the wage bill; the economic state of the enterprise; the value of production; and the flow of financial funds and their application. In workplaces with over 300 employees, additional information concerning performance and capacity of the plant is required.

Under legislation passed in 1977, the information provided to the *comité d'entreprise* must include an annual workplace *bilan social* (*CdT* 438-5). This summarises the position of the undertaking in the social area and must provide information on the following: employment, pay and benefits, health and safety, conditions of work, and the state of industrial relations. It must be endorsed and can be amended by the *comité d'entreprise* and must be made available to employees (*CdT* 438).

Thus, the French *comité d'entreprise* has extensive legal rights to information. However, a number of limitations exist. In contrast to Germany, the French *comité d'entreprise* has managerial employees in membership and is chaired by the employer. Moreover, there are weaker links with unions, which in turn have less capability and power than their German counterparts (Hege 1998; Pichot 1999; Dufour and Hege 2002). While the unions have a monopoly right to present candidates in first-round committee elections, the fact that density has fallen to less than 9 per cent (ETUI 1998) explains in part why the number of union candidates is shrinking. Trade union members provide 56 per cent of committee members, compared to 79 per cent in Germany. On balance, this has meant that the French *comité d'entreprise* has been less able to obtain and use company information (Sellier 1990, 1995; Hege 1998,).

Further legislation and special event disclosure

In addition to the legislation referred to above, in the area of collective redundancies, successive governments have seen fit to enact further measures. From the mid-1970s to the mid-1980s amendments were made to the *Code du Travail* mandating information and consultation in redundancy situations (Howell 1992; Jenkins 2000). This was augmented by further legislation in 2003 that allows plant collective agreements to lay down rules for information and consultation in redundancy situations involving ten or more employees. In addition, in 1989 and 1993, legislation made it obligatory on firms to draw up a *plan social*. This document must state the number of workers to be made redundant, their redundancy payments, training schemes, and possible relocation elsewhere in the company. If the *comité d'entreprise* feels that information provided in the social plan is inadequate, it may ask a tribunal to halt the dismissal procedure and require the production of a new plan. A number of important cases, involving firms such as Crédit du Nord, IBM France, La Samaritaine and Michelin, have interpreted the law favourably for employees but also stimulated demands for further legislation (Bledniak 1999; Jenkins 2000: 133–41).

In the case of takeovers or a change in control via the transfer of shares, judicial decisions have interpreted the *Code du Travail* to mean that an employer must inform and consult on the employment consequences of these matters. In addition, further legislation in 1989 stipulated that, as soon as a target company becomes aware of a takeover bid, it must inform the *comité d'entreprise*. The latter may then decide to invite the bidding party to present its case, outlining any possible effects on employment (*CdT* 432-1). However, in practice, successful legal challenges in the case of takeovers have been limited. One major problem here is that stock exchange confidentiality rules conflict with legislation on information to the *comité d'entreprises* (Commission des Operations de Bourse 1998).

The role of trade unions and collective bargaining

In the case of trade union collective bargaining, there were traditionally no statutory rights to information. Indeed, unions have had the legal right to operate in the firm only since 1968. Since then *delegués syndicaux* may be appointed according to the size of the workforce, and have the right to facilities and time off for the performance of duties, and protection against dismissal (*CdT* 132-2, 412-6, 412-20, 451). As in Germany, French unions have a monopoly on collective bargaining, and, for a collective agreement to be valid, it can only be concluded with a union. Moreover, where a union branch exists, it is illegal for an employer to conclude a works agreement with a *comité d'entreprise* (Bledniak, 2000). Any union affiliated to one of the five representative confederations has the right to conclude collective agreements or works agreements for all employees – including for non-unionised workers.

The 1982 Auroux laws, introduced by the Mitterrand government, had a number of somewhat contradictory purposes. One was to introduce a right of expression for employees; and a further purpose was to encourage collective bargaining. In the latter respect, the law introduced an obligation on employers to conduct negotiation every year at the establishment level on working hours and work organisation, and every five years at the industry level on job classification. The bargaining parties were encouraged to agree on necessary information to be disclosed (*CdT* 132-27). In practice, the legislation had a positive effect on the number of collective agreements at both national and enterprise levels. However, the unions had difficulty in leading plant-level negotiations, and in practice employers often chose to enhance the position of either the *comité d'entreprise* or the direct expression bodies. The same thing has occurred with the 1998 legislation on the 35-hour week, which also stimulated negotiations with unions and enhanced the flow of information to employees.

Nevertheless, French unions have indirect access to information through the *comité d'entreprise*, where they can be invited to assist and advise at meetings. Also, as in Germany, union influence extends through the training and expertise they provide to the *comité d'entreprise*. Union delegates must by law be invited to assist and advise the *comité d'entreprise* in all meetings with the employer. They receive information provided to committee representatives, including the annual *bilan social*, and they must be informed about training matters. Under the Auroux laws on the direct expression of employees, every three years union delegates have the right to give an opinion on the results of employees' expression rights, and their amended report is forwarded to the Labour Inspector (*CdT* 438-5). In multi-plant companies, the law protects the right of every representative union to appoint a 'central union delegate', which allows a union presence at the level of the central *comité d'entreprise* (*CdT* 412-12).

In sum, the abundance and inventiveness of French statutes relating to information disclosure is striking. As it stands, French law provides for substantial information to the *comité d'entreprise*. It also enjoins information provision via the *bilan social* and the right of expression. It provides some information directly to trade unions and some indirectly to them via the participation of union delegates in the *comité d'entreprise*. The approach is one that is largely process-driven, though there is also some event-driven disclosure. However, the institutions that might use the law are weak and have difficulty developing effective agendas. In turn, this means the system lacks the complimentarity and coherence of the German system.

The UK: towards Europe?

In the UK, the legal obligation on employers to provide information to employee representatives had its origins in the early 1970s, later than in Germany and France.

At that time, the emphasis was on disclosure for collective bargaining, and, despite the roll-back in auxiliary law in the Conservative years (1979–97), the legislation survived. In the 1980s and 1990s, there was a new emphasis on disclosure as part of joint consultation at work, reflecting both growing EU influence and the preference of Conservative governments and many employers for consultation over bargaining. The Labour government elected in 1997 introduced a new trade union recognition law and adopted European social policy, including EWCs. It also passed amendments to existing legislation on collective redundancies and transfer of undertakings, all of which contain event-driven disclosure provisions and extended the right to information disclosure for collective bargaining to the area of training (Employment Relations Act (ERA) 1999, s. 5). The government has also encouraged the development of so-called 'partnership' agreements between employers and unions that are also posited on a greater sharing of information (ERA, s. 30). More recently, and albeit reluctantly, the government has accepted the EU Directive on Information and Consultation rights in national-level undertakings (DTI 2002, 2004; Gospel and Willman 2003)

Disclosure for collective bargaining

Since 1976, employers have been obliged to disclose information, (a) without which a union would be materially impeded in collective bargaining, and (b) which it would be in accordance with good industrial relations practice to disclose. Bargaining must be about matters for which the union is already recognised. Moreover, the employer specifically does not have to provide the following: information supplied in confidence or that would cause substantial injury to the firm; information that would involve a disproportionate amount of work in its compilation; and original documents other than ones specifically prepared for the purpose of providing the information (Gospel and Willman 1981). If a union feels that an employer has failed to meet the statutory requirements, and after an attempt at conciliation by the Advisory Conciliation and Arbitration Service (ACAS), the Central Arbitration Committee (CAC) may make an award specifying the information to be provided. If the employer still refuses to disclose, the CAC may award improvements in the terms and conditions of the relevant employees. A Code of Practice lists items that might be relevant to collective bargaining, under the headings of pay and benefits, conditions of service, and performance and financial matters. A further list contains items that might cause substantial injury to the employer, such as cost schedules, price quotes, and details of proposed investments (ACAS 1977).

In the early years, there was an initial union enthusiasm for the procedure, but later the number of cases fell and they remained low throughout the 1980s; subsequently they have fluctuated considerably from the early 1990s onwards. However, over the whole period there have been only about twenty complaints to the CAC each year, and only two or three formal awards per year. The downward fluctuation reflects a number of factors. On the one hand, the decline after the early years might have reflected the indirect influence of the legal provisions on voluntary practice (Millward *et al.* 1992: 123–4). On the other hand, the later decline in usage also reflected disappointment with the provisions. A temporary increase in cases in the early 1990s might have reflected a pragmatic adjustment on the part of unions to the difficulties of the Thatcher years. The upward trend also seemed to have reflected a response from unions to the growing decentralization of business activities, the effects of privatisation and outsourcing, and the individualization of employment relations (Gospel and Lockwood 1999).

Overall, around half of union complaints have been held to be well founded. Complaints are more likely to yield information on terms and conditions of the represented group, and on labour costs and human resource budgeting; they are least likely to yield information on terms and conditions of other groups within the same organisation, and on financial matters and the overall state of the organisation. The most successful employer objection to information provision has been that the information did not concern a matter subject to collective bargaining, and that collective bargaining would not be materially impeded by non-disclosure. In addition, it is often claimed that the information was supplied to the employer in confidence (Gospel and Lockwood 1999).

The tests under the law are very restrictive. As noted, disclosure is limited to matters for which the union is recognised (Trade Union and Labour Relations Consolidation Acts. 181 (1); Central Arbitration Commission Award 8065). The test of 'good industrial relations' practice is vague, and the CAC has never acted as a trailblazer. The test of material impediment has also proved to be a major obstacle to unions that have previously operated without such information. Timing is a problem; the CAC may only adjudicate on a past failure to disclose, and may not declare what information should be provided in the future. Finally, the enforcement mechanism is weak, since the sanction neither forces disclosure nor provides for a punitive award.

Event-driven disclosure

More recent UK disclosure legislation has been event-driven and relates more to joint consultation than to collective bargaining. In response to EU Directives since the mid-1970s, employers have been obliged to disclose information to recognised unions and employee representatives in the event of both redundancies and business transfers. In both cases, the original law was amended in response to a 1994 European Court of Justice (ECJ) decision that the UK had failed properly to implement the Directives in that the right was only available to recognised unions. As a result of continuing criticism, in 1999, the Labour government introduced further regulations that give primacy to a trade union where such exists, but that also provide for other representatives in non-union situations (Gospel *et al.* 2003).

Where it is proposed to make twenty or more employees redundant, the employer must not dismiss any employee without first consulting with either a recognised trade union or employee representatives elected in advance, or *ad hoc* for the particular purpose. The information to be disclosed must cover the following: reasons for the redundancies; the methods of selection and implementation; and the calculation of redundancy payments. The employer must give a reasoned reply in 'good time' to any representations by employees. Where there are 'special circumstances' preventing compliance, the employer must nevertheless take steps that are feasible in the circumstances. If an employer fails to disclose and consult, the affected employees (but not the union) can present a collective complaint to an industrial tribunal for a financial settlement (TULRCA, 188(4), (7) and 89(4)).

In relation to business transfers, the employer must provide information on the following matters: the reasons for the transfer and its timing; implications for the employees concerned, measures the employer might take in relation to affected employees, and measures which the transferor envisages the transferee might take (TUPE 1981, 10). The employer is placed under a duty to inform, but there is not always an obligation to consult. The duty to furnish information is activated when a transfer is proposed. The duty to consult arises where an employer envisages 'measures' that will be taken in relation to any affected employees. In these circumstances, the employer has to consult appropriate representatives 'with a view to reaching agreement'. As with the redundancy provisions, if there are special circumstances, rendering it impracticable to disclose, the employer has to take such steps as are reasonably feasible (TUPE 1981, 10 (5) and (7)). If an employer fails in these obligations, the affected employees (but again not the union) can present a complaint to an industrial tribunal, which can award a financial settlement.

These event-driven provisions have several limitations. First, by their nature they do not allow for linkages to be made with other information, which might be germane to the prior business decision. Second, the obligation is to consult 'in good time' and not 'at the earliest opportunity'. As a result, employee complaints have often been that information provided by employers is too late. Third, the emphasis is placed on procedural justice for the individual, not collective entitlement claimed through a trade union; consequently, the redress is for the individual. Fourth, business transfers are not deemed to occur if there is a sale or transfer of shares, on the grounds that the employer remains unchanged. This is a real limitation, since economic control might have changed, and this might have important implications for employees. Finally, the obligation to inform and consult only applies to the measures that the employer envisages will be taken. If no measures are proposed, then no information or consultation is required. In addition, for the need to consult to arise, the employer must have formulated a definite plan or proposal on which it is intended to act, as opposed to mere forecasts. Furthermore, the obligation to consult is restricted to the subject matter of the proposed measures. In practice, in a developing situation, measures might only be envisaged at a late stage. In this situation, if there is insufficient time for effective consultations to take place before the transfer, the employer could not be criticised (*IPCS* v. *Secretary of State for Defence* (1987) IRLR, 373).

Following the Labour governments' acceptance of the Social Chapter, the EWC Directive was introduced in the UK. Under the Directive, management must draw up a report and meet with the EWC at least once a year to provide relevant information and to consult. The information disclosed must relate to the following: the economic and financial situation of the business; the likely evolution of the business, production and sales; trends in investments and employment; substantial changes in organisation, working methods, transfers of production, mergers, or retrenchment; and collective redundancies. In addition, in exceptional circumstances, such as a plant closure, there must be an extra *ad hoc* meeting for information and consultation as soon as possible. Redress for failure to inform and consult an EWC takes the form of a financial penalty.

The EWC Directive represented a move in the UK to a more process-driven approach, and in multinational companies has also provided a possible vehicle for unions to raise concerns and generate a management response. In practice, however, the information and consultation provisions are fairly limited, requiring only one annual meeting and the presentation of highly aggregated information in a special report. Moreover, management may withhold information which might be prejudicial to the enterprise. In practice, activities are often dominated by management, and employee representatives often feel they cannot participate seriously in decision-making (IRS 1998).

The UK: *plus ca change?*

The recent passage of the EU Directive on Information and Consultation in national level undertakings has introduced into the UK another process-driven procedure that is likely to be highly influential. The Directive will affect large enterprises (over 150 employees) by early 2005, and cover all undertakings with more than fifty employees by 2008, thus covering about 75 per cent of the UK labour force. In the Directive and related Regulations, consultation is defined as an 'exchange of views and the establishment of dialogue' (Article 2) – implying an ongoing process. Article 4(2) outlines the substantive areas: there is an obligation (a) to provide information on the general business situation of the undertaking; (b) to inform and consult on the likely development of employment and on 'anticipatory measures' that might threaten employment; and (c) an enhanced obligation to inform and consult on decisions likely to lead to substantial changes in work organisation or in contractual relations. Regarding item (c), consultation will be 'with a view to reaching an agreement' (Article 4) – implying an ongoing process of give-and-take. These are minimum mandatory topics and other matters can be covered. Consultation must take place at an 'appropriate' time, to enable employee representatives to prepare for consultation. It must also be 'at the relevant level of management and representation depending on the subject under discussion' – implying that there should be different levels of representation and consultation within an undertaking. In all cases, management is obliged to provide a reasoned response to representatives' opinions. Representatives are also to be given adequate 'protection and guarantees' to enable them to perform their duties (Article 7). On matters of confidentiality, information may be withheld if the employer considers it might seriously damage the undertaking, and representatives and 'any experts who assist them' may be made subject to an obligation of confidentiality. Sanctions for failure to comply will be 'effective, proportionate, and dissuasive' (Article 8). Employers and employee representatives may negotiate different arrangements before and after transposition – but these would have to respect the principles of the Directive (Article 5).

The Regulations that will transpose the Directive into UK law (DTI 2003; DTI 2004) conform to two broad and related principles that have long characterised the UK – voluntarism and adaptability to pre-existing institutions. The proposal is for a triggering process allowing employees to request information and consultation arrangements or, where such exist, to question whether they comply with the Directive.

Employees are allowed to request negotiations with their employers on the establishment of information and consultation procedures. The request must be made by at least 10 per cent of the employees in the undertaking, subject to a minimum of fifteen employees and a maximum of 2,500. If successful, the employer will be obliged to enter into negotiations with elected employee representatives to reach an agreement on information and consultation arrangements within the undertaking.

However, if such an agreement is in place and the request for a new one has been made by fewer than 40 per cent of the workforce, the employer may, instead of opening negotiations, hold a ballot of all the employees to ascertain whether the request is endorsed by at least 40 per cent of the employees. Where it is endorsed, the employer must enter into negotiations on a new agreement. Where employers indicate their intention to hold a ballot on a pre-existing agreement, an employee representative or employee (where there are no employee representatives) may complain to the CAC if they dispute that the claimed agreement satisfies the conditions above. Where the CAC finds the complaint well-founded, it will order the employer to enter into negotiations instead of holding a ballot. Pre-existing agreements may not consist of arrangements imposed unilaterally by management without any discussion with employees, and where employees have had no opportunity to signify their approval.

A key element here is that employers must make arrangements for employees to appoint or elect negotiating representatives. Negotiated agreements must be in writing, cover all the employees in the undertaking, and set out the circumstances in which the employer must inform and consult the employees. Moreover, agreements must either provide for the appointment or election of 'information and consultation representatives', who will be informed and consulted by the employer or provide that the employer informs and consults the employees of the undertaking directly. Agreements must be signed either by all the negotiating representatives or by the majority of them, in which case the agreement must also be approved in writing by at least 50 per cent of the employees or approved by 50 per cent of employees who vote in a ballot.

Where no agreement is reached within the six-month time limit or any agreed extended period, the fall-back is the application of the 'standard information and consultation provisions' which in effect copy over the requirements of Article 4 of the Directive. The employer is required to arrange for a secret ballot to elect one information and consultation representative for every fifty employees or part thereof, up to a maximum of twenty-five employees. The employer will then be required to provide information on the following: the recent and probable development of the undertaking's activities and economic situation; the situation, structure and probable development of employment within the undertaking and any anticipatory measures that might affect employment; and decisions likely to lead to substantial changes in work organisation or in contractual relations, including decisions covered by the legislation on collective redundancies and transfers of undertakings.

Enforcement is to be via the CAC, with the penalty being a fine on the employer for non-compliance. The employer is protected by a right of confidentiality on information disclosed to representatives and may withhold documents which might cause serious harm to the undertaking. Information and consultation representatives are entitled to reasonable paid time off to perform their functions, enforceable through employment tribunal claims. Employees are also protected against unfair dismissal or detriment by an employer when acting as representatives or otherwise exercising their rights under the proposed legislation (Hall 2005).

This is the first time that the UK's strategy for implementing an EU Directive has been agreed in tripartite discussions between the government, the Confederation of British Industry (CBI), and the Trades Union Congress (TUC). In the negotiations, the CBI's main objective was to protect existing company arrangements, whereas the TUC argued that arrangements that are not based on genuine agreement with the workforce must be capable of being challenged. In effect, the overall intent of the Regulations is a kind of legislatively-induced voluntarism, similar to the statutory trade-union recognition procedure, with the new legislation driving the spread of voluntary information and consultation agreements, reached either ahead of its coming into force, or as a consequence of its trigger mechanism being used.

One key concern is the reliance on employee representatives, which is central to the Directive, but fudged in the UK Regulations. Many firms in the UK rely on direct communication with employees (Millward et al. 2000). The entire framing of the discussion documents has focused on the positive impact of information provision and consultation on firm performance. On one interpretation, the UK Regulations imply that direct communication arrangements will satisfy the requirements of the Directive. If this is the case, unions, interested in extending employee representation, are likely to test this at the ECJ and cause continuing tension and uncertainty in UK labour law in this area.

In conclusion, therefore, the UK began with process-driven disclosure based exclusively on collective bargaining. Primarily under the influence of EU Directives, event-driven disclosure and consultation were later introduced. With the EWC and the Information and Consultation Directive and Regulations, there has been a reversion to process-driven disclosure, but based on consultation. The potentially far-reaching new Directive is posited on a long tradition of voluntarism.

Conclusions

It was argued in the introduction that information is a basic resource in enterprise decision-making. It is essential for all mechanisms that give employees voice and regulate employment relations. Though employers have an incentive to disclose some information to employees, informational asymmetry is pervasive in the employment relationship. In the legislation discussed above, this is indeed the assumption of national legislators, and the laws are posited on a belief that an adequate and timely flow of information will make consultation and negotiation more meaningful.

In the context of informational asymmetry and employer reluctance to disclose, there is a role for the law. The three different legal approaches to information disclosure reflect deep patterns of industrial relations and corporate governance in each country. The German arrangements reflect a system which values and promotes co-operative relations between stakeholders in an insider system of governance. Here, information disclosure is essential for the creation of trust, and encourages an employee collective agenda (Teubner 1998). In France, the law reflects a history of employer reluctance to disclose, especially to trade unions, in a situation where labour has never been an insider in governance and where there is less trust between the parties. At critical political points, governments have intervened to mandate disclosure and consultation in an attempt to give employees rights and to ease social tensions. However, the law has often been ineffective or had unintended consequences. In particular, employers have tried to turn disclosure to their advantage and to the disadvantage of trade unions. In the UK, the traditional approach was to privilege adversarial collective bargaining in a market system of governance and a voluntaristic setting. Disclosure legislation was originally introduced to facilitate union bargaining agendas. It was always limited, and its effective scope shrank with collective bargaining. More recently, EU membership has added two new dimensions: first, a different concept of event-driven disclosure for the resolution of specific problems, the establishment of individual rights, and the promotion of co-operative relations; and, second, legal rights for the establishment of process-driven works-council-type joint consultation arrangements. In the British case, these different approaches sit uncomfortably together.

A further conclusion is that legal supports and guarantees do affect information provision. Thus disclosure rights for the German works council give employee representatives good access to information, supplemented by information provided to employee representatives on company boards. The union plays a significant indirect role in information processing. In France, the legislature has tried repeatedly to make employers provide more information, especially for joint consultation. Such repetition itself suggests that these legal measures have had less effect on French disclosure practice. However, this is not to say that the law has been ineffective in France: it has given French employees and unions more resources than they would otherwise have had. In the UK, in the area of collective bargaining, the effect of process driven legislation has been more limited. On the borderline between collective bargaining and joint consultation, newer event-driven legislation has had some impact, though, to date, this has been limited.

Between the three countries, there are also differences in the coherence of the law. In Germany there exists an interlocking system which had its origins after the Second World War. By comparison with the other two countries, a system has been created that has proved to be coherent and complementary in its parts. Thus there has been little need in Germany to change the law on information disclosure by the addition of new requirements of an event-driven kind. By contrast, in France, layers of law have built up in a less coherent manner, reflecting a periodic desire by the legislature to develop consultative and bargaining institutions in the workplace and to create a more effective industrial relations system. The result is a set of laws that co-exist without reinforcing one another. In the UK, the law has developed under different influences – collective *laissez-faire*, the principle of procedural justice for individuals initiated by EU Directives, and now a more general set of process-driven obligations under the Information and Consultation Regulations. The latter is likely to lead to major changes.

In general, it would seem that disclosure for collective bargaining and for joint consultation are more likely to be additive where unions are already strong and can play a significant role in workplace regulation. The usefulness of the law depends on the existence of institutions that can use it. Germany is an example in this respect, with a close relationship between the works council, board representatives and the trade union in information receipt and processing. In France, where unions are weaker and have less effective ties with workplace bodies, the coherence between the law and institutional arrangements is less strong. As a result, periodically, the legislature has sought to intervene to promote greater coherence. In the UK, to date, there has been some confusion, but, with the passage of the new legislation, the UK will clearly move down the road to dual channels of representation via trade unions and works councils.

Acknowledgements

This chapter is produced as a part of the Leverhulme Programme on the Future of Trade Unions, Centre for Economic Performance, London School of Economics. We would like to thank Graeme Lockwood, King's College, London, who co-authored earlier articles, and Marina Bourgain, European University Institute, Florence, who provided research on Germany and France.

References

Advisory Conciliation and Arbitration Service (1977) *Code of Practice on Disclosure of Information to Trade Unions for Collective Bargaining Purposes.* London: HMSO.

Bertelsmann and Hans Bockler Foundations (1998) *The German Model of Codetermination and Cooperative Governance.* Guttersloh: Bertelsmann Foundation.

Bledniak, E. (1999) *Comité d'entreprise.* Paris: Dalloz, Encyclopedie Delmas.

Brody, D. (1998) 'Beyond exchange: the new contract of employment', *Industrial Law Journal* 27(2): 79–102.

Clark, J. and Hall, M. (1992) 'The Cinderella directive? Employee rights to information about conditions applicable to their contract or employment relationship', *Industrial Law Journal* 21(2): 106–18.

Collins, H. (2001) 'Regulating the employment relation for competitiveness', *Industrial Law Journal* 30(1): 17–48.

Commission des Operations de Bourse (1998) *Communications des societés financiers cotées vis-à-vis des salariés,* Paris: COB.

Cully, M., Woodland, S. O'Reilly, A. and Dix, G. (1999) *Britain at Work.* London: Routledge.

Daeubler, W. (1995) *Das Arbeitrecht, Leittaden für Arbeitnehmer.* Reinbek: Rowohlt.

Department for Trade and Industry (2002) *High Performance Workpaces: The Role of Employee Involvement in a Modern Economy: A Discussion Paper.* London: DTI.

Department for Trade and Industry (2003) *High Performance Workplaces – Informing and Consulting Employees.* London: HMSO.

Department for Trade and Industry (2004) *The Information and Consultation of Employees Regulations.* London: DTI.

Dufour, C. and Hege, H. (2002) *L'Europe Syndicale au Quotidien.* Brussels: Peter Lang.

ETUI (1998) 'Changes in trade union density in EU Member States since 1950'. *ETUI Information Bulletin, No. 1,* February.

Gospel, H. and Willman P. (1981)'The CAC decisions on disclosure of information', *Industrial Law Journal,* 10–22.

Gospel H. and Lockwood, G. (1999) 'Disclosure of information for collective bargaining: the CAC approach revisited', *Industrial Law Journal* 28(3): 233–248.

Gospel, H., Lockwood, G. and Willman, P. (2003) 'A British dilemma: disclosure of information for collective bargaining and joint consultation', *Comparative Labor Law and Policy Journal* 22(2): 101–23.

Hall, M. (1996) 'Beyond recognition? Employee representation and EU law', *Industrial Law Journal,* 25: 15–27.

Hall, M. (2005) 'A cool response to the ICE Regulations'. Warnick University, Working paper.

Hege, A. (1998) 'Works councils et comités d'entreprise. Histoires d'institutions et de representants. Quelques problemes de domparaison internationales des relations professionelles'. *Revue de l'IRES* 28: 9–42.

Howell, C. (1992) *Regulating Labor: The State and Industrial Relations Reform in Postwar France.* Princeton, NJ: Princeton University Press.

IRS (1998) 'Managers and unions are sceptical about European works councils', *Employment Trends* 5.

Jacobi, O., Keller, B. and Mueller-Jentsch, W. (1992) 'Germany: facing new challenges', in A Ferner and R. Hymancet, *Industrial Relations in the New Europe,* Oxford: Blackwell.

Jenkins, A. (2000) *Employment Relations in France: Evolution and Innovation.* New York: Kluwer.

Kenner, J. (1999) 'Statement or contract? – some reflections on the EC employee information (contract or employment relationship) directive after *Kampelmann*', *Industrial Law Journal* 28(3): 205–31.

Kleiner, M. and Bouillon, M. (1988) 'Providing business information to production workers: correlates of compensation and profitability', *Industrial and Labor Relations Review* 41: 605–17.

McMullen, J. (1992) 'Takeovers, Transfers, and Business Re-organizations', *Industrial Law Journal* 21(1): 15–30.

Millward, N., Bryson, A., and Forth, J. (2000) *All Change at Work? British Employment Relations 1980–1998, as Portrayed by the Workplace Industrial Relations Survey Services.* London: Routledge.

Millward, N., Stevens, M., Smart, D. and. Hawes, W. R. (1992) *Workplace Industrial Relations in Transition: The ED/ESRC/PSI/ACAS Surveys.* Aldershot: Dartmouth Publishing.

Morishima, M. (1989) 'Information sharing and firm performance in Japan', *Industrial Relations* 30: 37–61.

Morishima, M. (1991) 'Information sharing and collective bargaining in Japan: effects on wage negotiations', *Industrial and Labor Relations Review* 44: 469–85.

Muller-Jentsch, W. 2003 'Re-assessing co-determination', in Muller-Jentsch, W. and Weitbrecht, H. (eds) *The Changing Contours of German Industrial Relations.* Munich: Rainer Hampp, pp. 39–56.

Pichot, E. (1999) *Employee Representatives in Europe and their Economic Prerogatives.* Brussels: European Commission.

Sellier, F. (1990) 'Comites et syndicats. Situation française et comparaison France–Allemagne', *Revue de L'IRES* 3: 41–58.

Sellier, F. (1995) 'Specificites nationales et diversite des entreprises', *Revue de L'IRES* 19: 9–29.

Standing, G., and Tokman, G. (1991) *Towards Social Adjustement: Labour Market Issues in Structural Adjustment.* Geneva: International Labour Organisation.

Teubner, G. (1998) 'Legal irritants: good faith in British law or how unifying law ends up in new divergences', *Modern Law Review* 61: 11–32.

part **6**

Information and consultation in practice

In this final part of the book, two detailed case studies are presented. Taken together (and bearing in mind also the issues and dilemmas raised in Part 4) they offer some useful practical lessons for employers, employees and representatives with regard to the possibilities and problems attaching to information and consultation.

In Chapter 15, the B&Q case reveals how a multi-level system can operate in practice, and in Chapter 16 the Abbey National case gives useful insights into how consultation arrangements can work in situations where unionisation is relatively influential in terms of structures, but where membership stands at around 35 per cent.

These cases help to situate, and bring to life, the kinds of points, warnings and suggestions raised in previous chapters – most notably those by David Yeandle, by Marc Thompson and by Phil Beaumont and colleagues. The options which are, in varying degrees, explicit and implicit in these case chapters, can be further clarified by using the Decision Flowchart in the Appendix to this book.

15

Using a multi-level consultation framework: the case of B&Q

Mark Hall

This case study reviews the evolution of the multi-tiered information and consultation framework within the home improvement retail chain, B&Q. This information and consultation structure, known internally as the 'Grass Roots' process, dates back to 1998. Revised arrangements introduced in 2002 included formal elections for employee representatives and a consultative role in respect of planned business changes.

The company

The first B&Q store was opened in Southampton in 1969, since when the company has developed into the UK's best known DIY retail chain, with some 320 stores (including 90 warehouses) throughout the country employing more than 33,000 people. During the 1980s, B&Q grew rapidly, acquiring the Scottish DIY chain Dodge City and becoming part of the Kingfisher Group. In 1999, B&Q acquired the mail order company Screwfix Direct. Internationally, B&Q opened its first store outside the UK in 1996 – in Taiwan. In 1998, B&Q merged with France's leading DIY retailer, Castorama, becoming the largest DIY retailer in Europe. International expansion continued with the opening of a B&Q store in China in 1999 and one in Ireland in 2002. The company continues to expand domestically. During 2003, 17 new stores opened, creating 4,000 new jobs.

Industrial relations background

There is no trade union recognition within B&Q. Pay and terms and conditions of employment are determined on a national basis by senior management and signed off by the board. The company regards its pay and benefits package as 'advantageous' and consistent with its aim of being an 'employer of choice': pay for customer advisers in B&Q stores is reported to be in the upper quartile of the pay range of B&Q's competitors. Head office human resource (HR) staff report that the company has occasionally received approaches from one or other of the main retail unions for recognition, either on a nationwide basis or at particular stores, but that such requests have been declined.

Although it is a non-union company, B&Q accepts that some employees elected as Grass Roots representatives may be trade union members. In the 'rules regarding being a Grass Roots representative', posted on the company intranet, the answer to the question 'Does it make any difference if I am a trade union member?' is 'No. We respect people's personal, private rights to belong to political groups or trade unions. It is, however, inappropriate for a Grass Roots rep to use their position to canvass interest in or put forward any third party's opinion.' At least one of the six (non-management) employee representatives on the national Grass Roots forum belongs to a trade union.

According to head office HR staff, there has been some form of employee involvement arrangements within B&Q 'pretty much from the outset'. Prior to the introduction of the 'Grass Roots' initiative in 1998, the existence of store-level consultative committees, with the possibility of pursuing unresolved issues to divisional office level, provided a vehicle for some information and consultation activity, but this was reportedly very much of the 'tea and toilets' variety and dependent on local management attitudes to the process. The introduction of Grass Roots was intended to give more structure and scope to B&Q's employee consultation arrangements, and ensure its company-wide coverage and relevance through the establishment of a multi-tiered consultation framework operating at store, regional, divisional (in geographic terms) and national levels (see Figure 15.1).

As well as the Grass Roots structure there is a health and safety committee, which meets every two months and is chaired by a member of the main board. Although issues with health and safety implications are inevitably raised via the Grass Roots structure, they are referred to the health and safety committee for action. B&Q employees are also represented on the Kingfisher Group European Works Council (EWC), but there is no direct link between the EWC and the Grass Roots national forum – at present, the B&Q representative on the EWC is elected by means of a UK-wide election, not indirectly by the employee members of the national Grass Roots forum. However, given the growing international dimension to B&Q's activities, B&Q's head office management are at the time of writing considering the possibility of introducing a B&Q-specific transnational consultation forum.

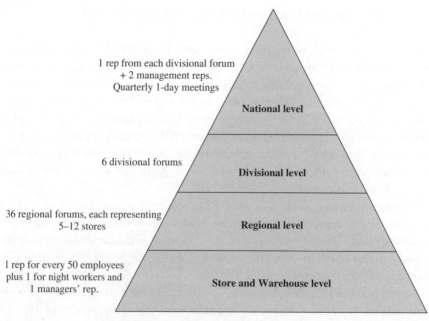

1 rep from each divisional forum
+ 2 management reps.
Quarterly 1-day meetings

National level

6 divisional forums

Divisional level

36 regional forums, each representing
5–12 stores

Regional level

1 rep for every 50 employees
plus 1 for night workers and
1 managers' rep.

Store and Warehouse level

Figure 15.1   B&Q's consultation structure

The company operates a separate grievance procedure, but if an issue is not resolved with line managers at store, regional or divisional level there is provision for it to be referred to the national Grass Roots forum for consideration.

Alongside Grass Roots, B&Q operates a range of other means of employee communications. These include regular day-to-day team briefings at store level; the use of focus groups to look at particular company issues; a monthly information bulletin, *In the Loop*, circulated to all employees; and *Talking Shop*, the company magazine. B&Q also carries out an employee feedback survey every six months, which is seen by senior management as an important barometer of shop-floor perceptions of the company as an employer.

The evolution of Grass Roots

B&Q first introduced Grass Roots in 1998 as a 'bottom-up' communication process. It operated primarily through store-based forums at which employees could raise issues of concern to them. Issues not dealt with locally could be passed up to Grass Roots forums established at regional, divisional and national level. Following a review of the system initiated by B&Q management in 2001, Grass Roots underwent a 'revamp' in the summer of 2002. Although the expected adoption of the EU information and consultation Directive was a factor in the decision to undertake the review, so too was feedback from the company's employees. B&Q's six-monthly employee feedback surveys suggested that the operation of the Grass Roots process had not resulted in a significant improvement in the number of employees who felt that their opinions counted. Discussions with employees, particularly those involved in Grass Roots, revealed a perception that issues raised via the Grass Roots process were sometimes not being dealt with quickly or thoroughly enough, and that there were inconsistencies in the way in which Grass Roots operated between different stores and in different regions.

Such concerns were reflected in a question raised by the Supercentre Central division at the national Grass Roots forum meeting in February 2002. This stated that 'The Grass Roots forum seems to be losing its credibility and impact, especially at national level. We need consistency of representatives at national level, commitment from senior managers to give quality, timely responses and rationale as to why we decide not to progress issues' (*Grass Roots News*, issue 15, Spring 2002). Pressure for changes in the Grass Roots system also reportedly reflected employee dissatisfaction over the 2000–1 review of the customer adviser pay structure, and the fact that this was not the subject of consultation.

The review paved the way for an enhanced role for Grass Roots, embracing more formalised consultation on planned business changes as well their existing role as a channel for employee views, suggestions and questions, and a more clearly defined role for employee reps as part of a more consistent and robust company-wide framework. Under the changes introduced in the summer of 2002, there are now more Grass Roots reps at store level (see below). They are now elected formally by secret ballot, whereas previously there was no single, consistent approach, with employee reps often being volunteers or asked to take on the role by management. In addition, training has been introduced for employee reps, as has an agreed allocation of time during working hours to carry out their Grass Roots duties, and the reps will stay in post for three years to ensure greater continuity. This package of changes to Grass Roots (see Box 15.1) was seen by B&Q's head office management as an evolutionary approach to strengthening the company's existing information and consultation 'arrangements, rather than something driven primarily by the Directive.

Box 15.1   Key innovations in the reformed Grass Roots process

- Grass Roots to be used for formal consultation on planned business changes in addition to its established communications role;
- management more proactive in using Grass Roots to address key business issues;
- more consistent and robust company-wide structure;
- store-level employee representatives formally elected;
- provision for representation of managers;
- training provided for employee reps;
- agreed time for reps to carry out their duties during working hours; and
- a greater emphasis on achieving positive results on significant issues.

Current arrangements

Grass Roots operates through a regular sequence of meetings at store, regional, divisional and national level, organised in the same format throughout the company. Meetings take place at each level on a quarterly basis, starting at store level and followed by meetings at successively higher levels so that, where appropriate, issues and ideas can be passed from store level up to national level. There is a formal nomination and election process for store-level Grass Roots reps. Representatives at regional, divisional and national levels are selected by and from the representatives at the level below. Grass Roots also operates within B&Q's head office departments and head office overall.

Store level arrangements

At store level, under the new Grass Roots arrangements, each B&Q Supercentre now has one rep for every fifty employees, up to a maximum of two, plus one rep for the night crew (where one exists) and one rep for the management team. In B&Q Warehouses, the maximum number of reps is three, plus one night crew and one management rep.

The nomination and election process for the current store-level Grass Roots reps took place in June–August 2002, supervised by the Involvement and Participation Association. Secret ballots to elect employee representatives took place where more candidates were nominated than the available places – which was the case in around a third of B&Q stores. Elections are normally held every three years, but the nomination/election process will also be triggered if an existing representative leaves, is promoted or needs to be replaced for any other reason.

The quarterly Grass Roots meetings at each of B&Q's 320 stores are chaired by the general/store manager. As well as the elected store representatives, any members of staff who wish to attend may do so. As specified in head office guidelines, a typical agenda will include:

- a training activity;
- an update on both the company's and the store's performance;
- discussion of store issues; and
- consultation on key company changes or initiatives.

Agenda items can be put forward either by staff or the company/management. B&Q head office provides pro forma agenda sheets for store-level meetings, together with a 'next steps' sheet for recording the action points from the meeting and highlighting any items that the store wants to forward to the next regional meeting for discussion. In terms of feedback from the meeting, Grass Roots reps are expected to report back directly to their colleagues, and the main action points from the meeting are posted on the store's notice board.

At the first store-level meetings held under the new arrangements – that is, in the autumn of 2002 – the elected store-level employee representatives decided which of them would represent the store at regional Grass Roots meetings. Head office guidelines outlined a range of methods, including informal discussion and 'mini selection' processes through which this could be done (which could also be used for the selection of staff representatives to the divisional- and national-level Grass Roots forums, and management reps at regional, divisional and national level).

Regional-level meetings

Regional Grass Roots forums typically cover between five and twelve stores. Separate regional arrangements cover B&Q's Supercentres and Warehouses. There are thirty-six regional Grass Roots forums in total. Chaired by regional managers, they consist of one employee representative from each store, plus one management representative from the region. A typical agenda for the quarterly meetings will include:

- a training activity;
- an update on both the company's and the region's performance;
- discussion of issues referred from store level;
- discussion of regional issues; and
- consultation on key company changes or initiatives.

The regional forum will agree key issues that their representative on the divisional forum will take forward to the next divisional meeting. The store reps on the regional forum are expected to report back directly to their stores on the outcomes of regional meetings.

Divisional-level meetings

Each regional Grass Roots forum chooses one of its employee representatives to attend one of six divisional forums – three covering Supercentres (Supercentre North, Supercentre Central and Supercentre South), and three covering Warehouses (Warehouse North, Warehouse West and Warehouse East). In addition, the divisional forums include one management representative from the division. The meetings are chaired by the directors of each division, supported by the divisional HR manager. A typical agenda for the quarterly meetings will include:

- training as required;
- an update on both the company's and the division's performance;
- discussion of issues unresolved at regional level;
- discussion of divisional issues; and
- consultation on key company changes or initiatives.

Again, the divisional forum will identify any issues to be referred to the national Grass Roots meeting. Key outcomes of divisional meetings are the subject of updates on the intranet, which are to be monitored by store representatives and information fed back by them to their colleagues.

National-level meetings

The national Grass Roots forum is made up of one employee representative from each of the six divisional forums plus two management reps (one representing Supercentres and one Warehouses). The quarterly one-day meetings are chaired in rotation by the managing directors of Supercentres and Warehouses, respectively, supported by head office HR staff. The agenda includes:

- an update on company performance;
- discussion of issues and questions referred from divisional meetings; and
- consultation on key company changes or initiatives.

Initially, the approach adopted to dealing with questions forwarded from the divisional Grass Roots meetings was to discuss them at the national meeting and then send them to the appropriate head office staff for written responses. However, the result was that responses to issues raised were slow to materialise, causing some frustration among employee reps at lower levels. Following a change in practice, draft answers to questions are now sought ahead of the meeting, so that the national Grass Roots representatives are able to discuss the answers rather than the questions and issues can be dealt with more quickly. The answers are subsequently published in *Grass Roots News – Your Questions Answered*, a printed pamphlet circulated to staff at their home addresses following each national Grass Roots meeting. Where the national Grass Roots meeting considers an answer to be unclear or otherwise unsatisfactory, it can be referred back to the manager concerned for further work. Feedback on the outcome of national Grass Roots meetings is also provided through team briefings at store level and the posting of action points on the company intranet.

Topics discussed via Grass Roots

B&Q sees Grass Roots as 'a process for communication and consultation in the business'. It '[provides] the opportunity to discuss substantial issues that are impacting on groups of staff or affecting the way we do business', and for a 'two-way exchange of information and ideas' (company literature).

Topics raised by employees

In terms of the 'bottom-up' aspects of the process, Grass Roots enables B&Q employees to pursue a wide range of questions and concerns, suggest ideas for operational improvements and make requests for the development, explanation or clarification of company policy. There are few 'no-go areas'. The guidelines on Grass Roots meetings on the B&Q intranet state that 'it is expected that personal issues are resolved directly with line managers so that Grass Roots meetings do not get clogged up with minor issues', and that 'some issues always remain outside of the consultation process, i.e. pay, terms and conditions decisions, individual disciplinary matters, etc.'.

Issues specific to particular stores, regions and divisions are dealt with at that level. Where appropriate, store, regional and divisional-level Grass Roots forums may decide to refer issues upto the next level for consideration. These must have general applicability at the higher level, but it is in the nature of B&Q's business that questions relating to many aspects of, say, customer service, operational procedures, HR policy or equipment provision will inevitably be relevant to most B&Q stores and employees.

A review of the four most recent editions of *Grass Roots News* at the time of writing (issues 14–17, covering Winter 2001 to Spring 2003) shows that employee questions on a wide range of issues have been answered by appropriate head office staff, up to and including board-level management. Each issue includes answers to between twenty and sixty questions forwarded from divisional Grass Roots forums. These relate to:

- employee 'gripes' or suggestions for improvements concerning in-store equipment, uniform, working practices, customer service issues and so on;
- queries about terms and conditions (for example, pay allowances, maternity benefits, pension provision);
- health and safety concerns; and
- (less frequently) questions about broader company policy (for example, concerning Kingfisher's de-merger plans, B&Q's approach to sponsorship, and the implications of the UK's adoption of the euro).

As has already been noted, employee grievances can also be referred to the national Grass Roots forum as the final stage of the company's grievance procedure. A recent case concerned the application of B&Q's business-wide provisions on meal and rest break entitlements for night crews. Following a change of management at a Warehouse store, it emerged that the night crew had been enjoying longer breaks than those specified in the company handbook. On being instructed to revert to the standard pattern of breaks, the employees concerned pursued a collective grievance through the appropriate procedure, arguing that the longer breaks represented established custom and practice, and were necessitated by the store's distance from local amenities. As the issue was not resolved in discussions with line management at store, regional and divisional levels, the employees' case was heard by the national Grass Roots employee representatives who concluded, without management involvement in the decision, that the standard pattern of breaks specified by the B&Q handbook had to be adhered to, and therefore rejected the employees' appeal.

Topics raised by management

According to head office staff, during the early years of Grass Roots, almost all the issues discussed tended to be those raised by employees. However, since the new Grass Roots arrangements were introduced, 'top-down', management-initiated items are reportedly beginning to feature more frequently on Grass Roots agendas.

One aspect of this is the inclusion on the agenda for all Grass Roots meetings of a briefing on company performance – and, as appropriate, the performance of the particular store, region or division within which the meeting takes place. Thus, at the March 2003 national Grass Roots meeting, Matt Tyson, the managing director of B&Q's Supercentres, gave a presentation on Kingfisher/B&Q's annual results, published the previous week. This highlighted the fact that the bulk of Kingfisher's profits had resulted from its home improvement operations, which was said to underline the case for the planned de-merger of Kingfisher's electrical businesses later in the year. Employee representatives commented that the B&Q's strong performance had positive implications for employment security.

As well as giving Grass Roots meetings a clearer business focus, a key objective of the changes introduced in 2002 was to enable Grass Roots 'to act as B&Q's formal consultation process when we are planning business changes'. This has yet to feed through systematically into the operation of the Grass Roots process. However, B&Q management did recently use Grass Roots to consult on options for a new store team bonus to replace B&Q's former profit-sharing scheme, designed to reward perform-ance against store-level sales, service and shrinkage measures. (An example of an Agenda from one meeting is shown in Box 15.2). Feedback forms from regional and divisional Grass Roots reps on what was a sensitive issue for staff reportedly resulted in significant modifications to the company's original plans. Revised arrangements for the new store team bonus were presented to the January 2003 national Grass Roots meeting by personnel director, Mike Cutt, and were 'given the green light' by employee representatives. According to Matt Tyson, the initial management proposals, discussed at all levels of the Grass Roots process, had been controversial, and he had made it clear to senior management colleagues that the new bonus scheme should not be rolled out across the business without having received the endorsement of the national Grass Roots forum.

Box 15.2   Agenda covered by national Grass Roots meeting, March 2003

- Business update: presentation and discussion of Kingfisher/B&Q annual results.
- Consideration of draft replies to 40 questions submitted by divisional Grass Roots forums. Issues raised included:

  - safety problems associated with in-store machinery;
  - suggested improvements to working practices;

- appropriateness of existing e-learning modules to staff needs;
- linking long service awards to additional holiday entitlement;
- requests for information about new statutory entitlements to parental leave/pay;
- in-store music system playlist;
- pay allowances;
- future prospects of Kingfisher pension scheme.

- Identification of key issues to report to B&Q board, and to health and safety committee.
- Discussion of operational issues relating to Grass Roots (training requirements and so on).

The Grass Roots process has not been used for statutory consultation over impending redundancies or under the Transfer of Undertakings (Protection of Employment) Regulations. In the context of sustained employment growth, very few redundancy issues tend to arise within B&Q, and where the TUPE requirements have applied this has been in relation to stores taken over from other companies.

Key operational issues

Training

As Matt Tyson points out, an enhanced consultation role for Grass Roots means that it is important to have properly trained employee representatives, who have good communication skills and are capable of obtaining and collating feedback on key proposals. The lack of training for employee reps was also something that came through strongly in the feedback received during the review of Grass Roots ahead of its 2003 relaunch. The emphasis on training also links with the new three-year mandate for employee reps. The company points out that, as well as ensuring better continuity, this means that 'maximum benefit will be gained from the training of each representative' (company literature).

Training is now available in a number of ways:

- an e-learning module on Grass Roots meetings provided by the 'B&Q University';
- the inclusion of short training activities during Grass Roots meetings at all levels; and
- specific training events for higher-level Grass Roots reps.

For example, the day before the March 2003 national Grass Roots meeting, representatives underwent a training session on presentation skills. Further training events will focus on influencing skills, self-awareness and understanding the business.

The company has also issued a handbook containing guidance for employee representatives on their role and the Grass Roots process.

A question raised at the March 2003 national meeting asked whether it was necessary to include a training activity during store-level Grass Roots meetings as it was difficult to find sufficient time to undertake this as well as to discuss important issues. The head office management view is that, given the developments in Grass Roots and the topics on which employee representatives may be consulted in the future, it is necessary to develop representatives' ability to undertake their role. However, management is seeking recommendations from the national reps as to the necessity and effectiveness of the training exercises currently being conducted at store level.

Facilities for employee reps

Under the new arrangements, Grass Roots reps are allowed time during their working hours to carry out their Grass Roots activities, by agreement with their general or store manager. Employee representatives also requested Grass-Roots-specific e-mail facilities to ensure a better flow of communication. These have since been set up.

Confidentiality

Both management and employee representatives report that, to date, the protection of confidential company information has not proved to be a significant issue in practice. At present, it is merely noted in the intranet guidance on Grass Roots procedures that employee reps will 'be required to keep sensitive information confidential', and occasionally the discussion of a particular issue may be identified as being confidential, primarily at national Grass Roots meetings. However, head office staff are aware that, as more company initiatives are put on to the agenda for consultation, confidentiality issues are more likely to arise. It may be, for example, that the discussion of some sensitive issues will be restricted to the national forum, and that more detailed confidentiality requirements may need to be introduced.

Top management commitment

B&Q head office staff believe that the fact that the national Grass Roots forum is chaired by a main board director – and that the company's CEO, Bill Whiting, has attended a number of its meetings – illustrates high-level management commitment to the process, and that this in turn has helped to raise the profile and impact of Grass Roots. In particular, as discussed in further detail below, key issues emerging from the Grass Roots process which require decisions at board level can be taken directly to the next weekly board meeting. B&Q's senior management recognises that this enables the employee reps to report concrete results to their colleagues at the lower level forums, and demonstrates to the workforce more generally that 'the Grass Roots process is working – that management is listening and action is being taken'.

Head office staff also point out that the roll-out of the changes to Grass Roots in 2002 was accompanied by major management push to raise awareness of the Grass Roots process. An extensive promotional campaign was carried out by the company to explain the new Grass Roots arrangements and their enhanced role within the company, to encourage good-quality representatives to come forward, and to launch the reconstituted forums effectively. This involved a significant investment of time and money, and was carried out through a range of channels, including in-store team briefings, posters, material on the company intranet, and a pamphlet (*Grass Roots is growing up*) circulated to employees. In addition, to try to ensure that the first forum meetings in the new cycle got off to a good start, B&Q's head office provided a structured agenda designed to encourage representatives to get to know each other better, and to talk about their reasons for becoming involved. According to Crystal Richards, B&Q's 'Great Place to Work' manager who co-ordinates the Grass Roots process, this proved particularly valuable at regional and divisional levels, where – unlike the store forums – people might not know each another but were being asked to choose someone to represent them on the next tier of the Grass Roots structure.

Impact of the changes

Matt Tyson, managing director for B&Q Supercentres, believes that the new arrangements are already producing better results than the old Grass Roots system. He cites the positive outcome of discussions on two issues raised recently via Grass Roots:

(i) Employee concerns about safety problems associated with the use of extensions on delivery trolleys have been raised at all levels of the Grass Roots process and were considered at the January 2003 national meeting. As a direct result, the next meeting of the B&Q board sanctioned a change in practice – the discontinuation of the delivery of trolleys with extensions – which added £250,000 to distribution costs.

(ii) Similarly, requests from employees for more e-learning facilities and for these to be made available on store PCs are reported to have contributed to a decision by the board to approve a £480,000 programme of investment in new PCs, most of which will have the capability of being used for e-learning purposes.

In Tyson's view, it is important to reach early conclusions on key issues raised via Grass Roots, in order to demonstrate the credibility of the Grass Roots process and generate momentum for its future development. Thus the national Grass Roots meetings need to be 'more proactive' in chasing prompt and thorough answers from head office management on the questions raised. He also stressed the importance of Grass Roots engaging effectively with management decision-making. To this end, he has introduced the practice at the end of national Grass Roots meetings of identifying three or four specific issues needing management action, which he then draws attention to in his subsequent report to the board. For example, at the national Grass Roots meeting held in March 2003, questions highlighting the need for transparency on pensions developments, and calling for a review of the appropriateness of existing e-learning modules to staff needs, were among those earmarked for drawing to the board's attention.

However, while resolving questions and problems put forward by employees continues to be a key role of the Grass Roots process, Matt Tyson emphasises that the value of Grass Roots to the company also lies in generating employee feedback on a wide range of business issues. Senior management therefore intend to be more systematic in their use of Grass Roots as a vehicle for consultation, presenting key company initiatives to Grass Roots reps ahead of communicating with the workforce as a whole, potentially extending to consultation over pay and reward issues, and other terms and conditions of employment.

In the view of one of the employee representatives on the national Grass Roots forum, the changes introduced in 2002, particularly the formal election of employee representatives, have enhanced both the effectiveness of the Grass Roots process, in terms of prompting management to act on employee concerns, and its credibility among employees. However, speaking after the March 2003 national meeting, the representative commented that there was still 'room for improvement'. Management 'could use us much more' to consult on 'meaty issues' in areas such as work organisation, store security, and pay and conditions.

Assessment and future prospects

Grass Roots is still a relatively new process, but clearly it has established a successful track record as a channel for employee views, questions and ideas, eliciting management responses and prompting the company to act on particular employee concerns. Moreover, in its current phase of development, following the changes introduced in 2002, it is evolving to take on an enhanced role. B&Q's head office management believe that the recent changes have contributed to raising the profile of Grass Roots within the business, among both management and workforce, and that employee representatives are exhibiting a growing professionalism and effectiveness in the way they operate. Writing in the Spring 2003 issue of *Grass Roots News*, Ian Morrice, managing director for B&Q's Warehouses, commented that the discussion at the recent national Grass Roots meeting he had chaired had been 'very purposeful and constructive', and that 'where investment has been needed...the board has been prepared to back your ideas with financial support'.

However, the new phase of Grass Roots's development is still in its early stages. In particular, in the light of the requirements of the EU information and consultation Directive, to be implemented in the UK in 2005, a key question is how its formal consultative role on employment, work organisation and contractual issues will develop. To date, management's use of the Grass Roots process to initiate consultation on upcoming business changes has been limited, with the consultation exercise on the new store team bonus being the principal example. But significant developments in terms of extending the consultative role of Grass Roots now seem to be under way. The main item on the agenda of the June 2003 national Grass Roots meeting was a forward plan identifying some twenty important business initiatives over the coming eighteen months on which head office management intends to inform and/or consult the workforce via Grass Roots, and setting out the timetable for doing so in terms of the quarterly cycle of store-level, regional, divisional and national meetings. The duration of national Grass Roots meetings may need to be extended to one-and-a-half days as a result. 'We'll be informing and consulting on key operations as well as HR issues', Crystal Richards explains, including topics such as childcare support and the task and communication strategy for stores: 'Very few are on the list because we'd be legally obliged to consult on them. Mostly it's a question of good practice.'

Crystal Richards professes: 'It has taken us by surprise how quickly Grass Roots is developing. We're on a steep learning curve, but we're determined to make the consultation process effective.' For B&Q's top management, a key indicator of success will be whether the development of the Grass Roots process is reflected in increased levels of employee engagement, as measured by the company's six-monthly employee feedback survey, which in turn have a positive impact in terms of store and company performance.

Box 15.3   The benefits of Grass Roots

According to B&Q, the benefits of the Grass Roots process are as follows. For staff:

- a channel for their views;
- an opportunity to give management employees' great ideas; and
- it keeps staff up to date about changes the company is making.

For Grass Roots reps:

- the opportunity to develop new skills;
- a chance to learn more about B&Q;
- gain wider contacts in the business;
- increase understanding that might help individuals in their future careers; and
- enables employees to demonstrate their ability to handle responsibility.

For B&Q:

- it gains more great ideas to run the business;
- a more involved and informed staff means a better deal for customers;
- better-quality decisions are made; and
- changes can be introduced quickly and smoothly, avoiding unexpected events.

16

Information and consultation in financial services: coping with partial unionisation

Mark Hall

Abbey National PLC was acquired by Grupo Santander in late 2004. Within the Abbey financial services company, consultation with employee representatives takes place at company and business area level, based on a long-standing recognition/partnership agreement with the Abbey National Group Union (ANGU). The agreement was updated in 2003 and the negotiation and consultation machinery adjusted to reflect changes in Abbey's organisational structure. Consultation over the impact of restructuring – a central requirement of the EU employee information and consultation Directive – has dominated Abbey's employment relations agenda since 2003. The UK's implementation of the Directive raises the question of whether Abbey's consultation arrangements may need to be adapted to embrace universal elections for employee representatives – participation in the existing machinery is restricted to ANGU representatives. However, both management and the union want to avoid disruption to the current procedures, which they regard as highly effective. See Box 16.1 for a description of the company.

Box 16.1   Company profile

Abbey National PLC, acquired by Banco Santander in 2004, is a leading personal financial services (PFS) company in the UK, with more than 18 million customers. It offers a wide range of services, both directly and via intermediaries, including mortgages and savings, bank accounts, loans and credit cards, long-term investments (including pensions and unit trusts) and insurance cover.

Abbey's roots date back to 1849, with the establishment of the National Freehold Land and Building Society. In 1944, it merged with the Abbey Road Building Society to form Abbey National. In 1989, it was the first building society to convert to plc status and to be floated on the London Stock Exchange. Subsequent acquisitions included the National & Provincial Building Society, Scottish Mutual and Scottish Provident.

In 2003, following the announcement of substantial losses, the company relaunched its business and brand. It shortened its name to Abbey and re-focused its strategy on its core UK PFS business. All other Abbey businesses and assets were placed in a portfolio business unit (PBU) and earmarked for sale or closure. In 2004, Abbey employed around 26,000 employees (full-time equivalent).

Employment relations background

The Abbey National Group Union (ANGU) is the only UK trade union recognised by the company. The union (see Box 16.2) represents and negotiates the terms and conditions of all UK-based Abbey employees excluding the 'director group' – the company's sixty most senior executives.

Box 16.2   The Abbey National Group Union (ANGU)

The Abbey National Group Union started life in 1977 as the Abbey National Staff Association. It obtained a certificate of independence in February 1978, affiliated to the TUC in 1998, and adopted its present name in 2001. It is a member of the Alliance for Finance, the umbrella group of finance sector unions.

At the end of 2003, ANGU had some 8,970 members (three-quarters of them women), almost all of whom are employees of the Abbey National Group. In recent years, ANGU's membership among Abbey staff (excluding executive management) has been around 30 per cent, but this density has increased towards 35 per cent as a result of restructuring. The union's top four full-time officials – the general secretary and three assistant general secretaries – are secondees from the company. There are around sixty ANGU lay representatives, including the union's chair and vice-chair, who work for Abbey and undertake union duties in addition to their jobs.

ANGU's single-employer character has been affected to some extent by the transfer or outsourcing of Abbey staff to other companies, and the sale of PBU businesses. The union does not always seek actively to retain such staff as members. Thus, while some ANGU members currently work for British Telecommunications plc (BT), ANGU would be content for them to join the established telecommunications sector unions. By contrast, ANGU has been

---

de-recognised by General Electric following the latter's recent acquisition from Abbey of First National Bank. Abbey's mortgage operations are undertaken as a joint venture with information technology services company EDS, but as this is majority-owned by Abbey, ANGU's position is the same as elsewhere within Abbey.

The basis of the relationship between the company and the union is a formal 'partnership' agreement that has been in place for a number of years and was updated in July 2003 (see Box 16.3). Both parties see their partnership as the natural development of a positive employment relations climate that dates back twenty-five years to the initial recognition agreement, and has 'delivered results' in terms of a progressive package of employee benefits. This includes a £5.50 per hour minimum wage, agreed in 2002; full parental leave rights for adoptive parents; various family-friendly and work–life balance policies including paid paternity leave; a job security agreement; a basic 35-hour week; and, most recently, an equal pay audit. The partnership also generates a range of joint statements and agreed policies. While both parties are committed to working together to resolve disagreements wherever possible, disputes do occur and the union will, for example, actively support individuals in cases against the company at employment tribunals. However, the union has never gone on strike or undertaken other industrial action.

Box 16.3   Key provisions of the partnership agreement

The partnership agreement between Abbey and ANGU was revised in July 2003.

The 'shared values and mutual objectives' of the two parties set out in the agreement are:

- 'to ensure the efficient and effective operation of Abbey which is in the best interests of employees, customers and shareholders
- to seek jointly ways that maximise Abbey's ability to manage change within the highly competitive environment of the financial services sector and, during a period of rapid technological change, remain a progressive and successful organisation
- to maintain and develop a strong partnership which fosters an environment within which sound employee relations may flourish
- to provide a framework for information sharing and consultation with employees.'

The specific goals of the partnership identified in the agreement include 'business success', employment security (see Box 16.4), corporate social responsibility, the creation of an 'open and honest working environment', and enabling Abbey to 'adjust its business at a speed that maintains or improves competitive advantage'.

Abbey recognises ANGU as the sole trade union for employees below director group level for the purposes of:

- individual representation (regarding disciplinary matters, managing employee concerns at work, employment continuity/job security and other work related matters);
- consultation with management; and
- collective bargaining.

The agreement provides that the company 'will meet all reasonable requests from the union for disclosure of relevant information for the purpose of effective consultation and for the conduct of collective bargaining except where such disclosure would be detrimental to the commercial interests of Abbey or the individual interests of employees. Abbey will meet its legal obligations to inform and consult with the union in such areas as:

- health and safety;
- recent and probable development of activities and Abbey's economic situation;
- situation, structure and probable development of employment and threat to employment; and
- decisions likely to lead to substantial changes to work organisation, employment policies or in contractual relations.

The agreement sets out the consultation and negotiation machinery that operates within the company (see Box 16.5) and includes provisions on mediation and arbitration following a failure to agree, facilities and time off for union representatives and 'check-off' (deduction of union subscriptions from members' salaries).

The July 2003 version of the partnership agreement made no changes in the underlying principles of the relationship, but included new material spelling out the objectives of the agreement (see Box 16.3), updated its terminology (for example, in relation to time off and facilities for ANGU representatives), and codified agreed practice that had evolved, notably in the area of employment security (see Box 16.4).

Box 16.4   Employment security

A key goal specified in the partnership agreement is 'to maintain employment opportunities for existing employees by providing a lifetime of jobs'. There is also a detailed employment security agreement between the company and the union, updated most recently in August 2003.

Box 16.4 (Continued)

The job security sub-committee of the JCNC provides the forum for 'communication, consultation and discussion between the company and ANGU on all matters concerning redundancy', including statutory redundancy consultation procedures. Monthly meetings of the sub-committee discuss all potential redundancies, TUPE transfers and other major reorganisations of work across the business. The meetings are chaired by group employee relations staff, and business managers present their proposals to ANGU. Proposals will often come to the sub-committee several times over a period of months as they develop. During consultation over redundancies and redeployment, ANGU officials seek to ensure that the business rationale for the proposed job cuts is sound, and that the selection criteria are appropriate and fairly applied. Once proposals are set to be implemented, ANGU ensures that officials are present at staff announcements to support their members.

The job security agreement outlines how staff will be treated if their jobs come to an end (or move to a different location beyond a reasonable travelling distance from home). Although continued employment is not guaranteed, the emphasis of the agreement is on redeployment within the company where possible. Affected employees are considered for other suitable jobs within Abbey ahead of other internal and external applicants, and financial support is provided with relocation or travel costs. The company seeks to match the skills of employees who are at risk of redundancy to any vacancies that are available. If staff are appointed to a new job that is not equivalent to their old one it will be offered on a trial basis. If the new position proves to be unsuitable, and Abbey still does not have an equivalent role to offer the staff concerned, they are entitled to leave with a redundancy payment. Where no suitable job is available, staff receive twice the statutory notice period, 3.25 weeks' severance pay for each year of service up to a maximum of 104 weeks, and outplacement support.

Specific problems with the application of the job security procedures may result in formal appeals. The agreement provides for these to be heard by a panel of three senior managers, including one from the HR division, who chairs the meeting. Employees may be represented by an ANGU official, or may be accompanied by another Abbey employee or a representative of another trade union.

The company's relationship with ANGU is managed by a partnership co-ordinator, a full-time member of the HR department (at the time of writing, Paul Day, a former chair of the union). The formal framework for the relationship – a group-level Joint Consultative and Negotiating Committee (JCNC) and several sub-committees – is outlined in the following section and includes a regular 'partnership meeting' in the form of the 'policies and procedures' sub-committee of the JCNC, which is used to discuss the logistics of the relationship and to provide a forum for updates on HR matters. Senior ANGU representatives are normally briefed by Abbey's chief executive following the announcement of the company's results, and ANGU and management representatives also take part in a range of other meetings and working groups to discuss particular projects, policies and other developments. Paul Day estimates that, on average, ANGU officials probably attend at least one meeting with management on four days out of five.

In 1996, the company established a voluntary European Works Council-type consultation body, the European Communications Forum. However, this body has not met for a number of years and, according to management representatives interviewed, the logic for having a European-level body has largely disappeared as a result of recent divestments in Europe.

The consultation and negotiation framework

The unified framework for both consultation and negotiation within Abbey is the Joint Consultative and Negotiating Committee (JCNC) and its sub-committees (see Box 16.5). The peak, group-level JCNC usually meets at least four times a year. There are also a number of sub-committees of the JCNC that undertake more detailed discussion of key issues such as health and safety, job security, and pay and conditions, as well as divisional or 'business area' sub-committees reflecting the business structure of the company. A crucial feature of the existing JCNC framework is that the employee participants are solely ANGU representatives. The union side of the JCNC is made up of the national officers plus representatives from the ANGU national executive committee. On the business area sub-committees, representation comprises one national officer plus employee representatives from the business area concerned, elected by ANGU members.

Box 16.5   The structure of the Joint Consultative and Negotiating Committee (JCNC)

The formal framework for consultation and negotiation within Abbey is the Joint Consultative and Negotiating Committee and its sub-committees.

The company-wide JCNC consists of up to five members representing management and up to five members from ANGU. Additional attendees are permissible by agreement between management and the union. The chair and secretary of the JCNC are appointed by management. Meetings are usually held at least four times a year, but additional meetings can be called by either side by giving two weeks' notice.

Box 16.5 (Continued)

Sub-committees of the JCNC undertake more detailed discussion of specific matters and/or matters affecting specific business areas. The scope of each sub-committee is agreed between the company and the union. There is a company-wide health and safety sub-committee, a job security sub-committee (where any potential redundancies or TUPE transfers are discussed), and a pay and conditions sub-committee(where most pay negotiations and activity on equal pay is undertaken). A policies and procedures sub-committee has the remit of keeping the overall partnership between the company and the union under review.

There are also a number of divisional or 'business area' sub-committees corresponding to Abbey's business structure, in which union representatives and senior management discuss matters affecting those businesses. The number and scope of the business area committees can and do change as a result of restructuring. However, between them they cover the company's entire UK-based operations. The current business area sub-committees, following reorganisation in mid-2003, cover:

- customer sales (branches, telephone and internet banking);
- customer propositions (marketing);
- customer operations;
- the IT division;
- central division, HR division and secretariat; and
- the portfolio business unit.

The agreement includes a template for the constitution of the sub-committees. Meetings are attended by up to five union representatives (national officers and representatives from the relevant business area) and up to five management representatives (normally including the director of the business area or a nominated representative and a group HR representative). The sub-committee chair and secretary are appointed by management. Meetings will generally be held four times a year, but their frequency depends on the matters to be discussed. Minutes of meetings are agreed by management and the union, and are reported to the following JCNC meeting.

The template states that matters for discussion at JCNC sub-committees 'may include business performance, plans and strategy, change management plans and progress, managing diversity [and] employee analysis (e.g. staff turnover levels)'.

With the agreement of both parties, matters discussed at the business area level can be referred to the JCNC.

The JCNC and relevant sub-committees are the forum for both consultation and collective bargaining, but the agreement does not differentiate between the two processes. Beyond referring to 'issues concerning employees', the agreement does not identify the subject matter for collective bargaining, nor does it identify topics appropriate for consultation.

In some larger business areas there are additional, lower levels at which regular consultation takes place. Within customer sales, for example, there are specific consultation meetings for the branch network and below that for each sales region. In the joint venture with EDS there is one committee for each of the three major sites.

The JCNC itself deals with group-wide issues and the annual pay review, as well as reviewing unresolved items from sub-committee meetings. Key union concerns are also raised here – that is, at the highest level within the organisation.

Outside the union-based consultation and negotiation structures, there are a number of company-wide communications initiatives that involve all employees in the business (see Box 16.6 for details).

Box 16.6 Wider employee involvement practices

Abbey operates a range of direct communications and employee involvement initiatives. Among other things:

- team meetings occur regularly to enable two-way communication between managers and their team members;
- the company's intranet system contains a wide range of information, from corporate announcements to departmental news. On occasions when there have been rumours or media speculation about takeovers, the company has used its intranet to explain to employees as much as it is able about what is happening;
- a majority of employees own shares in the business and/or save for share options, and therefore receive shareholder information about company performance;
- bonus payments are made to employees if the business performs at or above its targets, so information on performance is provided regularly;
- a staff TV channel includes programming, updated weekly, that advises employees in the branch network and other retail sites on issues affecting the business;
- a bi-monthly magazine is sent to all employees;
- significant announcements are cascaded to employees through the management hierarchy;
- evening 'Talk' sessions are held where executives answer staff questions; and
- Abbey undertakes and publishes annual employee opinion surveys.

Negotiation and consultation in practice

Broadly speaking, negotiation takes place within the JCNC and its policy sub-committees, while business area sub-committees are essentially a forum for consultation.

The bargaining agenda

Agreements reached at the group JCNC are communicated jointly to all staff by the company and the union. During 2001–3, examples of topics on which agreements were reached included:

- annual pay reviews;
- leave entitlement;
- car mileage rates;
- meal, out of pocket, call-out and branch key-holder allowances;
- the policy implications of a pilot on franchising branches;
- maternity returners' bonus (paid for two years to those returning from maternity or adoption leave);
- company policy on pension provision following the closure of Abbey's final salary pension scheme to new entrants;
- a charter on call centre standards, developed by a joint working group of union and company representatives;
- lifelong learning provision;
- late retirement; and
- employees' right to request flexible working patterns.

According to management and union representatives interviewed, annual pay reviews usually start in an informal and open way but are concluded by formal negotiations. The company compares salary ranges and anchor points within them with pay levels within the financial services sector more generally, to ensure they are aligned with the market. ANGU general secretary Linda Rolph believes that the union needs to be more rigorous in checking Abbey's market comparisons. The annual pay agreement is not put to a ballot of ANGU members for endorsement. The 'failure to agree' procedure – referral to mediation or arbitration – has not been used since the late 1980s.

Handling restructuring and redundancies

Since 2003, employee relations within Abbey have been dominated by the impact of extensive restructuring. While Abbey's UK PFS business remains profitable, losses on the sale and wind-down of businesses outside UK PFS led to total group losses of £984 million in 2002, and £686 million in 2003.

Since the second half of 2001, most members of the Abbey board, including the chairman, chief executive and finance director, have left; only two of the previous executive directors remain. The next level of management – the director group, the only employees that ANGU does not represent – has also undergone important changes. Following a review of the director group undertaken in the second half of 2003, a significant number of roles were removed or changed and, as a result, some executives left the company and others were brought in.

In the second half of 2002, as the scale of the financial problems facing the company became apparent, Abbey initiated a cost reduction programme under which each of the company's businesses was required to come up with significant cost-cutting plans. These entailed substantial redundancies or redeployments, affecting over 760 staff, according to union calculations at the end of January 2003. ANGU saw the redundancies as 'paying the price for the downturn in Abbey's profits, brought about by the wrong decisions being made at the top'. It sought to ensure that any management proposal for restructuring was 'robust' and had a 'clear business rationale'. Contested redundancies were dealt with under the job security agreement and the union reported a number of successes at job security appeals. Overall, ANGU leaders felt that their input had contributed to keeping job losses to a minimum.

Abbey's new strategy, announced in February 2003, has involved more substantial restructuring, including the disposal of non-core businesses to focus on mortgages, savings and investments, and the rationalisation or outsourcing of other operations.

The disposal of assets has included the sale of First National Bank to the consumer credit business of General Electric; Abbey National Bank Italy to Unicredito; and Royal Saint George Banque in France, also to General Electric. Dublin-based Scottish Mutual International and Scottish Provident Ireland were closed to new business in April 2003. In May 2003, Abbey announced that First National Motor Finance was to close to new business and would be wound down over the following two to three years with the loss of 650 jobs. In July 2003, the company announced the closure of the call centre and back office operation in Romford which services its private banking arm, Cater Allen, and the transfer of its work to offices in Sheffield and Bradford, affecting some 230 staff.

In May 2003, the company initiated a major restructuring of its branch network, involving a reduction in the number of management roles, the return of the role of branch manager, which it did away with four years previously, an increase of 600 customer-facing staff and about 250 net job losses. The changes required more than 2,000 employees to re-apply for the available jobs.

All the domestic changes outlined above were discussed with ANGU in line with established procedures, with regular meetings taking place on job security/organisational change. Through highly critical of past management strategies that had resulted in the restructuring plans, ANGU's approach to their detailed application was pragmatic. Linda Rolph points out that Abbey staff and the union have become used to an almost constant process of organisational change over many years, though the pace and scale of recent upheavals have been unprecedented. In respect of the branch network reorganisation, ANGU was heavily involved in discussions about the processes of re-applying for jobs/selection for redundancy. According to Linda Rolph, ANGU 'achieved significant changes in management's approach' in intensive talks involving weekly meetings with management, initially held outside the job security committee. How to ensure appropriate job matches for affected staff was reportedly the key issue.

However, the most contentious of Abbey's restructuring proposals has been the initial outcome of the company's 'sourcing review', announced in January 2004.

This reflected both the scale of the job losses involved (a total of 1,000–1,400) and the sensitivity of the issue of 'offshoring' for ANGU.

On 14 January 2004, Abbey announced that in future its customer operations business would be based around five core locations in the UK: Belfast, Bradford, Glasgow, Milton Keynes and Sheffield. The company argued that fewer but larger sites would release financial resources, allowing it to invest £25 million in the core locations over the next three years, and was part of its strategy to improve service quality and cost-effectiveness.

With Glasgow identified as one of Abbey's core locations, the company announced it would be consolidating its long-term savings and protection work there, and that its offices in Edinburgh would close by the end of 2004. The move affected 900 staff, including some 730 who worked for Scottish Provident, taken over by Abbey in 2001. Telephone banking operations are also being transferred to the core locations and, following the completion of a pilot scheme in India, some telephone banking work is transferring to India on a phased basis. As a result, Abbey's Derby and Warrington sites closed at the end of October 2004, and the telephone banking work currently carried out by customer operations staff in Bradford ceased.

During the preceding discussions with management, ANGU maintained its view that the transfer of jobs abroad would be 'wrong for employees, customers and the UK'. It issued a press statement expressing 'disappointment' at Abbey's decision to proceed with plans to transfer work to India. The union said it welcomed the company's investment plans and its commitment to jobs in Belfast, Bradford, Glasgow, Milton Keynes and Sheffield but 'we are against any work being offshored'. However, as the company had insisted on proceeding with this initiative, the union had negotiated a range of measures to minimise the impact on its members and maximise their opportunity for redeployment within the company.

ANGU similarly expressed 'disappointment' at the announcement of the closure of Abbey's operations in Edinburgh: 'ANGU are committed to supporting all of our members affected by this decision and in doing so we have negotiated enhanced support for redeployment within the company, which goes beyond our job security agreement with Abbey.'

According to Abbey management, discussions with ANGU on 'offshoring' began after the February 2003 results were announced and involved an 'open and honest assessment of the available options'. In the autumn, Abbey began a pilot programme involving the outsourcing of back office work to India in association with the US-based company MsourcE. In December, prior to the public announcement of the move, ANGU and the company issued a joint statement containing commitments by the company that:

- employees affected by offshoring or the 'co-location' of UK sites would have at least six months' notice if their job was to end;
- redundancies would be reduced by means of a recruitment freeze and the release of agency employees; and
- Abbey would 'make every effort to make another job available' to those affected, and provide help with relocation.

Coinciding with the public confirmation of the move, Abbey and ANGU announced that, following consultation, they had agreed enhanced measures to support individuals directly affected by the sourcing review, going beyond the standard arrangements contained in the job security agreement. Among other things, the company agreed that:

- a full relocation package will be available to those with redundancy payments of more than £10,000, and relocation costs of between £8,000 and £10,000 in other cases;
- additional travelling costs will be reimbursed over three years at 100 per cent for years 1 and 2, and 50 per cent for year 3;
- flexible working arrangements will be applied 'imaginatively and sympathetically'. Where business needs permit, staff will be allowed to work compressed hours (for example, working their contractual hours over four days per week rather than five, or nine days over two weeks); and
- company-provided transport to another site will be considered as an option where feasible.

The company also met informally with officials of the trade union Amicus to brief them on the background to the closure of its Scottish Provident offices in Edinburgh. Amicus had been recognised for some employees by Scottish Provident, but had been de-recognised by Abbey following acquisition, though Abbey management had agreed to continue an informal dialogue with the union in respect of former Scottish Provident employees. (Amicus, then known as MSF, had also been de-recognised by Abbey when it acquired Scottish Mutual in 1992.) Partial information about the sourcing announcement had leaked to the Scottish media a few weeks before the meeting with Amicus, and as a result the union had initiated a high-profile media campaign against the move. According to Abbey management, talks with Amicus ended prematurely and Amicus declined the company's offer to be present at the announcement to Edinburgh staff.

Key operational issues

Training

ANGU representatives who are non-secondees are usually sent on TUC courses for employee representatives. The company and ANGU are also attempting to identify company training that will develop the competencies that union representatives need.

Abbey's HR department recognises the need to raise managers' awareness of the types of issue requiring information and consultation, and improve their skills in respect of undertaking consultation, but Abbey's management development programme is not tailored specifically to handling consultation and negotiation.

However, some joint training has taken place for managers and ANGU representatives on partnership and consultation issues, to encourage best practice. Paul Day comments that the joint nature of such training – 'getting union reps and managers in the same room' – is important in reinforcing the partnership basis of the relationship.

Facilities and time off for employee representatives

ANGU's lay representatives have access to company facilities, such rooms for meetings and the use of information and communications systems, and are entitled to reasonable paid time off, subject to agreement from their line manager, to enable them to carry out their duties.

Problems are sometimes reported by local managers whose staff become ANGU representatives. Time off and reduced performance targets for the representative are not reflected in the targets for the business unit and the manager concerned, which can sometimes lead managers to resent the presence of an ANGU representative on their team. Moreover, the representatives' duties may sometimes focus on higher-level developments, so the reasons for their absence from the office may not always be apparent locally.

Agenda-setting

As noted, the partnership agreement does not identify 'no-go areas' for the JCNC and its sub-committees. According to HR managers, the nature of the relationship is such that the company is prepared to talk about 'more or less anything' except individual issues at formal meetings. Agenda items are identified by both management and union representatives.

Confidentiality

Neither HR management nor union representatives interviewed considered confidentiality to be a major problem. Paul Day notes that confidentiality is a worry for some line managers, but no problems had been traceable to breaches of confidence on the part of union representatives. Significantly, ANGU had not been blamed for the leak to the Scottish media of a company document on the closure of the Edinburgh offices ahead of the planned official announcement. Informing staff about acquisitions and disposals is potentially the biggest problem area, given the price-sensitive nature of the information involved. But, in general, the single-company nature of ANGU means that Abbey management is more willing than other similar companies to share information with union officials.

Feedback from consultation meetings

Reporting back to Abbey staff usually takes the form of company announcements to employees (discussed with ANGU) or the publication of joint statements on agreements reached via the JCNC. The outcomes of the negotiation and consultation processes are given prominent and extensive coverage in *ANGU News*, the union's bi-monthly magazine. Although only a minority of Abbey staff are members of ANGU, many non-union members reportedly rely on the union for information. However, ANGU cannot provide a formal conduit for information to all staff.

Consultation at workplace level

Local consultation is often informal in nature and depends on the level of activity of local union representatives and local management approaches. The business area sub-committees of the JCNC are organised along business-stream lines and do not relate to single geographical sites. The union's national leadership is involved directly in almost all consultation within Abbey. Where there is business/geographical alignment – for example, the mortgage centre in Southampton, local consultation is reportedly most likely to be effective and formal consultation meetings occur.

Assessment and future prospects

Abbey's long-standing, union-based negotiation and consultation arrangements have evolved over time and are reported by both management and union representatives to work highly effectively. The current partnership framework was updated comprehensively in 2003, and the coverage of the JCNC business area sub-committees was adjusted to match changes in Abbey's corporate structures. The monthly meetings of the policies and procedures sub-committee provide an important forum for the overall co-ordination of the company–union relationship. According to Paul Day, discussion during this meeting can cover any aspect of employment relations within the company, enabling both sides to 'fly kites' and engage in informal consultation.

The scale of recent and continuing restructuring within the company has provided a stern test of the partnership arrangements, but management representatives stress that Abbey has maintained its commitment to proceeding by consultation and has engaged in 'a very open dialogue' with ANGU about the pros and cons of the available options. Though highly critical of certain company strategies, the union too is largely satisfied by the way in which the negotiation and consultation machinery has operated. Although Linda Rolph comments that 'Abbey is no different from any other company in trying to do things without discussion if it can', the union points to the value in current circumstances of its job security agreement with the company, and to the additional safeguards it has secured in negotiations with the company for staff affected by Abbey's offshoring and co-location plans during 2004.

The strong commitment to partnership and consultation at group level is not necessarily replicated at branch office level. Both head office management and ANGU have some concerns that centrally-agreed policies may not always be implemented effectively at lower levels. Moreover, Abbey's December 2003 employee opinion survey, taken at a time of considerable uncertainty, suggests a generally unenthusiastic assessment on the part of employees. The majority of respondents agreed that the company kept them informed about its corporate strategy (61 per cent: 11 per cent more than the December 2002 figure) and was committed to improving communication with its employees (55 per cent; up 3 per cent). However, fewer than half of the respondents expressed satisfaction with their involvement in decisions affecting their work (47 per cent: down 6 per cent on the previous year), and only 36 per cent (down 3 per cent) thought the company was genuinely interested in involving employees in the process of change.

In terms of staff perceptions of ANGU, Linda Rolph comments that, while the old staff association used to be seen as a company 'puppet', ANGU is perceived as a more independent, effective body as a result of its TUC affiliation and its willingness to be critical of company plans. Abbey HR managers also believe that the union is 'respected by Abbey staff and acts effectively on their behalf'. Nevertheless, maintaining full coverage using ANGU's network of lay representatives is problematic, especially in newer establishments, and ANGU has little by way of full-time officer resources to plug gaps. Abbey management has also tried to encourage staff to stand as union representatives but it has sometimes proved difficult to find volunteers. During the present restructuring, the union has been critical of the scale of the job losses, but not entirely unhappy about the company's new strategy, which prioritises the core parts of the business that also tend to be the union's 'heartlands'. This will enable the union to focus on its own core areas of the business as well – and the level of ANGU membership as a proportion of all Abbey staff, traditionally only around 30 per cent, has been increasing as a result of changes.

A key issue for the future concerns the implications of the UK's Information and Consultation of Employees (ICE) Regulations for union-based consultation arrangements such as those at Abbey. Management initially felt that the EU information and consultation Directive might call into question Abbey's reliance on union-based procedures, and that the company was likely to have to establish arrangements to gauge the views of the 65–70 per cent of employees who are not ANGU members. But following assessment of the draft Regulations, and in the light of the major restructuring currently under way, Abbey favours retaining the existing arrangements. While the existing consultative structures are comprehensive, covering all employees but the most senior management, and could be adapted readily by moving to universal elections for employee representatives, there have reportedly been very few complaints about the current arrangements. Senior Abbey HR manager, Alison Rumsey, suggests that this may reflect a recognition that ANGU provides 'skilled negotiators' and a 'quality service'.

For its part, ANGU is firmly opposed to the participation of non-members in Abbey's consultative structures. Linda Rolph argues that the union-based system ensures that Abbey staff are represented effectively. Her worries about the prospect of non-union representatives include their performance, their independence, and the danger that they will pursue 'personal issues' rather than speak on behalf of their constituents. While ANGU should be well placed to maintain a leading role if universal information and consultation arrangements were to be introduced within Abbey, both management and ANGU are aware that opening up Abbey's consultative structures to non-ANGU representatives could provide an organisational foothold within the company for rival unions recruiting in the financial services sector, despite Abbey's sole recognition of ANGU.

Both parties take the view that it is unlikely that at least 10 per cent of Abbey's UK workforce would seek to trigger negotiations on new information and consultation arrangements under the ICE Regulations. Abbey's response to the introduction of the Regulations in March 2005 was therefore to try to stick with current arrangements in the belief that they have a proven track record and the broad support of staff.

part **7**

Conclusions

17

Conclusions

John Storey

Having journeyed through the twists and turns laid out in this volume, what judgement can we come to about the scope for adding value through information and consultation? The material presented makes it evident that one needs to consider for *whom* 'value is added' and it also highlights the question as to how it will be achieved.

So, to take the first issue: for whom is value added potentially achieved? The case for informing employees and consulting with them derives both from human engagement as a valued and valuable end in its own right, and for its potential in promoting more efficient and effective organisations. This latter aim (better performing organisations) is not just about higher revenues, but the potential for better hospitals and schools, more effective public services, better shopping experiences and so on – in other words, less waste and more service for all citizens. In turn, of course, higher revenues should not necessarily be dismissed, though there might be an understandable temptation to play them down if revenue distribution is skewed unfairly. Profitable enterprises should, other things being equal, secure employment, and enable a better quality of life. The extent to which margins do in fact lead to wider public good depends of course on other economic and political factors beyond employee involvement.

With regard to the second question: as to how it is to be achieved in practice, the material in the book also helps to answer some of the questions posed in relation to this and allay some of the fears raised at the start of the book. The case study chapters describing the contemporary operation of I&C in the UK make it clear that representative systems *can* work smoothly in Britain. Managers and workers are capable of negotiating and agreeing consultative systems. Trade union representatives can work with other employee representatives. Moreover, considerable evidence has been presented that seems to demonstrate that information and consultation – when allied with other HR systems – can not only operate smoothly but can also deliver real outcomes.

But we also learn that little, if any, of this happens automatically. It is possible to construct the most elaborate of representative structures and yet still not achieve active engagement. It is important to bear in mind that, despite all the understandable emphasis on getting the *structures* right (how many representatives; how should constituencies be drawn; at what level(s) of the organisation should consultation occur and so on) what will in the end matter more is how the *process* is handled by the participants. Even the most elaborate of democratic structures can evolve into an empty shell if the processes are not perceived as being meaningful by the interested parties. Experience to date suggests that a critical point of vulnerability is the communication between employee representatives and their constituents. If the grass-roots become disillusioned by the processes, then the whole edifice of the democratic structure becomes merely symbolic and ritualistic behaviour. Where this happens, employees become cynical about the processes and the machinery, and they withdraw from engagement – for example, by failing to vote and by failing to put themselves forward for election as representatives. Making the whole process meaningful is far more problematical than simply designing the machinery and the structure. In comparison, that is the easy part.

Experience and research suggest that information and consultation arrangements become moribund, or even fail outright, for a range of common reasons. These include lack of genuine commitment from senior managers; failure to consult at an early enough stage; a perception among employees that the machinery is a ritualistic talking shop; poor agendas; inadequate training; insufficient resources of time and information for representatives; poor communication of the nature and value and output from the information and consultation process; and, finally, a failure to evaluate periodically the processes and to take corrective action (CIPD 2004). The formula for success starts with ensuring the converse of each of the reasons mentioned above.

As pointed out already, the whole subject of employee information, consultation and involvement is far from new. But the new legislation may prove to be a catalyst in two senses: first, in helping to revitalise the idea; and second, in ensuring its application across a far wider proportion of the landscape than it has hitherto achieved. It seems possible, indeed, that some of the 'new territories' may come to embrace the idea and use it far more effectively than in the traditional settings, where the concept may have grown moribund. Just as the new democracies of Eastern Europe have prompted citizens to seize their democratic rights with a fervour exceeding many Western countries, so too might some new enterprise democracies yet prove to be the more vibrant, despite or because of, their late start.

Similarly, the fresh starters in the world of companies and other employing organisations have the potential to leap ahead dramatically on the employee involvement front. Conversely, organisations with long-standing mechanisms cannot afford to rest on their laurels.

The analyses in this book have also revealed that, while on the surface there might appear to be very substantial agreement between many of the interest groups, this masks some very different priorities and interpretations that persist at a deeper level. Some very old battles are still being fought. Yet it could be argued that the competitive landscape is changing so fundamentally that unless movement does take place in relation to employee engagement, then serious consequences will follow. To this extent at least, the issues on which this whole book are based can be seen as very fundamental indeed. Some of the rhetoric about 'High Performance Work-places' (HPWs) may be overblown. But, if even only a fraction of the many analyses of the new knowledge economy, for example, was to be correct, then, unless appropriate ways are found to inform, consult and engage with participants in economic enterprises, the other initiatives such as investment in R&D, investments in new ICT systems and so on will prove to be of little value. This does not mean simply adopting or complying with one model in a tokenistic manner. The real debate is not – or rather should not be – about that. Rather, the necessary debate concerns how to engage commitment, elicit trust (on all sides), how to allow the exchange of views, and to achieve innovation. That was the underlying agenda of this book. But, of course, in order to embark on realistic action it is necessary to recognise (rather than to ignore) and engage with (rather than dismiss) the realities of employment relations in Britain in the early 2000s.

Finally, although the DTI and others have chosen to 'sell' the information and consultation regulations on the back of the 'High Performance Workplaces' concept, it should by now be evident that simply following or installing machinery of the type prescribed in the Standard Provisions will not of course deliver anything approaching a HPW. As Marc Thompson's chapter in this volume (Chapter 6) makes clear, high-performance working can be found in the UK, and it can be shown to deliver results. But, as Thompson's chapter also shows, its realisation depends on an integrated array of human resource management and employment system arrangements. Authentic information and consultation practice is one crucial component. The pre-existing agreement illustrated in Appendix 2 reveals a detailed and well thought-through structure and process. Many organisations could benefit from copying many of its aspects. But, without the authenticity referred to above, such formulations will risk being reduced to mere ritualised empty shells.

Reference

CIPD (2004) *Information and Consultation: A Guide.* London: Chartered Institute of Personnel and Development.

appendix

IPA decision flowchart

Information and Consultation Flowchart

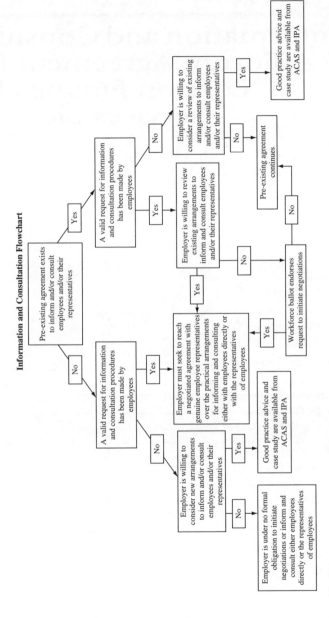

Source: Robert Stevens (IPA, July 2003)

appendix *2*

Information and Consultation Forum Agreement for London Financial · Services plc

CONTENTS

Date of Agreement

Parties

(1) London Financial Services plc ('the '**Company**'); and
(2) The persons whose names are signatories to this Agreement in their capacity as **Employee Representatives** of the **Information and Consultation Forum (ICON)** as elected and subject to this Agreement amended from time to time

1. Definitions

1.1 In this Agreement

The '**Company**'	means the Company and all or any of the subsidiary companies or division of Finance Co
'**Employee**'	means a permanent employee either part time or Full Time.
'**Employee Representative**'	means a permanent employee with at least two years continuous service elected under this Agreement.
'**ICON**'	Information and Consultation Forum.
'**Regular ICON**'	means Information and Consultation Forum (ICON) meetings normally planned for mid-November, March and July.
'**Special ICON**'	means Information and Consultation Forum (ICON) meetings where the Company is obliged to consult and inform employees, which does not form part of the scheduled Regular Information and Consultation Forum (ICON) meetings.

Framework

A. The parties acknowledge that the interests of the business and its workforce are better served if there is a forum through which, before certain final decisions are taken, employees can be informed about the performance and significant plans for the business and given the opportunity to engage in a dialogue with the **Company** to further the aims and objectives of the business.

B. The **Information and Consultation Forum** is not intended to be a collective bargaining or joint-decision forum but one through which the **Company** and the workforce can each better understand the challenges facing the business and their impact on it, including the workforce. Nothing in this Agreement is intended to limit the responsibility or rights of the **Company** to take final decisions and manage its business.

C. There are certain situations where the law requires there to be collective consultation between an employing Company and **Employee Representatives**, such as collective redundancies and transfers of undertakings.

D. The parties agree that bona fide activities of the Forum under this Agreement should be regarded as a normal activity of the business and that they both will operate this Agreement in a spirit of mutual co-operation and with respect given to their respective rights.

E. The parties believe and intend that this Agreement is a voluntary one, which complies with the requirements of Art 5 of the Information and Consultation Directive No 2002/14/EC ('the Directive').

F. The parties believe and intend that the **Employee Representatives** who are signatories to this Agreement are reasonably representative of the Company's workforce.

It is therefore Agreed as Follows

Establishment of the Information and Consultation Forum (ICON)

1. The **ICON** will commence operating with effect from March 2004 and will continue for successive fixed terms of 5 years each unless ended in accordance with section 33, 34 and 35 of this Agreement.

2. The **ICON** is intended to be an internal consultative body and therefore, subject to the circumstances referred to below, no external representatives will be permitted to attend **ICON** meetings. The **Company** may exercise its discretion to invite an external expert where it is of the opinion that the expertise of such an external expert may assist with the issues to be discussed at the **ICON** meeting.

ICON Composition

3. The **ICON** shall be comprised as follows:
   3.1 Representatives of the employees of the **Company** who are elected under this Agreement ('**Employee Representatives**') and
   3.2 two members of senior management as are nominated by the Chief Executive of the **Company**, (who will normally be expected to remain part of **ICON** for three years), the HR Director or his/her nominee and such other members of the management of the **Company** as are appropriate to attend, provided that the total **Company** management attendees do not exceed 5 at any time.

4. The **Employee Representatives** shall be elected by a secret ballot (in accordance with annex one) and shall hold office for 3 years.

5. The **Company** will procure the holding of elections for **Employee Representatives** in sufficient time for them to be in place by the start of **ICON** in April 2005.

6. **Employee Representatives** shall represent the views of employees, rather than their own views.

7. The **Company** shall appoint the Chairperson for **ICON**.

8. The HR Director shall act as the administrative secretariat of **ICON**. The functions of the **ICON** Secretariat shall be the day-to-day administration of **ICON** including:

   - arrangements for **ICON** Meetings (e.g. dates, venue, issuing invitations etc);
   - sending papers to **ICON** members in advance of meetings;
   - approving and arranging for the provision of facilities for **ICON** activities and meetings;
   - arranging for the taking of minutes of **ICON** Meetings;
   - processing the agreement of a joint communiqué following a **Regular ICON** meeting and distributing it to all affected employees;
   - liaising with the **Employee Representatives**' Spokesperson and his/her Deputy;
   - other administrative arrangements connected with **ICON**.

9. There will be a maximum of 7 **Employee Representatives** on **ICON**.

10. An **Employee Representative** for **ICON** must be an **employee** of the **Company**, which he/she represents, and have a minimum of two years continuous service with the **Company**.

11. **Employee Representatives** shall cease (with immediate effect) to be entitled to participate in any **ICON** meeting or have any rights under or in connection with this Agreement if they:

   - cease being employed by the **Company**, or
   - are removed from **ICON** in accordance with section 25 below.

12. Where, prior to the expiry of his/her term of office, an **Employee Representative** ceases for any reason to be entitled to participate in **ICON**, he/she shall be replaced by the individual with the next highest number of votes at the last election of the Employee Representative, and if there was a tie, by the one with the longest period of continuous service with the Company for the unexpired term of the ex-**Employee Representative's** term of office, subject to the individual still being employed by the company. Such a replacement shall not be entitled to any rights under the **ICON** Agreement until he/she has signed the document set out in Annex 2 under which he/she adopts and agrees to the terms of this Agreement as a party to it and has delivered it to the **ICON** Secretariat.

Organisation of Employee Representatives

13. The **Employee Representatives** shall elect (by a majority vote) from amongst their number a Spokesperson and a Deputy Spokesperson (to act in his/her absence) and who shall be the primary interface between the **Company** and the **Employee Representatives** on:

   - matters to do with the administration of **ICON**.

   The names of the **Employee Representatives'** Spokesperson and his/her Deputy shall be notified in writing to the **ICON** Secretariat.

14. There will be one **Employee Representative** for each 50 employees.

15. **Employee Representatives** shall be entitled to:

   - meet together (without the management representatives being present) for up to half a day immediately preceding a **Regular ICON** meeting at a time and venue approved in advance by the **Company**; and
   - liaise with their employees as necessary between **ICON** meetings. This will normally be by telephone or email, and at any other times, meetings shall only take place with local management's prior consent.

Regular ICON Meetings

16. The **ICON** shall meet 3 times each year, normally Mid-November, March and July. A typical agenda may well include the following items:

   HR Review

   - Training and Development
   - Health and Safety
   - Personnel (policies, practices and procedures)

Management Review

- Group developments
- Business as usual
- High level financial statistics

Corporate Review

- Current issues
- Compliance, IT, Administration, etc.
- Development

Meetings of ICON may also include other agenda items, which both fall within the scope of ICON (see section 23) and which are agreed between the Company and the Spokesperson.

17. **Regular ICON** meetings shall be attended by all management representatives and at least 25 percent of **Employee Representatives**. The dates shall, where practicable, be scheduled in advance for the year.

18. Prior to a **Regular ICON** meeting, the HR Director shall meet with the **Employee Representatives**' Spokesperson and/or his/her Deputy to agree an agenda for the next meeting. The **Company** shall use its reasonable efforts to make papers for the next **Regular ICON** meeting available to all participants at least 7 days ahead of the **Regular ICON** meeting.

19. Following a **Regular ICON** meeting, the **Company** and the **Employee Representatives**' Spokesperson and/or his/her Deputy shall agree the text of a communiqué to be communicated to employees.

Special ICON Meetings

20. The **Company** shall convene a **Special ICON** meeting in the event of a Special Event. This includes the following

- collective redundancies which require information and consultation under section 188 Trade Union & Labour Relations (Consolidation) Act 1992; or
- a transfer of undertaking which requires information and consultation under regulation 10 of the Transfer of Undertakings (Protection of Employment) Regulations 1981; or
- where the **Company** wishes to inform and/or consult with the **Employee Representatives** on an important matter substantially affecting the interests of employees and which cannot be postponed until the next scheduled **Regular ICON** meeting.

21. Those **Employee Representatives** attending a Special Meeting shall be entitled to attend subsequent meetings (without management being present) for the purpose of:

- formulating their response to the Special Event announced by the **Company**.

Such meetings must have the prior approval of the **Company**.

Report-back Meetings

22. An **Employee Representative** shall be entitled to reasonable time and facilities to liaise with employees.

This shall always be subject to the prior permission of local management, which shall not be unreasonably refused. To avoid doubt, situations where refusal may be reasonable include, but are not limited to, the operational requirements of the business, whether there is any disruption to the business, the urgency of the matter to be reported back and the amount of such time which the **ICON Employee Representative** has already taken for this purpose.

Scope of Regular ICON Meetings

23. The process at any **ICON** meeting shall be information and consultation, and not collective bargaining or joint decision-making. Consultation means an exchange of views and establishment of a dialogue between the **Company** and the **Employee Representatives**.

24. In addition to the subject matter set out in section 16 above, the **Employee Representatives** may submit to their Spokesperson and subsequently to the **Administrative Secretariat** agenda items for consideration to be included in regular **ICON** meetings. Any such item placed on the agenda is entirely at the discretion of the **Administrative secretariat**.

    The company may place additional agenda items as necessary.

Confidentiality

25. The **Company** may give to **Employee Representatives** some information, which is of a confidential nature. The **Company** will identify what information is to be treated as confidential and so not disclosed to anyone outside the **ICON** or used for a non-**ICON** related purpose. To avoid doubt, if the **Company** does not designate information as being confidential, **Employee Representatives** shall be free to disclose it to employees. It is an obligation of each **Employee Representative** under this Agreement that they fully observe such confidentiality. This obligation shall continue after an **ICON Employee Representative** ceases to hold such office or ceases to be employed by the **Company**. If any **Employee Representative** breaches such confidentiality (other than in situations protected by the Public Interest Disclosure Act 1998), he/she will be subject to investigation which may result in disciplinary action, and could result in the removal of the individual from ICON

26. The **Company** shall not be required to disclose to **ICON** any information, which falls into any of the following categories:

    - any information which is price sensitive;
    - information which is of a sufficiently commercially sensitive nature that, if disclosed to any person outside senior management, could risk causing any **Company** covered by this Agreement material harm or serious prejudice;
    - any information which has been given to any **Company** covered by this Agreement in confidence by a third party;
    - any information, the disclosure of which would be in breach of any law, Code of Practice, FSA requirement, or the rules of any other regulatory body.

Facilities for Employee Representatives

27. The **Company** will provide reasonable facilities to enable **Employee Representatives** to carry out their functions under this Agreement.

28. **Employee Representatives** shall be entitled to treat this appointment as part of their normal contractual terms and conditions of employment to attend meetings provided for under this Agreement.

29. **Employee Representatives** who incur travel or accommodation costs attending authorised **ICON** meetings shall be entitled to expense reimbursement under their employing **Company** expense policy as if the **ICON** meeting was an internal **Company** meeting as part of the performance of their duties.

Training for Employee Representatives

30. The **Company** will provide appropriate training to enable **Employee Representatives** to fulfil their **ICON** functions effectively.

Protection for Employee Representatives

31. **Employee Representatives** shall be entitled to the same protection (against dismissal or other victimisation) for carrying out their **ICON** duties, in good faith, as is provided for in UK employment protection legislation for **Employee Representatives**.

Amendment of Agreement

32. This Agreement may be amended in writing by the joint decision of both (1) The **Company** and (2) a majority of the **Employee Representatives** eligible to participate in **ICON**.

Termination of Agreement

33. The **ICON** may be disbanded at any time within a five year term by the **Company** serving 3 month's written notice (terminating this Agreement) on ICON **Employee Representatives,** If at the end of the 5 year term no such notice is served, **ICON** will run for a further 5 year term.

34. The **ICON** may be disbanded at any time by the **Employee Representatives** serving 3 month's written notice (terminating this Agreement) on the **Company**. If such notice is not served by the end of the 5 year term, the **ICON** will run for a further term of 5 years. Such a notice shall only be valid if it is approved in writing by at least two-thirds of all **Employee Representatives** eligible to participate in **ICON** and a copy of this approval is attached to the notice

35. The **ICON** may be disbanded at any time by the **Company** by the serving of 3 month's written notice terminating this Agreement on ICON **Employee Representatives**. But this provision shall only apply where LFS plc is taken over by any third party or transferred outside the LFS plc Group of companies. In this event there shall be discussions between the **Company** and ICON **Employee Representatives** over what structure will replace **ICON**.

Legal Status and Legal Proceedings

36. This Agreement is not intended by the parties to have legal effect.

Notices

39. Any notice to be served by **ICON Employee Representatives** on the **Company** shall be in writing and delivered to the HR Director.

40. Any notice to be served on **ICON Employee Representatives** shall be deemed served on all of them if it is served in writing on either:

   - all **Employee Representatives** entitled to participate in **ICON** by a letter delivered to their places of work; or

   - the **Employee Representatives'** Spokesperson and/or his/her Deputy by a letter to their places of work.

Miscellaneous

41. All references to **Employee Representatives** means those **Employee Representatives** who are elected to fulfil their respective roles and meet the requirements of sections 4, 10, 11, and 12 (as applicable).

Annex 1

Provisions relating to elections

1. The election of **Employee Representatives** shall be by a secret ballot in which all permanent employees located or based at the relevant location are eligible to vote.

2. The **Company** will provide reasonable facilities for elections.

3. Where an **Employee Representative** ceases to be on **ICON**, the individual with the next highest number of votes at the most recent election of the Employee Representative will automatically replace him/her as the official **ICON Employee Representative** for the unexpired term of the ex-**Employee Representative's** term of office, subject to the individual still being employed by the company. (see 6 below).

4. All employees with at least two years service shall be entitled to stand as candidates for **ICON Employee Representative**. But this is subject to candidates satisfying the criteria in section 10.

5. Elections shall be held on the basis of the candidates with the highest number of votes after one round of voting.

6. In the case of a tie, the result of a position will be decided by the candidate within the longest continuous service with the **Company**.

7. Prior to all elections the candidates shall be required to prepare a statement not exceeding 200 words, which the **Company** will distribute with the voting papers. Candidates are to explain who they are and give an outline on why they should be elected to **ICON**. The **Company** may refuse to distribute or edit out any material, which departs from this principle, or is defamatory, vexatious or abusive.

8. The votes in any election shall be counted under the scrutiny of one member of management and one nominated employee.

Annex 2

(Document to be signed by all new Employee Representatives)

THIS AGREEMENT IS BETWEEN:

   (i)   London Financial Services plc and

   (ii)   [   ] who is employed by LFS plc [   ] and is an **Employee Representative**

WHEREAS

   (a)   The **Company** entered into an Agreement with **Employee Representatives** dated [*date*] establishing an Information and Consultation Forum (**ICON** Agreement) on the terms set out in that document.

   (b)   [   ] has been validly elected to act as the **Employee Representative** on **ICON**

   (c)   The **ICON** Agreement requires newly elected **Employee Representatives** to become parties to it and to adopt its terms in full.

IT IS NOW AGREED AS FOLLOWS

1.   [   ] hereby agrees to become a party to the **ICON** Agreement in the capacity of an **ICON Employee Representative** and hereby adopts and agrees all the terms of the **ICON** Agreement (as amended) in force at the date hereof, a copy of which is attached hereto, with effect from the date when both parties will sign this Agreement.

2.   The **Company** recognises that Mr/Ms [   ] is hereby an **ICON Employee Representative** party to the **ICON** Agreement.

EXECUTED as a **Deed** by the Parties on dates set out below

....

For and on behalf of LFS plc   [*Date*]

....

Mr/Ms [**]**   [*Date*]

SIGNED...

Index